COMPLETE HANDBOOK
OF
CHURCH ACCOUNTING

COMPLETE HANDBOOK
OF
CHURCH ACCOUNTING

Rev. Manfred Holck, Jr., C.P.A.

with

Manfred Holck, Sr., C.P.A.

Prentice-Hall, Inc.

Englewood Cliffs, New Jersey

Prentice-Hall International, Inc., *London*
Prentice-Hall of Australia, Pty. Ltd., *Sydney*
Prentice-Hall of Canada, Ltd., *Toronto*
Prentice-Hall of India Private Ltd., *New Delhi*
Prentice-Hall of Japan, Inc., *Tokyo*
Prentice-Hall of Southeast Asia Pte. Ltd., *Singapore*
Whitehall Books, Ltd., *Wellington, New Zealand*

© 1978 by

Prentice-Hall, Inc.

Englewood Cliffs, N.J.

This publication is designed to provide accurate and authoritative information in regard to the
subject matter covered. It is sold with the understanding that the publisher is not engaged in
rendering legal, accounting, or other professional service. If legal advice or other expert
assistance is required, the services of a competent professional person should be sought.

. . . *From the Declaration of Principles jointly adopted by a Committee of the American Bar Association
and a Committee of Publishers and Associations.*

Library of Congress Cataloging in Publication Data

Holck, Manfred.
    Complete handbook of church accounting.

    Bibliography: p.
    Includes index.
    1. Church finance. 2. Church work--Forms,
blanks, etc. I. Holck, Manfred
joint author. II. Title.
BV773.H63   254.8   77-23882
ISBN 0-13-160895-9

Printed in the United States of America

To our wives
Lois and Bertha

About the Authors

Manfred Holck, Jr. has the rare distinction of being a clergyman and a Certified Public Accountant. He is also a noted lecturer on clergy income taxes, editor of the only financial newsletter for clergy, editor of a quarterly tax letter for clergy, publisher of *Church Management* magazine, and comptroller for the Board of Pensions of the Lutheran Church in America.

He is a member of the American Institute of Certified Public Accountants, National Association of Church Business Administrators, and the Society for Religious Organization Management. He holds C.P.A. certificates in Ohio and Texas.

He is the author of several previous books, including *Money and Your Church, Making It on a Pastor's Pay*, and *Tax Planning for Clergy*. His annual casette tape on the minister's income tax is used by thousands of clergy each year. A prolific writer, he has written many articles on clergy taxes, personal finance, and church finance for religious magazines and journals.

Manfred Holck, Sr. has had a long and distinguished career as an individual C.P.A. practitioner beginning in 1934. More recently he was associated wtih Barr, Howard, Boswell, and Holck, C.P.A.'s, and just prior to his retirement in 1969 was a manager for the Austin, Texas office of Touche Ross & Co.

He has served on the Board of Directors of the Texas Society of Certified Public Accountants, has been a Chapter President, and in 1976 received an honorary 40 years membership award from the American Institute of Certified Public Accountants.

Active in community affairs, he is a member of the Endowment Board of St. Martin's Lutheran Church and a volunteer consultant in the American Association of Retired Persons annual income tax advisory service to the elderly.

A Word From the Authors About How This Book Will Improve Your Church's Accounting And Financial Record Keeping System

This book will do two things for you:

1. It will tell you how to keep an easy, proven, practical set of church financial records.

2. It will show you how to tell your membership the way things really are at your church financially, with a simple, easy-to-understand system of reports.

If you have been unable to make much sense out of your congregation's financial records, here is the book that will clear away the fog. Not only will you find out just how to make some order out of all those church financial records, you'll also find out how to clear up the membership's confusion about what's going on—with a simplified set of bookkeeping records and a series of understandable financial statements, which are described in this book.

Chapters 13, 14, and 15 describe the possible systems. Chapter 17 shows how to make the report. And the chapters before, in between, and after support the system and clarify the reporting procedures. All of which will eliminate the financial confusion so frequently associated with church financial statements. The principles explained in this book can put your congregation's money picture into easy-to-understand layperson's language.

This is an accounting book, but it is a practical book, not just a theoretical book. It is a church accounting book; the first of its kind; a book that finally tells you how to control and manage your church's money efficiently, effectively, and according to generally accepted accounting procedures. It can be just about the most useful reference tool the congregational treasurer or anyone charged with the stewardship of the congregation's finances could possibly find.

Here, all in one volume, the *Complete Handbook of Church Accounting* puts together all the fragments of those systems (some good, some not so good) fre-

9

quently found in the back chapters of books on church finance and administration. Not just a few chapters are presented here, but an entire book about your congregation's financial record keeping system!

The accounting profession has never really defined what "generally accepted" accounting principles ought to be for churches. Consequently, every conceivable principle and system which is appropriate for churches has been described in this book. The *Complete Handbook of Church Accounting* eliminates the extraneous, codifies the essentials, and illustrates profusely and precisely just how your congregation can keep the best set of financial records possible—accurately, simply, completely. Without any loss of detail or recall capabilities, the systems you will read about in these 21 fact-filled chapters will make church accounting easier.

For example, just leaf through Chapters 13, 14, and 15. Here are three very carefully detailed church accounting systems. Nothing mysterious or complex about any one of them. One may be made to order for your congregation.

If you decide to use the first system, a formal fund accounting procedure, which is described in Chapter 13, you can turn out proper statements regularly, like clockwork—all debits and credits being equal (like any good accounting system), balance sheets carefully detailed for each fund, and nothing left to chance. It's a one-two-three system, adaptable by any parish. If your congregational treasurer has a knack for accounting (and most do!) and wants to do things properly, here's the complete, right-way system.

In Chapter 14, a second system is presented, equally as good but not as complex as the first, and those with a background in business organization accounting (profit making concerns) will find a familiar pattern. It's the usual debit-credit journals, ledgers, profit-loss statements, balance sheet, and so on system. It's not typical for churches (because they are non-profit), but for those so inclined, it works—even for churches. In fact, it's exactly the type of system you are most likely to inherit from the previous church bookkeeper. Since such a system is probably most familiar, it is the most frequent contender for first choice among church accounting systems. Yet, it is neither the most proper nor the least complicated system to use.

So, finally, there's a third, sort of a maverick, system, which is described in Chapter 15. Here's a method that will really take the rough edges off any congregation's financial record keeping and reporting procedures. From offering plate to audit, the system flows in exact and precise steps. Nothing is lost in the process, and all the pieces fit perfectly together. It's almost a fill-in-the-blanks method of doing the job.

Unlike either of the other systems, this third system requires no ledgers. There are only journals, and from them regular reports. It's the way to keep church financial records when you want a simple, unsophisticated method for keeping track of offerings and payments and then want to tell the membership where it's all come from and gone to.

So, this book is about church accounting, to be sure. But it is much more than just accounting principles and reporting methods. For example, it tells you how to apply those principles, how to keep the records, and how to report to the membership what's going on. The principles are important—of course they are —and they are carefully explained, but they are useful only as you put them to work in a good system. You'll also learn why it's important for two people to count the offering, why checks must be prenumbered, why no one signs checks in advance, and why a regular, consistent statement of assets, liabilities, and excess of revenues (or excess of disbursements, if that's the case) is important.

But even that's not all you will find in this book. You've really got to read through the whole book if you expect to utilize fully the system you've picked. There's not much point in going to all this record-keeping trouble if all you want to do is keep track of offerings and payouts and how much money is left over at month end. Your check book will (or it should) always tell you how much money is still in the treasury. An accounting system helps you analyze where all the money came from and how you used it, not just what happens to be left over after all the bills are paid. And then, it's how you go about reporting all of that which makes the difference. That reporting (and this book) will help you to clarify your impressions of what really happened last year and decide how to go about planning for next year.

So the concluding chapters offer all kinds of help in telling the membership just how things went. Church record keeping, no matter how sophisticated or simple the system, is a lost cause if you can't clearly and simply say how you are doing now, how you did last year, how things look in comparison to a year ago, or what you expect to happen considering what's gone on so far this year. Reporting is the way to tell the membership how it is with your church.

In the last chapters, therefore, you will find many suggestions on how to report and interpret the church's financial condition as revealed by your accounting system. There are aids here to make the seeming confusion of balance sheets logical and the frustrations of apparently meager "profits" encouraging. Financial reporting is as important as keeping the system. The one obviously comes before the other, but both are required for intelligent, meaningful church record keeping.

Even the annual audit is important. That's rather hard to understand when you consider the slip-shod way most church records are audited—a hand-picked committee of non-accountants thumbing through the cancelled checks and announcing that all is in order. But the audit is important, and in Chapter 18 you will find out how to make the audit procedure useful and meaningful for more effective church financial control.

Without good management and control, your system is doomed, no matter how good it is. The last chapter of the book explains how your church accounting system can be significantly improved through the right kind of administrative control. Good managers are needed in the church as well as in business enterprises.

An effective accounting system goes hand in hand with quality management. You will find out how it's done when you read Chapter 20.

This is a book of proven methods. It's a resource tool you will use over and over again. You may not even start reading at the beginning, although that's the best and logical place to begin to feel your way through the book. But once it is read, you will use it again and again for clarifying accounting transactions, using illustrative materials, improving your own system, or just finding out more about what church accounting is all about.

There's really no magic in any accounting system. But there can be confusion. The *Complete Handbook of Church Accounting* eliminates the confusion and resolves whatever mystery there may be. It makes the system work as it's supposed to work—for your church. In fact, this book will make the job of keeping your church's financial records a real joy.

So, read on, and you will be amazed at how the pieces of the church accounting puzzle all begin to fit together and how the job you have been elected to do may turn out to be much simpler than you ever imagined it could.

In sum, this book will do two things:

1. It will explain a church accounting system, and

2. It will suggest a way to report the results of the system.

And then, however you use this book, your congregation is bound to be better off for having had a more accurate system and a more intelligible report of what's gone on financially.

Manfred Holck, Jr.
Manfred Holck, Sr.

Table of Contents

Part One

Applying Proven Tools
And Techniques to a
Church Accounting System

Chapter One

Basic Principles and Routines: Necessary Procedures for Developing a Successful Church Financial Record Keeping System

There are more than 200,000 congregations in the United States —Protestant, Jewish, Roman Catholic—including your own. Membership in all of these groups is about 130 million people, including those who go to your church. And all of these congregations pour more than $5 billion into the economy annually by spending money on all kinds of projects and programs. And your congregation spent some of that money, too.

Typically these congregations are controlled by a church council, vestry, session, or official Board composed of leading citizens in the community, people who volunteer their time. The combined wealth and talent of those leaders is often impressive. Their influence in the community can often make a difference in the life of their congregations. Unfortunately, all of that experience is not always fully utilized by congregations. To the extent, however, that you can harness those abilities from your own members, you may dramatically improve the effectiveness of your congregation's outreach.

Many of those congregations, especially larger ones, employ staff, people who are paid for the services they render in keeping the church's program going. Except for the very smallest, every congregation typically has a pastor, usually a full-time employee of the congregation, paid for services rendered, expected to be the spiritual leader of the people.

There may be other employees who assist the pastor. Yet that pastor's ministry is supported most of all by all those volunteers who support and complement the work of ministry in that congregation.

All of these congregations, including your own, receive and spend money. Giving to churches in 1974, for example, was approximately $4.6 billion. And that money was spent on something, for not very much is traditionally saved or even kept for future projects. It was spent for goods and services and salaries and many benevolences.

All of this means that someone has to keep track of where all that money comes from and where it goes. A financial record keeping system of some kind must be utilized to do that. And someone must be assigned to do the work. The congregation's stewardship responsibility involves a proper accounting for and reporting of the financial activity of the church.

A person therefore is assigned that task. His title may be treasurer or financial secretary or something else. But someone is assigned the task; perhaps that is your job and that is why you are reading this book. With whatever title and whoever that person may be, familiarity with procedures for keeping church financial records is obviously going to be important. The purpose of this book is to help that person.

The Church Treasurer

Your church treasurer will normally be a volunteer already extremely active in the work of your church. Therefore, your church treasurer is probably quite familiar with what is going on in your congregation, how the money is collected, where it is supposed to go, and what kind of giving habits can be anticipated from the membership. Your church treasurer may or may not know very much about financial record keeping. Usually a business person is selected, typically an accountant is appointed. They would know. Often the treasurer does have an understanding of what is involved in keeping a set of financial records, sometimes not.

This book assumes only a limited accounting background. (This in no way is intended to insult you, if that's your job!) Of necessity it must. Treasurers of smaller congregations as well as of larger, well-financed congregations are expected to find assistance in these pages. But every reader comes to each chapter with a different understanding and experience. To assume too much competence may eliminate those readers whose congregations most desperately need some help in putting their finances in order. On the other hand, to assume too little competence by readers would only create a textbook of significant length but boring reading. A middle ground must be taken.

This book is therefore written on the assumption that your church treasurer, or whoever is charged with the stewardship of the congregation's funds, is a volunteer with little or no formal accounting background. To write otherwise would exclude the predominate majority of congregations and their treasurers.

Furthermore, we assume that your church treasurer is not an accountant, has no intention of ever sitting for the C.P.A. examination, but at the same time does understand something about the principles of church accounting and financial reporting or at least is eager to learn more.

In addition we assume that your church treasurer has been assigned the following responsibilities:

1. Keeping the congregation's financial records, corporate and individual.
2. Preparing meaningful and accurate financial reports.
3. Budgeting financial resources and needs.
4. Anticipating financial problems.
5. Managing, safeguarding, and maintaining the congregation's financial resources.
6. Complying, as required, with governmental reporting requirements.

1. Keeping financial records

Obviously your church treasurer is responsible for maintaining an accurate set of financial records for all money received, money spent, and money kept. In the smallest congregations the treasurer will do all of the work, keep all the records, make all the entries. Larger congregations may have a part-time bookkeeper or other volunteers who help keep the records. In the largest congregations an individual is probably hired to keep the books and do other clerical work as well.

But regardless of size, it is your treasurer's responsibility to see that accurate records are kept. The treasurer may do the job personally or hire others, but the point is that responsibility for those records is that of the treasurer. That requires at least a basic understanding of what bookkeeping is all about. It doesn't require a C.P.A. certificate. It does mean involvement, though, to make sure the records are being kept in good order. Probing, asking questions, suggesting change, these are all necessary if your volunteer treasurer with a hired staff is going to stay on top of the job.

The record keeping function is the responsibility of the treasurer, even if the work is done by others. A knowledge of what's involved is crucial. This book is an attempt to help in gaining that understanding for church treasurers.

2. Preparation of financial reports

Perhaps more important than any other responsibility, except for keeping accurate records, is your treasurer's responsibility for reporting the results of the congregation's financial activity. Unless accurate, timely, concise, understandable reports are prepared for the membership, the treasurer's work will be suspect and the stewardship of the congregation can be rightfully questioned. It is important to let the members of your congregation know how their money is being used.

Therefore, as your treasurer puts together a system or improves on the one you already have, the following characteristics of that system will be important to review.

Financial statements presented to your membership for reporting on the congregation's activities must be:

1) *Understandable.* Anyone taking the time to read your congregation's financial statements must be able to comprehend quickly and easily precisely just what has happened. Unfortunately, many church financial statements are simply too complicated or incomplete to give a true and inclusive record to the reader.

2) *Concise.* A lengthy detailed statement is almost worse than none at all. No one will understand it. Worse yet, a minute detail will be questioned and the thrust of the report wasted by conversation on inconsequential matters. Short, to the point, complete—such is the format of a useful statement.

3) *Inclusive.* Every activity, organization and function represented in dollars should be part of the report. The reader of your church's financial statements should be able to grasp the scope of your congregation's full range of programs without getting lost in the detail. No function or program or activity involving money must be deleted from the report. It is inclusive of the whole gamut of congregational activity—church, women, men, youth, church school, endowments, plant, benevolences, etc.

4) *Comparative.* Financial statements are generally meaningless without some base of comparison. A budget of the previous year's or month's activities, trends in other congregations, plans for future activities, percentages, these are all representative. A column of numbers with a total can be incomprehensible without a focal point for comparison.

5) *Timely.* Six months after the fact may just be too late to read a statement and take any meaningful action on it. Financial statements must be distributed to readers as soon as possible after the end of the period reported. Delays in taking corrective action could be disastrous.

Financial statements must communicate accurately what has happened. Your church treasurer cannot hide income or disguise expenses or bury facts. Straightforward, candid reporting is required—unbiased, factual, accurate. Every fund must be accounted for somehow, every donor satisfied that gifts given for specific or general purposes have been so used; in short, all income and all expenses must be accurately reported.

This is nothing more than you would discover in any business financial report. It must also be in every church financial statement you read as well. The part-time, temporary, and volunteer nature of your treasurer's job or even the inexperience of your treasurer are no excuse for a less than accurate and understandable report. Church financial reports must have the characteristics listed above. Again, this book should help your church treasurer achieve that goal.

Financial statements should communicate everything that readers need to know about the congregation in an understandable way in order for them to make required decisions. Are the statements so done that a person of normal intelligence without an accounting background who takes the time to study the report can understand it?

Too often a church board of professional business people will insist that the congregational financial statement should conform to the format of a business. That may be all fine and good if only business people were supposed to read and understand and take action on the report. But congregations involve people such as yourself, people from all walks of life, and all of them have a say in how their money is going to be used. They should be able to understand how it is being used as well. A church financial statement cannot be delivered in the traditional format of accountants. It simply won't be understood.

3. Budgeting financial resources

Another responsibility for your church treasurer is supervising the preparation of the church budget. That is more than just looking at last year's results, tacking on a cost of living percentage, and suggesting the total for spending next year. Budgets can be complex or rather simple, but they are supposed to be meaningful plans for charting the direction of your congregation's program next year and perhaps for years beyond that, too.

More will be said about budgets and their function in other chapters, but primarily they are a format for laying out where the money is coming from and how it will be spent. A budget approves a plan for programming based on available resources. It must be realistic, well planned, used, and anticipate the unexpected.

4. Anticipating financial problems

Another function of your church treasurer is to "out-guess" the experts and anticipate all the possible ways in which the congregation's money may be spent, whether planned or unplanned. Is the boiler ready to go out? Funds must be budgeted. Will costs for electricity go up again? Utility budgets must be advanced. Will the church lawnmower hold out for another year? Are church school supplies adequate? Will the curriculum change? Is the parsonage roof still in good shape? Your church treasurer, with the help of other members to be sure, must not only plan for the future, but forecast the future as well. A formidable job, to say the least!

5. Resource maintenance

Your congregation has assets which must be safeguarded and maintained; it is your treasurer's job to do so. Perhaps those assets are no more than the cash in the bank. If so, that too needs to be protected with proper controls over spending, depositing, and investing.

If your congregation has a building, then that is an asset that must also be protected. Your treasurer should make certain that insurance coverage is adequate, unexpired, and regularly increased to provide for inflation's boost in the cost of the replacement construction. A property committee will normally look after maintenance, but safeguarding the asset through insurance is your treasurer's responsibility.

Other investments need protection, too. Endowment funds must be adequately invested to protect principal and to earn income; certificates of deposits, shares of stock, bonds must all be kept under lock and key.

Internal control requires proper safeguards over the handling of cash, to be certain that unauthorized persons don't have access to funds, that the offerings are properly protected, counted, deposited, and that all temptation to misappropriate funds by any employee or member is carefully removed.

Excess cash may not be your congregation's "problem," but where seasonal offerings at Christmas and Easter exceed spending demands at those times, your treasurer must see that those funds are properly invested to secure maximum financial return in the meantime. As will be explained later, when all of the congregation's excess cash funds from all sources are combined, there may be opportunity to secure higher than usual rates of interest on investments. Your treasurer has the responsibility of gathering those funds and of putting them to work for the benefit of the congregation.

6. Governmental reporting requirements

Congregations, fortunately, are not exposed to a myriad array of reporting forms for the Federal government. In fact, at present, payroll reports are about the only governmental forms required from congregations. There are no income tax returns, not even informational returns. Quarterly Forms 941 or 941E plus the annual W-3, W-2, W-4 and 1099's are about all that is necessary for your church to be concerned with (plus any state or local forms). However, in Chapter 21, government reporting requirements, especially payroll reports, will be discussed more fully.

Thus, the treasurer's role in a congregation is substantially similar to that of a treasurer for a commercial enterprise. Accurate financial records must be kept and proper reports filed. Responsibilities do differ, however, from those of a business treasurer since congregational requirements for record keeping are in fact much less complicated, and the amount of activity often considerably less. Still, the techniques and responsibilities for proper accounting remain virtually the same no matter what the institution.

Stewardship vs. The Profit Motive

The basic difference between a business enterprise and your congregation is in their reason for being. The business must secure a profit to remain in business. Its income must always exceed its expenses, at least eventually, or more so than not. It can obtain cash through borrowings and sale of equities. It is responsible to no one except the owner for making a profit, and what it has to sell may or may not benefit the community.

Your congregation, on the other hand, exists to serve its membership and the community. Profit is not important, it is not even part of the reason for being. Instead, your congregation uses monies received for specific purposes designated by the donors. It intends to spend everything received and it must account to every donor with respect to the proper use of those gifts.

Thus, your congregation's cash flow, for example, is important. Your treasurer will always be concerned about cash balance because only if your congregation has cash available from gifts can it purchase goods and services and pay for the social responsibilities it has assumed in the community. Your treasurer will be concerned about the cash in every fund, received for whatever purpose, and will report on every gift and payment from all of them. Your congregation is accountable to every donor for every gift.

Consequently, your congregation's financial statements can be voluminous as every fund and special gift is accounted for. A business has only one fund, normally, money received from sales or services and disbursements required to gain those funds. A congregation, on the other hand, still has the responsibility to account to each donor and for each of several possible funds. It is not surprising therefore that congregational financial statements are often so complex compared with the relatively less complicated business summary of receipts and disbursements from operations.

Furthermore, there has been considerable discussion over the years about meaningful disclosure and comparability between commercial organizations, so that statements, formats, and accounting principles for businesses have been more clearly defined. Unfortunately, though, congregations have no common ground, no single set of principles, no one source of authoritative description of how to keep their financial records or report the results to interested readers or conform to any consistent comparative reporting technique.* Perhaps this book will offer guidelines toward that objective.

*However, see the AICPA final report on accounting principles and reporting practices for nonprofit organizations that are not covered by existing audit guides. This 1978 report includes suggested procedures for many nonprofit organizations, including religious organizations.

The primary difference between commercial accounting and church accounting is that one is interested in attaining a profit, the other in accounting for funds received. Yet that difference requires substantial modification of generally accepted business accounting techniques for church accounting purposes.

Accounting Differences Between Business and the Church

While there are many similarities between accounting procedures for business and congregations, accounting principles for churches do differ from those for commercial organizations in these important ways:

1. Cash vs. accrual accounting.
2. Fund accounting.
3. Fixed assets, depreciation.
4. Transfers between funds, appropriations for future projects, investment income.
5. Contributions, pledges.

Each of these differences are discussed fully in the next several chapters.

Chapter Two

A Church Accounting Primer:
An Introduction to Accounting Principles,
Techniques, and Procedures Useful for
Keeping Church Financial Records

If your congregational treasurer is an accountant or a bookkeeper or someone who knows the difference between a debit and a credit, that person may want to skip over this chapter.

But not every church treasurer is familiar with church accounting terminology or procedure, which, of course, is why we have written this book. Sometimes treasurers are drafted for the position because they were willing or had the time or had a knack with money or no one else would take the job, not because they knew anything about church accounting. This is a chapter for those treasurers (and other lay leaders) who know little or nothing about posting, footing, and balancing across, the difference between a balance sheet and an operating statement, not to mention what a debit or a credit really is.

If you have selected a willing volunteer as treasurer, someone more knowledgeable about selling cars or teaching high school English or singing cantatas than about accounting, this is the chapter for both of you (even if *you* are a C.P.A.)! This chapter will give your treasurer a basic understanding of what accounting is all about and you an understanding of what your treasurer must know to keep your congregation's records straight.

How to Keep the Debits Separate From the Credits

The starting point for any financial record keeping system is a clear understanding of what's a debit and what's a credit. Simply put, a debit (Dr.) is always an entry on the left side of an account, a credit (Cr.) is an entry on the right side.

Accounting systems use "accounts" for indicating the many increases and decreases that result from the exchange of values in a business transaction. Think of an apothecary balance. Both sides are in perfect equilibrium when there are no weights on either side. They are also in equilibrium when equal weights are placed on each side.

Thus, when all debits equal all credits in an accounting system, the system is said to be "in balance." If there is only one account, then the sum of all transactions on the debit (left) side are equal to the sum of all the transactions on the credit (right) side. If there are many accounts, each account may not necessarily be in balance between its own debits and credits, but the sum of all the debits in all of the accounts will be equal to the sum of all the credits in all of the accounts.

From a practical point of view, though, the net difference in each account between debits and credits will be either zero or a debit balance (if debit entries exceed credit entries) or a credit balance (if credit entries exceed debit entries). Then the sum of all those debit balances will be equal to the sum of all those credit balances and the accounts will be in balance.

Then, when transactions occur, an entry must be made in the appropriate accounts. For every transaction there must be at least one debit entry and one credit entry, each for the same amount. In complex entries, there may be only one entry on either side and many entries on the other side. But the sum of all the debits for any transaction must equal the sum of all the credits for the same transaction.

Accounts may be increased or decreased by debits and credits depending on the normal account balance. Thus:

Accounts	Normal Balance	To Increase	To Decrease
Assets	debit	debit	credit
Liabilities	credit	credit	debit
Fund Balance/Net Worth	credit	credit	debit
Income	credit	credit	debit
Expense	debit	debit	credit

Assets are things or values owned such as cash, land, buildings, furniture, receivables, stock certificates. Asset accounts are increased by debits, decreased by credits.

 Liabilities are values owed to others, such as notes payable, accounts payable, mortgages. These accounts are increased by credits, decreased by debits.

The Net Worth or Fund Balance accounts are the difference between assets and liabilities. To be solvent an organization must have more assets than liabilities, thus the Net Worth or Fund Balance account normally has a credit balance and is increased by credits, decreased by debits.

When income is received, the assets of the organization increase; so does the Net Worth. Thus, income accounts normally have credit balances and are increased by credits (thus in effect increasing Net Worth) and decreased by debits.

Expenses have exactly the opposite effect on the account balances as income. Money spent decreases assets and decreases Net Worth. Thus expenses are increased by debits and decreased by credits.

Now, putting all that together in an example, and using what accountants call "T" accounts, consider the following:

SAMPLE TRANSACTIONS AND THEIR ENTRIES TO "T" ACCOUNTS

Assume:

1. A $10,000 mortgage was secured.
2. Land was bought for $10,000.
3. Offerings received totaled $1,000.
4. A $100 desk was purchased.
5. A $200 utility expense bill was paid.
6. A $300 payment was made on the mortgage.

Debit Balance Accounts   Credit Balance Accounts

ASSETS   LIABILITIES

	Cash		
1)	10,000	10,000	2)
3)	1,000	100	4)
		200	5)
		300	6)

	Mortgage Payable		
6)	300	10,000	1)

FUND BALANCE

	Land	
2)	10,000	

Fund Balance	

Figure 2.1

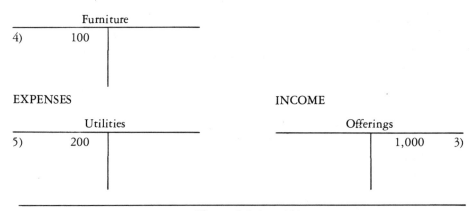

Furniture

4)	100	

EXPENSES

Utilities

5)	200	

INCOME

Offerings

		1,000	3)

Figure 2-1 (cont'd.)

All transactions assumed have been debited and credited to the appropriate accounts and keyed for identification. Debits are recorded on the left side of each "T" account, credits on the right side. Furthermore, the sum of all debit entries is equal to the sum of all credit entries. And the debit and credit balances of each account are likewise in balance.

TO VERIFY DEBITS AND CREDITS

Sum of Debits and Credits

Debits (Dr.)	Credits (Cr.)
$10,000	$10,000
1,000	100
10,000	200
100	300
200	10,000
300	1,000
$21,600	$21,600

Account Balances

	Debits		Credits
Cash	$ 400	Mortgage payable	$ 9,700
Land	10,000	Fund Balance	-0-
Furniture	100	Income	1,000
Expenses	200		
	$10,700		$10,700

Figure 2.2

Trial Balances

	Beginning		Closing Journal Entry		Ending	
Account	Dr.	Cr.	Dr.	Cr.	Dr.	Cr.
Cash	400				400	
Land	10000				10000	
Furniture	100				100	
Mortgage payable		9700				9700
Fund Balance		-0-	200	1000		800
Income		1000	1000			-0-
Expenses	200			200	-0-	
Totals	$10700	$10700	$1200	$1200	$10500	$10500

Figure 2-2 (cont'd.)

Notice that the Fund Balance account before adjustments and closing journal entries has no entries or balance. Recall that this account represents the difference between assets and liabilities, but it can only be used to show that value when entries are made to it. No entries are recorded from the original assumed transactions.

Income and expenses are neither assets nor liabilities. The income is not owned, although it has been earned; the expenses are not liabilities because they show an amount already paid on some debt. Thus the income and expenses can only represent part of the Net Worth or Fund Balance.

In order to prepare financial statements that accurately reflect the Net Worth or Fund Balance of the organization, an additional journal entry must be made. The income and expense accounts must be "closed" into the Net Worth or Fund Balance account with the following type of entry:

Journal Entry	Dr.	Cr.
Income	1000	
Net Worth/Fund Balance		1000
Net Worth/Fund Balance	200	
Expense		200

Various financial statements must be prepared once all of the transactions for the period have been recorded and necessary adjustments and closing entries prepared.

FINANCIAL STATEMENTS

Statement of Revenues, Disbursements & Transfers

Income	$ 1000
Expenses	200
Net Increase (Decrease)	$ 800

Balance Sheet

Assets		Liabilities	
Cash	$ 400	Mortgage Payable	$ 9700
Furniture	100	Fund Balance	
Land	10000	Net Worth/Fund Bal.	800
Total	$ 10500	Total	$ 10500

Changes in Fund Balance

Beginning balance	$ -0-
Additions: Income	1000
Deductions: Expenses	200
Ending Balance	$ 800

Figure 2.3

Obviously this is drastically simplified to what may be encountered in an actual situation. But understanding how the debits and the credits are utilized to keep the accounts straight is important.

In church accounting, as in any accounting function, it is important to produce complete, accurate, orderly and timely financial information required for the proper handling of receipts and disbursements, to provide church officials with the financial information needed to plan budgets and programs, and to keep the membership informed of the use of t heir contributions. These preliminary, although elementary, steps are the beginning of that process.

The method by which all of this is accomplished is the use of a series of record books, hence the phraseology "bookkeeping." The financial record books must be kept.

In the typical situation these will include the cash receipts journal, the cash disbursements journal, the general journal, and the general ledger. Journals are books of original entry. All transactions and changes are recorded in these books first. Then appropriate totals from the journals are posted or copied into the general ledger, the book of final entry.

Journal books are usually sheets of varying widths and numbers of columns bound into a notebook. The record of transactions is continuous in each journal in chronological order. Ledger books may also be single sheets bound into a book with each page used for an account. Ledger forms usually have three columns—for debit and credit entries and for a balance amount. Ledger sheets are kept permanently since they represent the permanent status of every account at specific periodic intervals in the life of the organization. A ledger record is an historical record of the financial activity of that account. Some accounts, such as cash, may have a great deal of activity; other accounts, such as land, may have only one entry for all the years that an organization is in operation.

In subsequent chapters of this book, these principles are followed. In fact, in order to understand the illustrations in some chapters, it is necessary to have this basic understanding of what record keeping is all about.

Obviously, only if careful records are kept of the congregation's financial transactions will the membership and others know what is going on. A good accounting system serves the needs of the members and all segments of the church. It helps members to be informed individually of their giving commitment and progress toward fulfilling that commitment. It reveals for the leaders of the congregation the relationship between the budget and income and expenses. It serves as a periodic reminder to the congregation of its mission and purpose for being. It reports income received, money spent. It is easy to understand and use by those responsible for keeping the records. And it produces reports that clearly reveal the congregation's financial activities, strengths, and weaknesses. Small or large congregations must adapt a system that suits them best, neither too complex for a simple transaction or too simple for a complex procedure.

And that continues to be the stated purpose of this book—to provide those illustrations and explanations of systems which offer any congregation alternative choices for developing a record keeping system best suited to their needs and the capabilities of those responsible for keeping the record books.

If you still don't know a debit from a credit, you had better go back to the beginning of this chapter and start out once more from there. Knowing the difference is critical to understanding church accounting and reading this book.

Chapter Three

Cash Basis vs. Accrual Basis Accounting:
Simplicity vs. Greater Accuracy:
How to Gain the Most From a Cash
Basis Accounting System

Business organizations almost always keep their records on an accrual basis while congregations invariably report their results on a cash basis. This chapter explains why.

Cash basis reporting records each transaction only as cash is received and paid out. Month-end results simply reflect cash received and cash spent. It's like your own checkbook. The cash you had at the beginning of the month, plus what you deposited during the month, less what you spent is your checkbook balance at the end. Accrual basis accounting, on the other hand, does the same, of course, but goes one step further. It also records amounts owed to others and due from others. It more accurately reflects the financial condition of the enterprise.

Since cash basis accounting is much less complicated, congregational treasurers often use that system rather than the accrual basis. Larger congregations, however, may use some sort of modified accrual basis simply to reflect a bit more accurately liabilities and/or anticipated gifts already pledged but not received. Smaller congregations will generally stick to a pure cash basis system. But it is important to understand the differences in order to know why record keeping and reporting may differ between commercial and church organizations.

For example, compare the two statements for Christ Church in Figure 3.1. One statement is on the cash basis, the other on the accrual basis.

CHRIST CHURCH
Statement of Income and Expenses
Twelve months ending December 31, 19__

	Cash basis	Accrual basis
Income:		
Offerings	$ 25,000	$ 25,000
Pledges due but not paid	-0-	1,000
Interest income	2,500	3,000
	$ 27,500	$ 29,000
Expenses:		
Salaries	$ 12,000	$ 12,500
Payroll taxes	700	720
Insurance premiums	600	900
Other costs	10,000	10,000
	$ 23,300	$ 24,120
Excess of income over expenses	$ 4,200	$ 4,880

Figure 3.1: Comparison of cash basis and accrual basis accounting systems financial reports.

CHRIST CHURCH
Balance Sheet
December 31, 19__

	Cash basis	Accrual basis
Assets:		
Cash	$ 3,000	$ 3,000
Pledges not yet paid	-0-	1,000
Interest receivable	-0-	500
	$ 3,000	$ 4,500
Liabilities:		
Accounts payable	$ -0-	$ 300
Payroll taxes payable	-0-	20
Salaries payable	-0-	500
	$ -0-	$ 820
Fund balance:	$ 3,000	$ 3,680
	$ 3,000	$ 4,500

Figure 3.2: Comparison of cash basis and accrual basis fund balance sheets.

As is obvious, the systems each give a different result because not all of the accrual basis transactions are cash transactions.

Pledges due during the year but not yet paid are considered income on the accrual basis even though the cash has not been received. Interest income due on securities and thus earned but not yet received is income on the accrual basis, but not on the cash basis. Salaries and payroll taxes due at the end of the month but not yet paid are expenses for accrual basis accounting even though no cash has been paid out. (If payday is Friday and the end of the month is Wednesday, wages earned through Wednesday are an expense even though they will not be paid until on Friday.) Insurance premiums are due but have not been paid.

As a result of all this, the cash basis and accrual basis fund balances are different, too. In theory the accrual basis is more appropriate because it more accurately reflects income and expenses for the current period. The cash basis statements make no mention of these potential assets and liabilities and thus would not accurately portray the true financial status of the fund. So, why use the cash basis method then if it is not as accurate?

When the Cash Basis Is Appropriate

The most significant advantage to the cash basis system is its simplicity. There is just no easier way to keep a set of financial statements, especially for non-accountant treasurers.

Since transactions are recorded only as cash is received or paid out, a check-book is often the only record needed. In fact, if check stubs are carefully kept and include all necessary information about checks and deposits, these plus a few files may be all a smaller congregation needs to keep its finances in order. In a cash basis system the checkbook is an entirely appropriate substitute for any other financial record. In some congregations it may be *the* system.

Even in larger congregations, however, a cash basis system may be used just because it is less complicated. In those congregations more than a checkbook may then be required because of the increased activity and potential complexity of the system, but transactions still are entered only as cash is actually received or paid out.

Look back at the illustrated comparison between cash and accrual basis financial statements. It is appropriate to ask, after reviewing such a comparison, what difference does it really make? In that situation will anyone do anything differently because the records are kept on a cash or accrual basis?

Well, accrual accounting, as indicated before, does state the financial position of a congregation much more accurately by reflecting bills due and unpaid pledges not yet collected. All costs and all income expected can be shown in the appropriate period. But what assurance is there that those pledges are really going to be paid? Of course, the bills will be paid, but the anticipated income may never show up. How reliable, therefore, is the accuracy of the accrual basis statement?

In time, whatever income the congregation expects to receive will probably be received, but is it worth the time and effort to record anticipated income, only to have some of it never materialize, thus requiring adjustments to income every year for the no-shows? Considering the extra effort and possible costs of an accrual system, a congregation must ask, is it worth the price to have statements that reflect not only cash transactions but also show promised income and unpaid liabilities?

Chances are, say the strongest advocates of a cash basis system for smaller congregations, that over the years the net effect on income is not material. Unrecorded income is collected the next year anyway, each year, and tends to offset any unrecorded income in that year. Unpaid bills are paid in each subsequent month. Thus, a consistent adherence to the cash system will probably produce comparative statements not materially different from those on an accrual system.

The Accrual Basis Is Useful, Too

The obvious disadvantage to the cash system, as was pointed out, is not reporting income not yet collected and bills not yet paid. When income and disbursements are recorded only when received or paid, pledged income due now but not yet received and unpaid bills on hand are simply not reflected on the financial statements, even though they are assets and liabilities of the congregation. Thus, the purpose and the advantage of accrual basis accounting is to record that income and those liabilities.

Where such amounts are insignificant to the financial statement accuracy, a cash basis system still offers the least complicated procedure. But where such uncollected income or unpaid bills might materially distort the financial statement, the accrual basis is obviously the more appropriate system of financial record keeping to use. For that reason congregations do use it, especially where the church treasurer is familiar with accounting techniques and procedures.

Also, as congregations realize the importance of using realistic budgets to control spending, accurate financial statements become even more crucial. Using a budget for this purpose is discussed in a subsequent chapter, but accrual basis accounting provides the actual income and spending data which is more useful for comparative analysis of month to month activity than is the cash basis.

Combinations, Modifications, and Reporting, Using Cash and Accrual Basis Systems

Where the accrual basis is considered important, congregations may modify a cash system to develop accurate financial statements on a full or modified accrual basis. For example, financial records can be kept on a cash basis but adjusted at the end of each period using a worksheet. Statements would be prepared directly from the worksheets on an accrual basis without changing the cash basis system of record keeping.

Or the accounting system itself can be modified to record some transactions on a cash basis, others on an accrual basis. Consistency from one period to the next is especially important then. For example, all other records can be kept on a cash basis except that unpaid bills can be recorded on the accrual basis without recording uncollected income. Or, a cash basis system can be used with unpaid bills totaled at the end of each month and entered into the records only then or by using a worksheet and not even recording the bills formally in a journal. But all unpaid bills on the last day of the month are payables and would appear on the balance sheet as liabilities even though they were paid on the first day of the next month.

Or the books can be kept open a few days after the end of the month with bills paid those five or six days considered costs for the previous month. Accounts payable would not appear on the balance sheet. Instead cash would be reduced. (That system may be acceptable for internal reporting, but would be inadequate for reports to banks or others.)

For most congregations the cash basis system of keeping financial records will be entirely adequate for the reasons cited. But a fair and more accurate method of record keeping is the accrual system. Where unpaid bills and uncollected income is not normally a material item at month or year end, a complete cash basis system is preferred simply because it is less complicated and much easier for the non-accountant to maintain.

Accrual accounting will be required if the true cost of programs is to be measured or comparisons to budget are an important part of financial planning. A tight budget cannot be adequately evaluated if all unpaid bills and anticipated income are not included in the financial statement. Furthermore, congregations which have an annual audit by a C.P.A. must use the accrual basis, or at least their financial statements must reflect accruals even if the records are not kept that way. Otherwise a qualified opinion would be required, as explained in a subsequent chapter.

CHRIST CHURCH
Statement of Income and Expenses
Worksheet—Cash to Accrual basis
For the year ended December 31, 19__

	Cash basis	Adjustments		Accrual basis
Income:				
Contributions-pledged	$ 50,000	$ 5,000	1.	$ 55,000
Other offerings	5,000			5,000
	$ 55,000	$ 5,000		$ 60,000

Figure 3.3: Worksheet for reporting operations on an accrual basis using a cash basis accounting system.

Expenses:

Salaries	$ 20,000	$	2,000	2.	
			(3,000)	2.	$ 19,000
Benevolences	10,000				10,000
Payroll taxes	600		20	3.	620
Insurance premiums	1,000		700	4.	
			(200)	4.	1,500
Other costs	20,000		1,000	5.	21,000
	$ 51,600	$	520		$ 52,120
Excess of income over exp.	$ 3,400	$	4,480		$ 7,880

Figure 3.3 (cont'd.)

CHRIST CHURCH
Balance Sheet
Worksheet—Cash to Accrual basis
December 31, 19__

	Cash basis	Adjustments		Accrual basis
Assets:				
Cash	$ 6,900			$ 6,900
Pledges receivable	-0-	$ 5,000	1.	5,000
	$ 6,900	$ 5,000		$ 11,900
Liabilities:				
Accounts payable	$ -0-	$ 3,700	2,4,5.	$ 3,700
Taxes payable	-0-	20	3.	20
	$ -0-	$ 3,720		$ 3,720
Fund balances				
Beginning	$ 3,500	$ (3,200)	2,4.	$ 300
Excess income over exp.	3,400	4,480		7,880
Ending	$ 6,900	$ 1,280		$ 8,180
	$ 6,900	$ 5,000		$ 11,900

Figure 3.4: Worksheet for converting cash basis accounting system balance sheet to accrual basis.

Explanation of adjustments in Figures 3.3 and 3.4.

1. Pledges due by December 31, but unpaid.

2. Wages earned but unpaid $2,000, wages paid this year but applicable to last year $3,000.

3. Payroll taxes due for this year but not yet paid.

4. Insurance premiums due this year $700, premiums paid this year but due last year $200.

5. Other unpaid bills due this year.

Chapter Four

Using Fund Accounting Techniques: How to Identify the Source and Use Of All Contributions, Gifts and Incomes

Fund accounting is unique to non-profit organizations such as churches, colleges, universities, and governmental units. It is not used in industry, business or by any organization interested in generating a profit. Because most business persons are so used to reading financial statements of commercial enterprises, they often have a difficult time understanding the use of fund accounting. Profit oriented readers will frequently insist that a congregation's financial records be kept the same way as their own business. To do so, however, is incorrect and can be misleading to members of a congregation.

What is fund accounting? (Subsequent chapters illustrate the principles of fund accounting in detail.) It is a system of financial record keeping in which separate records are kept to identify the source and use of all gifts restricted by donors. Unrestricted gifts are generally lumped together in one fund, but the system is such that there is an accounting for the use of all contributions and income. Financial statements will normally include a separate accounting, even separate balance sheets, for each fund or restricted gift.

Once the concept is understood there is really nothing difficult about fund accounting. Most congregations limit their record keeping to one fund anyway, but even with several funds, the entire report can be rather simple once the principles are understood. Your congregation has a responsibility to account for the use of gifts given by its many donors. It has a stewardship responsibility to use those funds in an appropriate way. A fund accounting system makes that process much less difficult.

For example: Contributions to your church building fund should be kept separate from funds donated for current operating expenses. You know that, and your members will insist that it be done. After all, the church building fund is a restricted fund, therefore accounting procedures must make certain that contributions are used for the purpose intended, that is, to build a building.

Or, your congregation may receive bequests or specific gifts for endowment purposes, that is, the income generated from the investment of those gifts is all that is available to your congregation to spend. A proper accounting must be made of the principal and the income to be sure that the original gift is not dissipated and that the income is used for the purpose designated. A separate endowment fund makes that accounting possible.

Or, members and friends contribute money to a memorial fund upon the death of someone they know. Such gifts are given for a specific purpose to a specific fund. A fund accounting system will provide an accounting of the use.

Thus, fund accounting is a way to keep track of gifts, to make certain donors' wishes are carried out, and to report in financial statements the source and use of all gifts received whether restricted or unrestricted. Furthermore, separate funds may be designated by your official Board for special projects from gifts without any restrictions. Fund accounting provides the means for reporting the use of such separately designated monies.

Typical funds used by congregations include these:

1. General Funds
2. Restricted Funds
3. Plant or Fixed Asset Funds
4. Endowment Funds
5. Board-Designated or Quasi-Endowment Funds

General Fund

Your congregation may call this fund by a different name, such as, current fund, unrestricted fund, operating fund, all of which mean the same kind of fund. The purpose of a General Fund is to accumulate and account for all unrestricted gifts. Generally all financial transactions for your congregation will be recorded in this fund unless you have some kind of restricted gifts. Then another fund would have to be used also.

If your congregation receives none or very few restricted gifts, fund accounting may be limited to just one fund in which a separate accounting of the restricted gifts is also noted.

But the General Fund is that fund which pays all operating bills, salaries, utilities, etc. It also receives the offerings and is always the principal fund for any congregation using a fund accounting system.

Restricted Funds

A Memorial Fund, an Altar Fund, a Kitchen Fund, a Lawnmower Fund, these are typical restricted funds. A donor gives a gift expecting it to be used to purchase a specific item or pay for a specific program. With fund accounting a separate fund is created to account for the use of this gift.

Since your congregation may receive gifts for many specific purposes, it is not practical to have a different fund for each gift. Thus all such special gifts are placed together in one restricted fund. An accounting must still be maintained for each gift, but this is done much more efficiently within the framework of one special Restricted Fund.

Most restricted gifts are for some particular purpose, project, or program in addition to the normal activities of the congregation. Such restricted gifts must be so used. But a building fund program requiring many gifts and being a very specific part of the congregation's ongoing program may well be kept separate from the many smaller special interest restricted gifts. A building fund, therefore, may properly be a restricted fund all its own into which all building fund contributions must be placed and from which all payments for a building are disbursed.

Plant Funds

Congregations which insist on recording the cost of fixed assets will probably use a Plant Fund or Fixed Asset Fund or Land and Building Fund or some such. Since such assets may not be considered available for the general use of the congregation (that is, they must be used for worship or education and cannot be sold without congregational action), they are put into a separate fund and so designated. Additions to and deductions from such funds are then carefully and accurately accounted for. Contributions received for additions or improvements to the building facilities would be recorded in this account rather than the general fund. A separate capital improvements budget for the Plant Fund may even be established separate from the ongoing general operating fund budget.

While fixed assets are generally not restricted as to use by any specific donor, a separate accounting in a Plant Fund may be helpful simply to keep an historic record of the cost of the church building.

A separate Plant Fund for a congregation however may not really be practical. Historic costs are not particularly significant for accounting purposes. If depreciation is taken (and arguments against taking depreciation in a congregation are listed in a subsequent chapter), a separate fund confuses the matter and complicates the record keeping. Most readers will simply not comprehend the use or significance of a separate Plant Fund. Few congregations, except the very largest, will benefit from the use of such a fund in their accounting system.

Endowment Funds

Whenever the term "Endowment Fund" is used, it refers to gifts received which have been so restricted that only the income generated from the principal can be used. A congregation receives a $50,000 bequest, for example, with the stipulation that the income from the fund be used to provide scholarships for members preparing for the ministry. That is an endowment fund.

A large gift given to a congregation to be used for construction of a new church building is not an endowment fund gift since the entire gift is to be used for a specific purpose. It is a restricted gift. Income generated by the principal of that gift, until it is used to pay for a building, will also be restricted for use in the same building project.

An endowment gift to support the salary of a minister of visitation, for example, is an endowment fund gift. The income from the fund will be a restricted fund item to pay for the salary.

Thus your congregational treasurer must determine what is an endowment fund gift and then be certain that principal and income from those funds are used only for the purposes intended. Fund accounting provides the means for keeping all of that record keeping in order.

Gifts to the Endowment Fund will all have legal restrictions that prevent any alteration of use by the official Board of your congregation or even by the congregation itself. Gifts received which permit discretionary use by the official Board or the congregation are not endowment funds, but general funds.

Board-Designated Funds

Quasi-Endowment or Board-Designated Funds are those monies which the official Board has specifically set aside for purposes of its own choosing. Since the Board can reverse its decision and use the funds for any other purpose as well, such funds are not endowment funds nor restricted funds. They are still general funds, but for one reason or another the Board has set them aside for its own purpose to be used as it designates.

Such funds could just as well remain in the general fund, thus simplifying record keeping significantly. If such funds are set aside, though, to be invested so they will earn income while awaiting use in some special project, a savings account would accomplish the same purpose very well, all still in the general fund, and without the necessity of setting up a special fund.

Fund accounting is difficult enough to comprehend. Complicating the issue by adding an additional and unnecessary fund seems inappropriate, though it can certainly be done. But such a fund carries no specific restrictions and the Board is accountable only to itself (or to the congregation if the fund was in fact established by congregational action) for the fund's use. Such funds can be transferred back to the general fund at any time for any purpose. Thus, maintaining the funds in the general account can offer equal protection and separation, but with less complication than in a special separate Quasi-Endowment Board-Designated fund.

While Figure 4.1 is an extremely simple example of financial statements for a fund accounting system, it can be seen quite quickly that a proliferation of funds

---

ST. JOHN'S CHURCH
Statement of Income, Expenses and Transfers
For the year ending December 31, 19—

General Fund

Income: Contributions	$ 50,000	
Investment income (from endowments)	5,000	$ 55,000
Expenses: Salaries	$ 20,000	
Administration	28,000	
Maintenance	5,000	
Other costs	5,000	58,000
Excess of expenses over income		$ (3,000)
Fund balance, beginning, Jan. 1	$ 8,000	
Transfers to other funds	(1,000)	7,000
Fund balance, end of year, Dec. 31		$ 4,000

Restricted Funds

Income: Contributions	$ 6,000	
Investment income (from endowments)	800	$ 6,800
Expenses: Altar flowers	$ 500	
Pastor's discretion	200	
Other expenses	1,500	2,200
Excess of income over expenses		$ 4,600
Fund balance, beginning, Jan. 1	$ 1,000	
Transfer from other funds	1,000	2,000
Fund balance, end of year, Dec. 31		$ 6,600

Figure 4.1: Example of typical operating and balance sheet statements for a fund accounting system. NOTE: In order to avoid confusion in the use of terms, the word "income" is used throughout this book for all receipts, revenues, and other sources of income received, except transfers. The word "expenses" is used generally to include all costs, disbursements, expenditures, expenses or other outflows of funds, except transfers.

Endowment Fund

Income: Contributions	$ 10,000	
Investment income*	2,000	
Gain on sale of investments	1,000	$ 13,000
Expenses: Administrative costs		200
Excess of income over expenses		$ 12,800
Fund balance, beginning, Jan. 1		50,000
Fund balance, end of year, Dec. 31		$ 62,800

*Income restricted for specified term for addition to Endowment Fund rather than general use.

ST. JOHN'S CHURCH
Balance Sheet
December 31, 19___

General Fund

Assets: Cash	$ 3,000
Pledges receivable	1,000
	$ 4,000
Fund Balance:	$ 4,000

Restricted Funds

Assets: Cash	$ 7,400
Liabilities: Scholarships payable	$ 800
Fund Balance:	6,600
	$ 7,400

Endowment Fund

Assets: Cash	$ 2,800
Securities (market $62,500)	60,000
	$62,800
Fund Balance:	$62,800

Figure 4.1 (cont'd.)

and transfers between funds could complicate an already complex accounting system rather drastically. Thus congregations using fund accounting will want to limit the number of funds and the transfers or borrowings between funds.

Too much detail in a fund account statement will also only confuse readers. It is easy enough to follow the activity in the illustration, but a full year's activity in an average congregation could involve many transactions and many accounts. It will be necessary, therefore, for your treasurer to take extra precautions, if this system is used, in preparing a set of financial statements that will be understandable, particularly with a large number of accounts. Obviously, for your treasurer, yourself, and other members of your congregation, knowing what to look for and how to follow transfers between funds is important to an understanding of what fund accounting statements are all about.

The illustrated statements are typical of fund accounting financial reports. Accountability for each fund is clearly shown, even though a clear picture of the total activity is a bit difficult to determine without a careful analysis, as noted in the previous paragraphs. But the principal advantage of fund accounting is the ability to show the activity in each fund separately and clearly.

If your church treasurer used this system this way, then every church member should be able quickly and easily to determine precisely what has happened with current contributions, special restricted contributions, and the congregation's Endowment Funds. And that's what your congregation's financial statements are supposed to tell.

Relationships between funds is obvious, also. The use of Endowment Fund income, as required by donors, is clearly reported. In the example, income restricted to scholarships is so designated and listed as a liability of the restricted fund. Income available to meet current operating expenses is all included in the General Fund statements including investment income from endowment gifts intended for that purpose. As will be explained later, a transfer is not involved because the income is unrestricted and thus was never part of the Endowment Fund, although the principal clearly is.

The General Fund statements thus report that contributions and other income were inadequate to meet the costs of the program this year. Fortunately a healthy fund balance from the previous year provided the additional funds needed to care for this year's program. Nevertheless, the congregation had anticipated income from the endowment fund to help meet those costs, at least in part. A transfer was made to Restricted Funds for some special purpose.

Investment income from endowments which is restricted to use for scholarships is shown as income for the Restricted Fund, not the Endowment Fund. While Endowment Fund investments may have generated that income, the income is not for endowments, but for scholarships, a restricted purpose. Thus it appears in that fund's statements. Furthermore, since the scholarships are apparently not yet paid, the Balance Sheet for the Restricted Funds shows a payable amount reflecting the fund's liability and commitment to that purpose. Recipients have been selected, perhaps, but for whatever reason, funds have not been disbursed.

It is one thing to report the financial activity of a congregation, it is another to communicate what went on. Unless these statements also accomplish the latter objective, the report will not have achieved its purpose. As accurate as a financial statement may be, unless it is simple enough for the members of a congregation to read, it cannot be used by the membership to make intelligent decisions on future action, much less to know what has gone on in the past.

Chapter Five

How to Simplify Church Accounting: Don't Record Fixed Assets And Don't Use Depreciation *

There is considerable difference of opinion on how to account for a congregation's purchase of land, buildings, and equipment and then whether or not to take depreciation. Some church treasurers will insist on capitalizing all assets, others don't record the purchase at all, except to pay for it. Some treasurers insist on taking depreciation with or without funding, others ignore the matter entirely. The question is indeed one where accounting principles for congregations can be quite different from those for commercial enterprises and yet be entirely correct.

The problem arises because a congregation and a commercial enterprise purchase assets for different reasons and finance those purchases in quite different ways. Your congregation, for example, will go out among the membership to raise money to pay for a building it needs. A business, on the other hand, will likely borrow money to build and then sell enough merchandise or services to pay for it. If income from sales is inadequate to pay for the building and the cost of operations, the company goes bankrupt. Your congregation, though, has its building mostly paid for probably. It does not need to worry about selling merchandise to pay the costs.

Thus depreciation becomes important for the business in order to recover the costs of that building as a charge against future income. Since congregations don't finance their buildings that way, there is really no need to match income and expenses with respect to the purchase of a building. It is quite unnecessary for your congregation to be concerned with depreciation.

*Adapted from *Church and Clergy Finance,* Vol. 6, No. 14 ("Is Depreciation Appropriate in Church Accounting?" by Manfred Holck, Jr.), published by Ministers Life Resources, Minneapolis, MN, used with permission.

Furthermore, to depreciate a church building built many years ago and obviously worth much more now than then (at least more expensive to replace now) seems somewhat ridiculous to many. Also, to take depreciation on a building (thus charging current income) which was paid for with contributions would seem to some as a double charge. For what purpose is the charge than? If, however, depreciation is also funded with money set aside for replacement, then it might be justified.

Furthermore, from our point of view, there seems to be no real purpose achieved by recording fixed assets at all. Where a plant fund is in use, it can be done, of course, but it complicates the accounting process. Normally, a congregation will raise money to build a building, borrow some to pay the balance and perhaps even set aside certain current funds to pay for the costs. Once paid for, though, the mortgage will be amortized out of current or building fund offerings. But the cost of the asset as an asset is not important to the congregation (its value is important for insurance purposes, however).

The status of a congregation's various fund balances requires an accounting, but not the cost of assets already paid for. Obviously, there is no unanimity on how assets and depreciation are to be recorded, if they should be at all. But let us suggest a way that seems best and least complicated for your congregational treasurer to use if you decide that assets should be recorded in a Plant Fund and depreciation taken.

Recording Fixed Assets

Your congregation may follow one of several ways of handling the purchase of fixed assets and accounting for the cost. You may write the cost off entirely against income as expenses (which is the way you have probably been doing things), capitalize the costs by recording them as assets instead of expenses, or write the cost off against income and also capitalize.

The least complicated method, as suggested above, is just to pay for the asset out of income as an expense and neither capitalize the assets nor bother with depreciation. That has the advantage of being very easy to record and understand. Furthermore, the balances of your congregation's various funds continue to represent cash and liquid assets, assets you can use. Since the cost of buildings cannot be converted into cash (unless you sell the building, which is not likely), their value has no importance to funding the congregation's program. Expensing the cost of assets, therefore, is sufficient.

The primary disadvantage to this procedure is that the cost of that asset will not appear anywhere on the congregation's financial statements after the year of purchase. Furthermore, writing the cost of buildings and improvements off against income tends to fluctuate income and expenses rather drastically, making realistic year-to-year comparisons difficult.

CHRIST CHURCH
Statement of Income and Expenses
For the year ended December 31, 19__

General Fund

Income: Contributions	$ 50,000
Expenses: Building remodeling	$ 10,000
Other costs	45,000
	$ 55,000
Excess of income over expenses	$ (5,000)

Building Fund

Income: Contributions	$ 50,000
Expenses: Cost of new building annex	$ 150,000
Excess of income over expenses	$(100,000)

CHRIST CHURCH
Balance Sheet
December 31, 19__

General Fund

Assets: Cash	$ 7,000	Fund Balances:	
		Beginning, Jan. 1	$12,000
		Excess of expenses	
		over income	5,000
		Ending, Dec. 31	$ 7,000

Building Fund

Assets: Cash	$ -0-	Fund Balances:	
		Begin, Jan. 1	$100,000
		Excess of expenses	
		over income	100,000
		End, Dec. 31	$ -0-

Figure 5.1: Financial statements with fixed assets expensed and not capitalized.

In Figure 5.1 a current fund surplus at the beginning of the year was actually used to pay for the remodeling of the existing church building. But a comparison with last year's income might show a much larger amount than this year because of the special effort to raise funds for the remodeling. Expenses this year will obviously be more than last year and probably more than next year, too, because of the remodeling costs.

The building fund has over the years apparently accumulated funds for the new building annex, so while expenses exceeded income for the current year, the previous balance was actually used to help pay for the building. The Balance Sheet shows nothing left in the Building Fund and only the current balance in the General Fund. There is no record of the cost of the new building or the remodeling shown on the Balance Sheet at December 31.

A second method of recording the transactions for the purchase of fixed assets is simply to capitalize the cost. Instead of expensing the cost of the building it is recorded as an asset. Using the facts of the previous example, the operating statement and balance sheet will now appear as in Figure 5.2

Obviously, the asset value for the existing building, $500,000, must now also be shown on the Balance Sheet. No expense appears in the current operations for the new building or the remodeling, only a transfer of funds. The cost is capitalized in the Plant Fund.

The main advantage to this procedure is that the cost of all assets is now

---

CHRIST CHURCH
Statement of Income, Expenses and Transfers
For the year ending December 31, 19___

	General Fund	Building Fund	Plant Fund
Income: Contributions	$ 50,000	$ 50,000	$ -0-
Expenses: Other costs	$ 45,000	-0-	-0-
Excess of income over expense	$ 5,000	$ 50,000	-0-
Transfers	(10,000)	(150,000)	$160,000
Excess of transfers over income and expense	$ (5,000)	$(100,000)	$160,000

CHRIST CHURCH
Balance Sheet
December 31, 19___

Assets: Cash	$ 7,000	-0-	$ -0-
Old building & land			500,000
New building annex			150,000
Remodeling			10,000
	$ 7,000	-0-	$660,000

Figure 5.2: Financial statements showing capitalization of fixed assets.

Fund balances:

Beginning, Jan. 1	$ 12,000	$ 100,000	$500,000
Excess of transfers over income	(5,000)	(100,000)	
Transfers from other funds			160,000
End, Dec. 31	$ 7,000	$ -0-	$660,000

Figure 5.2 (cont'd.)

shown on the Balance Sheet each year. Any member therefore can tell at a glance the cost of buildings, land, and equipment. However, the Balance Sheet amount does not necessarily reflect the value of those assets. And that is a principal disadvantage of the procedure.

Fair market value, if available, could also be listed by footnote and for insurance valuation purposes. If your treasurer is accustomed to reading business financial reports, it is likely that capitalization of fixed assets costs will be suggested as the appropriate procedure for your congregation. The method does lend itself to taking depreciation.

The primary disadvantage to this procedure is confusion by readers because of the added complexity of the statements and misunderstandings about the function of transfers.

A third method is to combine the previous two systems into one. The advantage of that is to show the payment for the cost as part of the operations for the year as well as to maintain an historical cost record. Such a system however is not an acceptable accounting procedure, and depreciation would be impossible since costs have already been written off against assets.

CHRIST CHURCH
Statement of Income and Expenses
For the year ended December 31, 19__

	General Fund	Building Fund	Plant Fund
Income: Contributions	$ 50,000	$ 50,000	
Expenses: Building remodeling	10,000		
Building construction		150,000	
Other costs	45,000		
	$ 55,000	$ 150,000	
Excess of income over expense	$ (5,000)	$(100,000)	-0-

Figure 5.3: Example of financial statements of a congregation where fixed assets are written off and capitalized.

CHRIST CHURCH
Balance Sheet
December 31, 19___

Assets: Cash	$ 7,000		
Land & buildings (old)			$500,000
Remodeling			10,000
New building			$150,000
	$ 7,000	-0-	$660,000

Fund Balances:			
Beginning, Jan. 1	$ 12,000	$ 100,000	$500,000
Excess of income over expense	(5,000)	(100,000)	
Building and improvements capitalized			160,000
	$ 7,000	$ -0-	$660,000

Figure 5.3 (cont'd.)

Figures 5.1, 5.2, and 5.3 all report the use of separate funds for current operating funds, plant funds, and building funds. Figure 5.4 shows how financial statements would appear with only one fund when fixed assets are accounted for in

CHRIST CHURCH
Statement of Income and Expenses
For the year ended December 31, 19___

	Procedures for recording fixed assets		
	Expense on purchase	Capital- ization	Expense and capital- ization
Income: Contributions	$ 50,000	$ 50,000	$ 50,000
Building Fund	50,000	50,000	50,000
	$ 100,000	$100,000	$ 100,000
Expenses: Remodeling	$ 10,000	$ -0-	$ 10,000
New building annex	150,000	-0-	50,000
Other costs	45,000	45,000	45,000
	$ 205,000	$ 45,000	$ 105,000
Excess of income over expense	$(105,000)	$ 55,000	$ (5,000)

Figure 5.4: Financial statements for congregation with only one fund with fixed assets recorded in three different ways.

CHRIST CHURCH
Balance Sheet
December 31, 19___

Assets: Cash	$ 7,000	$ 7,000	$ 7,000
Land & bldgs. (old)		500,000	500,000
New buildings		150,000	150,000
Remodeling		10,000	10,000
	$ 7,000	$667,000	$ 667,000
Fund balances:			
Beginning, Jan. 1	$ 112,000	$612,000	$ 612,000
Excess of income over expenses	(105,000)	55,000	(5,000)
Building costs capitalized	-0-	-0-	60,000
	$ 7,000	$667,000	$ 667,000

Figure 5.4 (cont'd.)

different ways. The one fund approach is probably the least difficult to understand and the easiest to use. Separate funds are useful when large amounts are involved or more complicated accrual basis accounting is used or simply because of the personal preference of your treasurer.

Cash basis congregations will simply find the immediate expense or write-off approach the least complicated procedure when fixed assets are purchased. It may also be the best understood. Accrual basis systems and larger congregations would capitalize assets. No system should use the third suggestion as illustrated in Figure 5.3 for the reasons previously cited. If members of your congregation are to understand financial statements, then your treasurer should use the least complicated method possible to convey congregational financial activity to the membership.

In any event, small costs should be expensed anyway, say equipment items costing less than $100 or $500. It is much easier to do things that way than to try to keep track of the many smaller equipment items your congregation may purchase from time to time.

Recording Depreciation

There is virtually no good reason that we know of for your congregation to be concerned with recording depreciation on financial statements. And that's true even if you use the accrual method of accounting and capitalize your fixed asset costs anyway. The only reason a congregation might consider using depreciation is that the church treasurer or some business man in the congregation is familiar with depreciation and thinks it must be done here, too. When expenses must be matched against income, as in a commercial business activity, depreciation makes sense (it's important for tax purposes, too). But a congregation is not in the business to make a profit. It must match contributions against budgeted expenses, to be sure, but depreciation serves no useful purpose to accomplish those objectives.

Furthermore, your congregation probably paid for its buildings through special fund raising activities aimed at securing the cash needed to build. Even replacement or remodeling of those facilities may be done by raising more money from donors. You simply don't need a depreciation charge to recover costs from future contributions.

Depreciation has nothing to do with a decline in the value of an asset, although some people associate the term with that valuation. Furthermore, to depreciate an asset which has increased in value, as have most church buildings, makes little sense either.

Finally, and perhaps of most importance to your church treasurer, recording depreciation for a congregation can be complicated and confusing. It seems to us that if it's not required and serves no particularly useful financial purpose, depreciation may as well not be considered.

It might be argued that depreciation must be taken to show the cost of assets. Otherwise readers may never know the true costs of their building or equipment. If your congregation wanted to keep income down and make the costs of a program more realistic with respect to facilities used, depreciation would do that.

Depreciation does help in keeping the pattern of spending level from year to year. As noted, expensing the full cost of assets could create significant spending variations from one year to the next. Years with large costs for equipment would be unrealistic in comparison to total costs in years when equipment purchases were low. By capitalizing the costs and then depreciating them, your treasurer would be able to show a more level cost of operations.

When accrual methods of accounting are used in commercial enterprises, depreciation is a required procedure. Some argue that the same rule should be applicable for churches. However, we still know of no valid reason why any congregation needs to bother with the complexities of taking depreciation. Of course, it may be done, but no useful purpose, it seems to us, is accomplished by doing so.

It may be desirable, of course, for your congregation to fund the replacement of existing assets. Certainly efforts will be taken to raise money for new projects and even for replacements, but it is possible to fund replacements without too much accounting difficulty and without taking depreciation. Figure 5.5 shows a procedure that can be used both to record depreciation, if that still seems to be a congregation's desire, and/or fund replacement costs. Depreciation is charged as an expense against the General Fund in the operating statement. When a separate

Plant Fund is maintained, thus adding to the complexity of the accounting function, then the depreciation charge is appropriate against that fund by a transfer from the Plant Fund to the General Fund. Furthermore, if depreciation is to be funded for replacing the costs of the assets, funds must be transferred to the Plant Fund from the General Fund. Each transaction will cancel the other.

FIRST CHURCH
Statement of Income and Expenses
For the year ending December 31, 19__

	General Fund	Building Fund	Plant Fund
Income: Contributions	$ 50,000	$ 50,000	$ -0-
Expenses: Other costs	$ 41,000		
Depreciation	5,000		
	$ 46,000		
Excess of income over expense	$ 4,000	$ 50,000	$ -0-

FIRST CHURCH
Balance Sheet
December 31, 19__

Assets: Cash	$ 16,000		
Investments		$ 150,000	
Savings account for replacement of assets			$ 5,000
Land & Buildings			550,000
less: Reserve for Depreciation			(25,000)
	$ 16,000	$ 150,000	$ 530,000
Fund balances:			
Begin, Jan 1	$ 12,000	$ 100,000	$ 530,000
Excess of income for expenses	4,000	50,000	
Transfer to Plant Fund	(5,000)		5,000
Depreciation transfer from Plant Fund	5,000		(5,000)
	$ 16,000	$ 150,000	$ 530,000

Figure 5.5: Financial statement with several funds, assets capitalized, separate plant fund maintained, depreciation taken and funded.

Thus, in the changes in fund balance of the General Fund these items must be shown: excess of income over expenses which increases the fund, transfer of funds (cash) to a savings account in the Plant Fund for a decrease in the General Fund, and transfer of the depreciation cost to the Plant Fund thus increasing the General Fund balance.

Changes in the Plant Fund correspond with an increase in the fund for the cash to a savings account for replacement of assets and a decrease for the depreciation change. The Balance Sheet will show these changes as well as a Reserve for Depreciation for depreciation charges.

An examination of Figure 5.6 will quickly reveal how one fund can simplify the accounting process. The combined statement of income and expenses reveals an excess of $54,000 in income over expenses. Depreciation for $5,000 has been charged. The fund balance as noted is simply increased by that excess.

FIRST CHURCH
Statement of Income and Expenses
For the 12 months ending December 31, 19—

Income: Contributions		$ 100,000
Expenses: Other costs	$ 41,000	
Depreciation	5,000	46,000
Excess of income over expenses		$ 54,000

FIRST CHURCH
Balance Sheet
December 31, 19—

Assets: Cash		$ 16,000
Savings account for replacement of assets		5,000
Investments—Building Fund		150,000
Land & Buildings	$ 550,000	
less: Reserve for Depreciation	25,000	525,000
		$ 696,000
Fund Balance:		
Beginning, Jan. 1		$ 642,000
Excess of income over expenses		54,000
		$ 696,000

Figure 5.6: Financial statements with only one fund, depreciation expensed, replacement of assets funded, assets capitalized.

Assets are listed, too, taking into account the depreciation charge and the funding of replacement costs. The Reserve for Depreciation reflects accumulated depreciation. Total cash of $21,000 has been divided so that a separate $5,000 savings account has been established to provide future funds for replacement of assets.

If depreciation must be taken or replacement costs provided, these procedures suggest a way to get the job done.

Depending on how you handle the recording of fixed assets, you may or may not want to record depreciation. If assets are expensed in full with a total write-off when purchased, depreciation cannot be taken although a replacement fund can be established. If assets are capitalized, then depreciation may be taken to reflect costs against future income. Replacement funding is also possible. If assets are expensed and capitalized, depreciation is not possible although funding can still be recorded.

But the whole question of depreciation should be removed from church accounting consideration for all the reasons cited above. It can be done, of course, as shown, and your treasurer may still consider the procedure necessary, but it does complicate the recording process and it may unnecessarily confuse those who are interested in knowing how their congregation's finances are progressing. Depreciation actually serves no real useful purpose in church accounting.

Chapter Six

Precautions:

Avoiding Transfers Between Funds, Funding Future Projects and Recording Investment Income Properly

Yet another area of difference between congregational and commercial organization accounting principles and procedures relates to recording transfers between funds, making appropriations for future projects, and using capital gains and losses (realized or unrealized) as investment income.

Transfers Between Funds

Treasurers of congregations which elect to use a formal fund accounting system with more than one separate fund, must be familiar with procedures for recording transfers between those funds. Transfers will be equipped, for example, if general funds are to be placed in plant funds (such as with funding depreciation) or for investment in a Board-Created Quasi-Endowment Fund. Examples of transfers have already been shown in previous illustrations.

But the indiscriminate or incorrect use of transfers by your treasurer would be very confusing and actually misleading to members of your congregation. This is particularly true in the transfer of funds between the General Fund and the Endowment Fund, as will be shown.

Normally, transfers between funds must be shown either in a Statement of Income, Expenses and Transfers or on the Balance Sheet changes in fund balance section. Transfers should not be shown as part of income or expenses since they affect only fund balances.

To show transfers on a financial statement otherwise is simply misleading. Your church treasurer's objective in preparing financial statements is to show the members what has happened, financially, over the past year. And that presentation is to be made in as simple a way as possible. Unless the membership understands what has happened, there is little point in going to all the trouble of preparing a statement.

Thus, transfers, to be shown for what they are, are not included either as income or expenses, but as a change in fund balance. For example, the transfer of excess General Fund monies to a special fund is not an expense to the General Fund or income to the Special Fund. It is a transfer of funds which were originally recorded as income in the General Fund Statement of Income, Expenses and Transfers.

Depending on the type of financial statements that your treasurer prefers, transfers may be shown in several ways providing they are not misleading to your members. Figures 6.1 and 6.2 show acceptable procedures.

FIRST CHURCH
Statement of Income, Expenses and Transfers
For the year ending December 31, 19___

	General Fund	Special Fund	All Funds
Income: Contributions	$ 50,000		$ 50,000
Expenses: All costs	45,000		45,000
Excess of income over expenses	$ 5,000		$ 5,000
Transfers to Special Fund	(4,000)	$ 4,000	-0-
Excess of income after transfers	$ 1,000	$ 4,000	$ 5,000

Figure 6.1: Reporting transfers on a Statement of Income, Expenses, and Transfers when Balance Sheet statement of changes in fund balances is not used.

Most readers of financial statements will look first at the bottom line, but this may or may not be the correct figure to read in order to get a picture of what has happened. In Figure 6.1 it is obviously the wrong amount to look at to determine the congregation's progress. The results of the period's activities are on the line "Excess of Income over Expenses" and not on the last line.

A better presentation of the facts is shown in Figure 6.2. The bottom line in the statement of operations is in fact the result of the period's activities. A careful reading of the Balance Sheet, especially the changes in fund balances section, will reveal for the reader additional important information as to the use of those excess funds.

FIRST CHURCH
Statement of Income, Expenses and Transfers

For the year ending December 31, 19___	General Fund	Special Fund	All Funds
Income: Contributions	$ 50,000		$ 50,000
Expenses: All costs	45,000		45,000
Excess of income over expenses	$ 5,000		$ 5,000

FIRST CHURCH
Balance Sheet
December 31, 19___

	General Fund	Special Fund	All Funds
Assets: Cash	$ 8,000	$ 10,000	$ 18,000
Fund balances:			
Beginning, Jan. 1	$ 7,000	$ 6,000	$ 13,000
Excess of income over expenses	5,000	-0-	5,000
Transfer of funds	(4,000)	4,000	-0-
Balance end, Dec. 31	$ 8,000	$ 10,000	$ 18,000

Figure 6.2: Reporting transfers when a Balance Sheet and a statement of changes in fund balances is used.

Any transfers of funds must be made according to the predetermined uses for those funds. General funds, for example, cannot be transferred unless the congregation has given authorization for the use of general income for other than general operating purposes. Restricted funds income can be transferred and used only according to the wishes of the donors. Endowment Fund income, as will be shown, when restricted to Endowment Fund use, cannot be transferred. Building Fund money is not for General Fund use. Benevolence monies are only for benevolence purposes. Thus a congregational Board cannot arbitrarily transfer at its own discretion monies between funds. And when it does make a transfer, it must be carefully and accurately reported.

Appropriations

Congregations often accumulate surplus funds or fail to expend funds budgeted and raised for special programs. In order to maintain the identity of those funds committed for special projects or programs, a congregation may use the appropriation procedure.

An appropriation is not an expenditure. It is not a transfer either. It is simply the designation of a portion of the fund balance for a special project. If a restricted fund is to be established for the project, then a transfer is appropriate. As long as the money remains in the same fund, but is kept separate in order to identify it for future project use, it is an appropriation.

Generally, the use of appropriations in church accounting is only confusing. It is not necessary and can complicate the record keeping procedure as well as the reporting techniques of the congregation. The impression which readers too often gain from such reporting is that the funds have already been spent, when in fact they haven't. Appropriations are one technique often used by congregational Boards for giving the impression that more has been spent than is actually the case.

Nevertheless, if a congregation persists in appropriating funds or at least in setting aside funds for special projects, the procedures for doing so and reporting the activity are indicated in Figure 6.3.

CHRIST CHURCH
Statement of Income and Expenses   First Year
For the year ending December 31, 19___

	General Funds	Special Funds	All Funds
Income: Contributions	$ 50,000	$ 5,000	$ 55,000
Expenses:			
Special Project	-0-	-0-	-0-
All other costs	40,000	3,000	43,000
Excess of income over expenses	$ 10,000	$ 2,000	$ 12,000

Balance Sheet
December 31, 19___

	General Funds	Special Funds	All Funds
Assets: Cash	$ 12,000	$ 13,000	$ 25,000
Fund balances:			
Begin, Jan. 1	$ 6,000	$ 11,000	$ 17,000
Excess of income over exp.	10,000	2,000	12,000
Appropriation for special project	(4,000)	-0-	(4,000)
	$ 12,000	$ 13,000	$ 25,000

Figure 6.3: An example of the correct way to show the use of appropriations.

Statement of Income and Expenses   Second Year
For the year ending December 31, 19___

Income: Contributions	$ 60,000	$ -0-	$ 60,000
Expenses:			
Special Project	3,500		3,500
All other costs	41,000	1,000	42,000
	$ 44,500	$ 1,000	$ 45,500
Excess of income over expenses	$ 15,500	$ (1,000)	$ 14,500

Balance Sheet:
December 31, 19___

Assets: Cash	$ 31,500	$ 12,000	$ 43,500
Fund balances:			
Begin, Jan. 1	$ 12,000	$ 13,000	$ 25,000
Excess of income over exp.	15,500	(1,000)	14,500
Appropriation no longer			
required	4,000	-0-	4,000
	$ 31,500	$ 12,000	$ 43,500

Figure 6.3 (cont'd.)

As noted, funds for a special project were set aside as required. Actual costs in the following year, however, were less, as shown, and reduced the amount added to the fund balance. The previous appropriation, however, must then be added back to the fund balance since the project is completed and the total cost has been reflected in the current year's activity.

Investment Income

If your congregation has endowment fund and other investment portfolios, you must make proper accounting to the membership for investment income, as well as for the principal of the funds. Again, the importance of reporting accurately and precisely what has happened is crucial to an adequate stewardship of the congregation's funds.

There are two types of income generated by investments: income from interest and dividends, and income from the sale of securities. Traditionally investment income from interest and dividends has been considered income, while gains or losses from the sale of securities has been considered an addition to or reduction of fund principal.

Investment income may be either restricted or unrestricted depending on its source and on any restrictions placed on such income by the donor of the principal fund.

Unrestricted interest and dividend income is part of the General Fund and must be reported as income from investments. This includes income from unrestricted General Fund investments, special funds whose income is unrestricted, and Endowment Fund income where income may likewise be unrestricted.

Restricted income is reported as income to the fund for which the money is restricted. Thus, interest or dividend income from endowment funds which require that earnings be added back to the principal of the fund for a period of time, are endowment fund income and must be listed as such. Income from endowment funds to be used for special projects is income for the special projects fund, not the endowment fund. It is inappropriate and confusing to report such income first as endowment fund income and then transfer it to a special project fund.

When investments are sold, a gain or loss is realized against the original cost of the security. For endowment funds such gains and losses have generally not been available traditionally for other uses but rather are added back to or subtracted from the fund balance. A separate listing for realized gains and losses on the sale of securities is often a permanent account in the endowment fund. There is a legal question involved in the propriety of using such gains in other ways.

Unrealized gains and losses on securities, that is the difference between the market price and the cost of the security, is traditionally not shown or recorded in any way on a congregation's financial statement. A notation regarding the market price may be made on the balance sheet, but the cost amount is usually reflected in the fund balance. At least that is true when the market value is more than cost. If the market value is less than cost, the balance sheet figure may then actually be adjusted downward with a corresponding decrease in the fund balance.

Figure 6.4 shows the proper way to record interest and dividend income, realized gains and losses, and unrealized gains and losses on a congregation's financial statements.

To the casual reader of these statements, the following facts stand out:

1) The General Fund spent $7,000 less than it received in income. Income consisted of contributions and unrestricted investment income from some of the securities in the Endowment Fund.

2) Income restricted to additions to Endowment Fund principal was $4,000. This amount was added to the Endowment Fund in accord with the stipulations of the donor of the principal amount. Securities sold netted a $1,000 gain. The market value of the Endowment Fund portfolio is $6,000 less than cost.

3) Contributions were made to Special Funds. Securities, whose principal and income are restricted for special programs and which were not intended to be for Endowment Fund purposes, produced $3,000 of income. (It is not clear from the statement that this entire $3,000 income came from these special fund sec-

urities. Endowment Fund income restricted to special programs may be included in this total.)

4) The congregation has an Endowment Fund worth $146,000 (not including cash) plus securities restricted for use in special programs valued at $70,000, cost $60,000.

5) Fund balances reflect changes due to the excess of income over expenses for the period.

Such is the way your members might analyze these statements. Income from investments is clearly shown in the proper fund regardless of the funds in which the securities are recorded. Realized gains and losses are recorded as income or expenses, unrealized gains are noted by comment, and unrealized losses are reflected in fund balances.

This is a conservative, safe, generally accepted way to record income from investments for congregations which do have significant endowment or special interest funds.

One further comment on the use of endowment funds. Considering the toll which inflation has taken on the purchasing value of investment income, there are those who suggest using at least realized gains from sales to supplement general fund investment income. Barring restrictions to the contrary, it seems to me that it is perfectly legal, although you will want to seek your lawyer's advice. In fact, where the "total return" concept is used, unrealized gains are even transferred to and used in the General Fund.

FIRST CHURCH
Statement of Income and Expenses
For the year ending December 31, 19__

	General Fund	Endowment Fund	Special Fund	All Funds
Income:				
Contributions	$ 50,000	-0-	$ 10,000	$ 60,000
Investment income	2,000	$ 4,000	3,000	9,000
Gain on sale of investments	-0-	1,000	-0-	1,000
	$ 52,000	$ 5,000	$ 13,000	$ 70,000
Expenses:				
Operating costs	45,000			45,000
Excess of income over expenses	$ 7,000	$ 5,000	$ 13,000	$ 25,000

Figure 6.4: An example of statements showing the use of investment income and realized and unrealized gains and losses on securities.

FIRST CHURCH
Balance Sheet
December 31, 19___

Assets:				
Cash	$ 8,000	$ 2,000	$ 1,000	$ 11,000
Investments at cost:				
—less reserve for decline in market value of $6,000		146,000		146,000
—fair market value $70,000			60,000	60,000
	$ 8,000	$ 148,000	$ 61,000	$ 217,000
Fund balances:				
Begin, Jan. 1	$ 1,000	$ 149,000	$ 48,000	$ 198,000
Excess of income over expenses	7,000	5,000	13,000	25,000
Decline in fair market value of securities	-0-	(6,000)	-0-	(6,000)
End, Dec. 31	$ 8,000	$ 148,000	$ 61,000	$ 217,000

Figure 6.4 (cont'd.)

Chapter Seven

Recording Contributions and Pledges: Easy But Not Obvious In a Church Accounting System

Church accounting is also different from commercial enterprise accounting with respect to accounting for sources of income. Your congregation, for example, depends upon contributions from members and interested friends for virtually all of its support. A commercial enterprise depends upon income from sales and services to customers to pay for expenses and to return a profit to the owners. Thus, accounting for contributions and pledges is a unique feature of fund accounting for congregations.

Contributions

It would appear to be a rather simple matter to record contributions, and it is, if there are no special contributions. But most congregations will receive contributions with all kinds of restrictions and requests for special purposes. These must be carefully accounted for and appropriate use made of the gifts. A proliferation of special contributions may be an accounting headache, but if that is the way your members make their contributions, then your treasurer will have to keep the financial records accordingly.

Unrestricted contributions are really no problem, of course. They are recorded in the General Fund as income and used for whatever purposes the Board designates (within the confines of congregational approval, naturally). Such contributions, however, can only be reported in the General Fund and may not be reported directly in any other funds. Sometimes such a procedure is followed (using other funds) in order to hide financial problems in other funds or to suggest that more must be given to the General Fund because it receives so little in comparison to costs. But it is improper to record unrestricted gifts anywhere except in the General Fund. Transfers may be made as approved from the excess income after expenses are noted.

Restricted contributions offer additional problems. Non-current restricted contributions are given for some special program or project that is not customarily part of the congregation's ongoing concern, but funds for which will be expended eventually, if not promptly. Such gifts are not intended to be endowment gifts. A separate restricted fund account can be used to account for such gifts and their use.

Restricted contributions for current purposes, on the other hand, are more of a problem. These are contributions that can be used to meet the current expenses of the congregation even though they are restricted to a specific use. The difficulty in accounting for such funds is in the member's understanding of what is going on.

A gift for scholarships is a restricted special gift. A gift to remodel the church library is a restricted special gift, also. But a gift to fund payment of the pastor's salary for one year or to pay the bill for Sunday bulletins is a current restricted gift. Just how such gifts are to be reported on the congregation's financial statement, to be certain a proper accounting has been made and that the gift has been used for that purpose, is important.

When a separate restricted current fund account is maintained, restricted current contributions and the related expenses would be reported in that fund. The General Fund statement, however, would reflect only unrestricted contributions and related expenses. Readers would not easily be aware, then, of total costs for the current program since contributions and costs were listed in two different funds.

A transfer to the General Fund of an amount equal to the expense covered would be appropriate. In that case, the contribution would still be recorded in the restricted account, but the expense would appear in the General Fund along with all the other current expenses. Funds to cover the expense would be transferred and appear on the General Fund statement as a transfer following the amount of excess expense over income. Since the transfer is not a General Fund unrestricted contribution, however, it cannot appear as a contribution to that fund and in the restricted fund also.

Or the income transferred might be recorded as income in the General Fund providing it is properly listed in the restricted fund as simply an addition to that fund and not as a contribution. This may seem to be a small point, but if readers are not to be confused, contributions should be reported only once and only in one fund.

Or the income and expenses may all be reported in the General Fund, providing proper notations are made indicating how much of the fund balance remains as unexpended restricted contribution. Obviously, frequent transfers between funds or improper listing of accounts only confuses the congregation and adds to the complexity of communicating church financial information to the membership.

Perhaps the most helpful way to report current restricted gifts within the restricted fund and yet convey a clear picture of total current operations is to use a columnar report such as shown in Figure 7.1.

REDEEMER CHURCH
Statement of Income and Expenses
For the year ending December 31, 19___

	General Fund Un-restricted	Current Restricted	Total Current	Endow-ment Fund	Total all funds
Income:					
Contributions	$ 50,000	$ 20,000	$ 70,000	$ -0-	$ 70,000
Investment income	1,000	-0-	1,000	2,000	3,000
	$ 51,000	$ 20,000	$ 71,000	$ 2,000	$ 73,000
Expenses:					
Salaries	$ 10,000	$ 18,000	$ 28,000		$ 28,000
All other costs	40,000	-0-	40,000		40,000
	$ 50,000	$ 18,000	$ 68,000		$ 68,000
Excess of income over expenses	$ 1,000	$ 2,000	$ 3,000	$ 2,000	$ 5,000

REDEEMER CHURCH
Balance Sheet
December 31, 19___

	General Fund Un-restricted	Current Restricted	Total Current	Endow-ment Fund	Total all funds
Assets:					
Cash	$ 3,000	$ 2,000	$ 5,000	$ 4,000	$ 9,000
Investments	-0-	-0-	-0-	38,000	38,000
	$ 3,000	$ 2,000	$ 5,000	$ 42,000	$ 47,000
Fund balances:					
Begin, Jan. 1	$ 2,000	$ -0-	$ 2,000	$ 40,000	$ 42,000
Excess of income over expenses	$ 1,000	2,000	3,000	2,000	5,000
End, Dec. 31	$ 3,000	$ 2,000	$ 5,000	$ 42,000	$ 47,000

Figure 7.1: Example of statements showing presentation of restricted and unrestricted General Fund contributions.

That statement clearly differentiates between restricted and unrestricted contributions and expenses but shows total contributions and expenses for current operations as well. There is no need to make transfers or otherwise mix the restricted and unrestricted funds using this format.

Pledges

If your congregation receives pledges from members, there is always the question of what to do about uncollected pledges at year end. Are these assets? Should they be included in income this year or wait until paid next year and recorded then?

If the pledge will definitely be collected and it is material in amount, then normally it would be recorded, providing the congregation is on the accrual basis of accounting. Cash basis congregations would record as contributions only pledges actually paid, since receivables would not appear on a balance sheet.

The normal procedure and that which we would recommend, is to record as income only those contributions actually received. Pledges would be recorded only as information and would not affect income one way or the other. Anticipating the payment of pledges cannot be done very accurately and at best is only a guess anyway. Besides, most congregations will soon discover that a certain percentage of pledges will never be paid no matter how diligent the effort to collect. That loss ratio must then be built into income planning for each year.

Furthermore, most congregations will urge members to complete their planned giving by December 31 anyway, or the end of the congregation's fiscal year, to take advantage of tax regulations. Even so, with experience, congregations will soon discover the collectability of pledges made for any year.

Recording and Reporting Other Contributions

Contributed services from volunteers are not recorded on a congregation's financial statement. Recognition of such services and even a value can be noted in a footnote or special presentation, but the value of such services are not normally recorded on financial statements of congregations.

Non-cash contributions such as stocks or bonds or valuable antiques and paintings should be recorded, however, at fair market value, the same as if the item were purchased. The entry would increase the assets of the congregation and the balance of the particular fund involved.

Part Two

The Church Budget:
Keystone in the Modern
Financial Reporting System*

*Portions reprinted from *Annual Budgeting* by Manfred Holck, Jr., copyright 1977 Augsburg Publishing House, used by permission.

Chapter Eight

Understanding the Church Budget: How to Plan for the Effective Use of a Church Budget

I suppose your congregation can get along perfectly well without a church budget. Many congregations do. At least there is no accounting requirement that you have a budget. Your congregational constitution probably makes no requirement for a budget, and there is obviously no legal requirement for a church budget. Besides, your congregational treasurer may be rather comfortable with the way things are going, even without a budget. Most treasurers have a feel for the trend of costs anyway. A budget would not seem necessary.

In fact, a church budget, used as it should be, will only mean more work for your congregational treasurer. A budget means more time, more statistical analysis computation, more effort in keeping up with the financial records of the church and reporting of the results. There is a lot more involved in managing the affairs of a church when a budget is properly used.

What's a Church Budget For?

A church budget is an appropriate church document. Few members will really object to its use. Certainly most congregations have traditionally used budgets, some better than others, of course. It's too bad, but a lot of congregational budgets are used for nothing more than to window-dress the financial statements with an aura of acceptability. Many, however, are used as important tools of financial management. Thus, to use a budget, most congregational leaders would agree, is proper, appropriate, and generally encouraged. Yet, that alone does not make a budget necessary or useful.

An effective church budget involves a proper understanding of what is involved with policy making for your congregation. Just how is the planning, programming and controlling done? If done right, significant dollars can be added to the church coffers. At least good money management can be achieved through the effective use of a church budget.

A Preliminary Plan of Action

First, there must be *stated policies* which your congregation has established. These are the objectives, the goals of your congregation, how you are going to do things. The congregation must set out the policies it expects your official Board to follow; thus the Board can determine how and when salaries are to be paid, for example, what a church secretary will do, how money will be raised, debts paid, the lawn mowed. Policies set the parameters within which the Board administers the functions of the congregation, especially the staff, volunteers, and workers.

Second, *planning* is an attempt to find the best way to implement those policies. All planning, therefore, is intended to accomplish the objectives of the congregation, reflect the thinking of the congregation's leaders, and generally set the specific direction in which the congregation will move. Planning may be short term (scheduling a special activity for next Sunday) or long term (developing a five year spending plan) or something in between. No matter what the length of time involved, planning a budget is an attempt to develop a blueprint, an overall plan for fulfilling the objectives set by the congregation.

Third, *programming* is the process of spelling out in detail precisely what that planning is going to be all about. A program is a specific agenda for a specific project that has previously been planned to fulfill the congregation's purpose for being. It is scheduling that special program for Sunday and developing the procedures for getting that five-year plan down on paper. Programming is the place where the job finally gets done.

Finally, the budgeting process involves *controlling spending* of the congregation, of course. That implies the development of a process for making sure that all of those policies, plans and programs are done the way they are supposed to be done. Using the budget to control spending can be a complex process of evaluation, comparison and correction of deficiencies and discrepancies. But no matter how difficult, it is critical to a successful budgeting process.

Seven Good Reasons Why Your Congregation Needs a Budget*

The use of a church budget has several important advantages.

---

*Adapted from *Church Management: The Clergy Journal*, Vol. 52, No. 4 ("What's a Church Budget For?" by Manfred Holck, Jr.), published by Church Management, Inc., Hopkins, MN 55343, used with permission.

1. First of all, too much congregational spending is done emotionally, on the spur of the moment, impulsively, especially when there is no budget. An emotion-packed plea for money for a director of music or for a church redecoration project or a new furnace can utterly bankrupt an otherwise productive church program by siphoning off dollars desperately needed for existing programs, no matter how worthwhile those other projects may be.

Without a budget, no one has any idea how much money will be needed to keep the church program going. And worthwhile as any on-the-moment program may be, unless your congregational leaders are aware of what the diversion of funds to other programs will do to existing programs, they may blindly applaud the plea, agree with the need, and vote hundreds of dollars away from projects already approved and just as worthy. A budget helps your leaders to implement approved and funded projects which have been previously agreed upon.

2. Whenever your congregation puts a budget together, it must plan rather carefully. At least, if you expect to make the budget realistic, your budget makers must know something about the history and activities of the congregation and where it expects to go. In the process, your leaders will find out about the weak spots, the strong places. You will quickly learn what has been done, what is being done, and what is not getting done. An organization is strengthened when it plans a useful budget.

3. Furthermore, a good budgeting procedure will get a lot of people involved, and that's good. It's good because the more people who know what is going on in the congregation, the better. There is the opportunity for more ideas and better cooperation toward implementing programs and accomplishing the mission of the congregation. If planning is done properly, just about any member who wants to should be able to get in on the planning action.

4. A budget always involves commitment by the membership. Once adopted, it sets out a plan for spending which the membership has approved. At least that is what should happen. Conscientious members will see that it does. For there is nothing gained in approving unrealistic spending goals if there is no chance at all for financial support. A budget requires commitment and awareness of what the congregation says it is going to do.

5. If a budget is used properly, it will require an appropriate accounting of where all the money has come from and where it has gone. Actual experiences should be compared to budgeted amounts to be certain the congregation is doing what it said it intended to do. Better resource conservation and meaningful allocation come about because a budget is used to monitor spending.

6. A combination of good accounting, reporting and budget comparisons can generate significant confidence from the membership in the congregation's leadership. When reports make sense, when goals are explained and adhered to,

when a congregation knows what is going on without the uncertainty of unanswered questions or incomprehensible reports, it will be much more amenable to suggestions for change, improvement, and outreach. A positive reaction to financial statement reporting is more likely when a budget is part of that information.

7. Furthermore, whenever your congregation goes out to borrow money or raise money to meet new goals or otherwise seek the financial support of members and nonmembers, a history of careful resource allocation preparation is impressive. It is simply good management technique to budget carefully. Good budgeting procedures imply that other financial procedures are being followed with equal care.

Don't get the idea that a church budget will solve all of your financial problems. It won't. But it is a good beginning. Now you will have to wrestle much more realistically perhaps with making the painful decisions about how the congregation's money will finally be spent. Besides, not every budget will be used the way it is supposed to be used. Some won't be used at all, even after all this effort. And some just may not work.

Use your church budget well, however, and your congregation will be able to spend its money better, besides knowing how its money is actually being spent in comparison to how it wanted the money to be spent.

Planning the Budget*

Two basic functions of a church budget are (1) to set realistic goals and objectives for the coming year or years, and (2) to monitor the financial activities of the congregation during the term of the budget. The first function is as important as the second, for without realistic goals a budget may be ineffective for monitoring costs.

The plan of action for developing and using your congregation's budget must, therefore, include adequate preparation, appropriate comparisons with the financial statements, timely preparation of financial statements for comparison to budgets, and action by your official Board where deviations from the budget are significant.

Every congregation will develop a plan for budget preparation to suit its own needs. But to be effective, that preparation should adhere closely to the ways in which most successfully managed congregations plan their budgets.

A budget should not be prepared by only one person. The process should be a joint effort, actually involving as many people as is practically possible. If the budget is to be a plan of action by which the congregation's program and outreach during the next year is determined, then it must involve the membership all the way from its inception to its final outline as well. Of course, that may not be the

*Adapted from *Church and Clergy Finance*, Vol. 7, No. 9 ("Your Church Budget: A Plan of Action," by Manfred Holck, Jr.) published by Ministers Life Resources, Minneapolis, MN, used with permission.

easiest way to put a budget together, but it certainly is a necessary procedure if the budget is to represent what your congregation wants.

Listing objectives: Thus, a list of objectives and goals must be agreed upon. Before any dollars are attached to the costs of any programs, your congregation must agree on where it wants to go, what it intends to do, and whether or not existing programs should be continued, expanded, or discarded. Maybe you will only re-evaluate what you already have. Maybe you will toss something out which no longer serves a useful purpose although it may have done so in the past. Maybe you will keep the things that are working well and attempt to develop new ideas to replace what hasn't turned out so well in the past.

One way to develop that scheme of goals is to form a large budget planning committee, a committee that can dream dreams they never thought possible to achieve in your congregation (and maybe they still can't!) A good cross section of the membership can be called together for one or two meetings just to brainstorm where the congregation should be going. Perhaps as many as forty people could attend.

But, prior to that first meeting, someone should prepare an accurate fact sheet about where the congregation has been and what it is doing now. That's so the entire committee will have the same basic information and assumptions about what has been going on. Figure 8.1 shows the kind of information that may be most helpful.

FACTS YOU SHOULD KNOW ABOUT YOUR CONGREGATION BEFORE THE BUDGET IS MADE

A. *Membership*

	Number	Increase	Percentage
This year			
Last year			
3 years ago			
5 years ago			
10 years ago			

B. *Age range*

	Number	Percentage
Young to age 35		
Middle: age 36-59		
Older: age 60+		

Figure 8.1

C. *Weekly Giving Patterns by Families*

Weekly gift	Number	Percentage	Weekly	Annually
Over $75	_____	_____	_____	_____
$50 to $74	_____	_____	_____	_____
$25 to $49	_____	_____	_____	_____
$10 to $24	_____	_____	_____	_____
$5 to $9	_____	_____	_____	_____
less than $5	_____	_____	_____	_____
No gifts	_____	_____	_____	_____

D. *Budget Summary*

	Last Year	This Year	Percentage Attained Last Year	Percentage Attained This Year
Revenues				
Current	$_____	$_____	_____	_____
Special	_____	_____	_____	_____
Benevolences	_____	_____	_____	_____
Other	_____	_____	_____	_____
Total	$_____	$_____	_____	_____
Disbursements				
Current	$_____	$_____	_____	_____
Special	_____	_____	_____	_____
Benevolences	_____	_____	_____	_____
Other	_____	_____	_____	_____
Total	$_____	$_____	_____	_____

E. *Cash deficits, if any.* If so, how much? $_____ this year; $_____ last year.

F. *Pledge response last year.*

	Pledged	Budgeted	Percentage Pledged
Current expense	$_____	$_____	_____%
Special programs	_____	_____	_____
Benevolences	_____	_____	_____

G. *Number of family units:* last year_____, this year_____.

H. *Indebetedness:* $_____ . Amount due this year $_____ .

I. *Potential Resources:*

1) *Giving family units:*

	Number of Giving Units		Giving Units Equivalents
Husband & wife	_____	@ 1 =	_____
Single employed	_____	@ 1 =	_____

Figure 8.1 (cont'd.)

Wife only members   _____ @ ½ = _____

Two denominations   _____ @ ⅓ = _____

Retired   _____ @ ¼ = _____

    Total   _____ _____

2) Average family incomes (giving units)

    Our congregation $ _____

    Our community $ _____

3) Total resources:

    Family income giving unit equivalents times average family income equals total

        potential resources $_____ .

    Giving potential (the following percentages times potential resource listed above):

If everyone gives this percentage of income,	Then, potential income is this amount:
15%	$_____
10%	_____
8%	_____
5%	_____
3%	_____

Last year's Percentage
(Annual congregational income
divided by last year's
potential resource):   _____ %

Figure 8.1 (cont'd.)

Knowing all of this—what resources are possible and what the congregation's financial history has been—can be most helpful to your budget planning committee as it attempts to make its decisions about next year's program.

A planning resource worksheet: At the first meeting of that larger committee, but before any of these facts are made available to the membership, the members should be given an opportunity to fill in their individual copies of a Planning Resource Worksheet as shown in Figure 8.2. This is a listing of all those things those members think their congregation should be doing now or sometime.

CHECKLIST FOR PLANNING RESOURCE WORKSHEET

	O.K. ____	Needs Attention	No Need	Don't Know
Christian Education 1. Sunday Church School program meets needs of the congregation and community?				

Figure 8.2

	O.K.	Needs Attention	No Need	Don't Know
2. Vacation Church School program?				
3. Release time program?				
4. Training programs for prospective teachers?				
5. Fulltime personnel needed?				
6. Audio-visuals under responsible direction?				
7. Subsidies for training schools and retreats?				
8. Library facilities for the membership?				
9. Adult counselors for youth activities?				
10. Promote church colleges and church vocations?				
11. Promote reading of official denomination publication?				
Evangelism				
1. Instruction and orientation for new members?				
2. Assimilate new members into congregational life?				
3. Use local news and broadcast media?				
4. Outreach to Church School parents?				
5. Reach new people in community promptly?				
6. Effective use made of materials provided by the church?				
7. Contacts maintained with our youth in colleges and armed services?				
8. Periodic congregational fellowship gatherings?				
9. Leadership trained in evangelism?				
10. Members prepared for witnessing in daily life?				
Ministry				
1. Staff sufficient for present and expected opportunities?				
2. Pastor relieved of administrative detail?				
3. Organized voluntary service program?				
4. Good working facilities for entire staff?				
5. Salaries of entire staff reviewed annually?				
6. Congregation regularly informed through parish newsletter?				
7. Periodic evaluation of program & outreach?				

Figure 8.2 (cont'd.)

	O.K.	Needs Attention	No Need	Don't Know
Property				
1. Housekeeping (e.g., cleanliness, heating, etc.)?				
2. Bulletin boards and signs?				
3. Custodial?				
4. Repairs made promptly?				
Worship				
1. Present hours of services adequate?				
2. Attendance by family units stressed?				
3. Hymnals in adequate supply and repair?				
4. Music leadership and staff?				
5. Organ and instruments on regular maintenance?				
6. Choir supplies and facilities?				
7. Ushers friendly, helpful and attentive?				
8. Members cordial to one another and to visitors?				
9. Religious art, music, and drama appreciation cultivated?				
10. Frequency of the Sacraments?				
Social Ministry				
1. Congregational program of Christian service?				
2. Service to emotionally disturbed (in the community)?				
3. Service to physically handicapped (blind, deaf, etc.)?				
4. Laity trained to visit and aid the sick, shut-ins and aged?				
5. Special transportation assistance?				
6. Laity serving as volunteers in local institutions?				
7. Interpret social problems?				
8. Hospitality to international students?				
Stewardship				
1. Stewardship education a year-round concern?				
2. Stewardship is understood to be total life commitment?				

Figure 8.2 (cont'd.)

	O.K.	Needs Attention	No Need	Don't Know
3. Effective use is made of time and abilities of members?				
4. Children's pledges encouraged and offering envelopes used?				
5. Proportionate giving stressed?				
6. Our congregation is moving toward increased benevolence support?				
7. Mission education programs sponsored?				
8. Visits made to new members for information and pledge?				
Finance				
1. Prepares inclusive budget in view of expressed objectives for the congregation?				
2. Gives oversight to all financial affairs of the congregation?				
3. Attends, through the treasurer, to the prompt payment of all obligations?				
4. Benevolence monies are forwarded each month to the proper agencies?				
5. "Overage" giving considered?				

How to use the Planning Resource Worksheet

Each participant on the special committee appointed to assess congregational needs should have a copy of the checklist. Working independently, each member will check off appropriate responses. Is the present program O.K.? Does it need attention?

Responses are summarized and listed for a subsequent meeting of the group. Costs are then assigned for correcting or improving those programs thought most in need. A priority of listing is agreed upon.

The checklist, summary, cost estimates, and priority listings are then used by the Church Council to evaluate congregational needs for a proposed budget.

Figure 8.2 (cont'd.)

The first meeting: By using a worksheet similar to that illustrated, your committee can be most creative at this first meeting. Each committee member can rate all of those programs in which each believe the congregation should be involved.

The results of that evaluation will quickly tell your official Board how the membership sees the congregation's programs.

Money, of course, is not a consideration at the moment although it obviously will be for implementing any new programs. However, at this first meeting the membership should be encouraged to be creative, freely expressing their attitudes about what they think is and should be happening in their congregation irrespective of the costs.

You will quickly learn that such an activity will use up at least a full evening's meeting. But it can be an exciting time!

Then, prior to a second meeting, selected members should compile the results of that first session. It should be easy enough to summarize most of the responses from the form used. Comments may be reproduced on a separate sheet also for distribution to the group at the second meeting, if that seems helpful.

The second meeting: At a second meeting the committee can get down to the brass tacks of attaching dollar values to all of those dreams. Again, unencumbered by any total anticipated income from offerings, the committee can calculate, as accurately as possible, the basic costs for all the programs thought most desirable by a majority of the group. Dollar costs for every program mentioned could be determined, but a realistic appraisal of available resources will quickly indicate that only a small number of programs can be implemented. Thus concentration on the more popular suggestions may be the most useful.

It may also be useful to try to agree on some priority listing for all of those suggestions. Sometime someone is going to have to list a proposal of programs and costs that fits into anticipated resources. At this second meeting, therefore, dollar amounts and some consensus on priority can be determined.

The third meeting: A final and perhaps third meeting of this planning group may be useful to develop a formal proposal or series of proposals to be used to challenge your congregation to a generous response in giving. Because only as your congregation is willing to support the program with money will it be able to implement any of these ideas. Thus, a set of proposals, as shown in Figure 8.3, may be developed as a challenge to the membership before pledges or commitments for the new year's program are received.

But this is not the budget, not yet. This is simply a proposal. Budgets are best set only when resources are known. So you must wait until the annual fund raising activity (Every Member Response program) is completed before putting a budget in order. A realistic budget will not exceed known resources.

Congregations are challenged by proposals, not by budgets. Thus, final spending budgets should not be formally adopted until the congregation has had a chance to indicate its support for a proposed program. A total response for the venture part of that illustrated budget may suggest that as the final budget,

A PARISH PROPOSAL

	Minimum	Needed	The Venture Program	Purpose
Parish Extension				
Benevolences	$ 9000	$ 10000	$ 13000	To share with others
Other Benev.	1000	1800	2100	More sharing
Parish Expansion				
Christian education	1000	1200	1500	A Sunday School program
Evangelism &				
Social Mnstry	100	200	300	To witness of faith
Youth	100	200	300	A youth program
Communications	50	150	400	To tell others about our church
Anything else	100	200	300	If needed
Parish Ministries				
Worship & Music	300	400	500	A music program
Staff salaries	15000	17000	20000	As contracted
Supplies	600	700	800	As needed
Leadership training	100	150	200	To train leaders
Building Maintenance	1000	1500	2000	Repairs
Insurance	1500	1500	1500	As required
Utilities	2000	2000	2000	As required
Car allowance	1500	2000	2500	For pastor's calling
Staff benefits	1000	1200	1400	Pensions & Health
Contingency	1000	1000	1000	For emergencies
Parish Development				
Equipment	500	700	800	New equipment
Building projects	2000	3000	5000	Redecoration
Property debt reduction	2400	2400	5000	Mortgage payments
TOTALS	$40250	$47300	$60600	

Figure 8.3

perhaps. A pledging response at the minimum proposal clearly indicates *that* as the program to be used for the coming year.

Thus, the planning committee makes its proposal, the congregation responds through a fund-raising effort (for suggestions on how you can raise more money for your congregation, see our book *Money and Your Church*), and only then does a committee put the budget together.

Finally, this same large committee can come together once more and decide on a budget, if that is the procedure your congregation prefers. It may be better, at this point, however, to have the Finance Committee take all of this data and all of these ideas to develop a specific budget. Matching available resources with proposed programs will not be an easy task no matter which committee assumes the job. The next chapter tells how to build the budget.

Chapter Nine

Building the Church Budget:
Using Proven Techniques to Develop
A Useable, Flexible Church Budget;
Program Budgets; Zero-Based Budgets;
Capital Budgets; Line Budgets;
And Other Budgets

Specific Steps

Your congregational Finance Committee should consider taking the following steps toward putting your church budget in shape.

1. Review the *objectives and goals* of the congregation as previously agreed upon in planning the budget. Perhaps a refinement of those goals or a more realistic assessment of what seems appropriate for the congregation could be summarized for purposes of a concise statement of the mission of the congregation.

2. Determine the *costs* to achieve all of the proposed programs that have already been suggested. Programs considered for the highest priority by that Planning Committee can now be reviewed with respect to actual costs. A more detailed analysis is now required to be certain that estimates will not be seriously overspent if the programs are committed to the budget. Furthermore, when possible, a series of costs should be developed for each program, depending upon the

degree of implementation expected when costs must be reduced because of limited resources.

   3. Estimate the expected *income* of the congregation from the results of the fund-raising activity. Other income may also be presumed above that which has been pledged or committed. Only income that can reasonably be expected to be received should be listed. The tendency for congregations to be too optimistic can be disastrous. A realistic budgeting of income may be more important than the budgeting of expenses. There must be realism in the anticipation of income, otherwise the budget will really have no meaning.

   4. *Reconcile* anticipated income and expenses. Since there are always more programs desired than there is money to pay for them, the process of reconciling income with anticipated expenses is crucial to the success of the budgeting process and the continuation of the congregation's financial stability. Even the most optimistic income estimate should probably be reduced by 10% or 15%. A contingency of up to 10% of total costs may be added to expenses to cover unexpected items. Expenses cannot exceed income, obviously, unless the congregation has cash reserves it can use. There is no margin for error. Thus a conservative approach that underestimates income and overestimates the potential costs of program provides a balancing of income and expense that may offer the greatest chance for success.

   5. *Recommend* to your official Board a budget for the year, income and expense. The Board will review the proposal, take appropriate action, and then present it to the congregation for vote and approval.

   Steps such as these are important for developing a budget. Congregations can, of course, skip around them or ignore them altogether, but successful budgets are put together in a deliberate and planned way. Besides, full participation by as many people as possible in the whole process (Planning Committee to Finance Committee) generally assures the Board of having a budget that will be approved and supported by the congregation without undue disagreement. After all, when so many people have had a hand in putting the thing together, the results will be more agreeable to the most people.

The Budget-Making Process*

   Typical budgets are developed for a year at a time. Annual costs for doing business are determined, totaled, and approved. Year-end comparisons then are made between what was actually spent for the year and what was budgeted.

   But that kind of comparison may simply be too late to take any corrective action for items that exceed the budget significantly. By the time the year is over, there's not much that can be done, except to watch that kind of spending a bit more carefully in the next year.

---

*Adapted from *Church* and *Clergy Finance*, Vol. 7, No. 13 ("Specific Steps Toward Developing the Church Budget," by Manfred Holck, Jr.), published by Ministers Life Resources, Minneapolis, MN, used with permission.

Typical budgets are divided into monthly segments or at least quarterly segments. Then, actual spending for each month or each quarter can be carefully compared with a budget for that year. That kind of comparison may make it possible to take corrective action before the end of the year. At least the problems become obvious long before the year is already over.

A simple division of the annual budget by twelve is one way to develop a monthly budget, but it may not be the most realistic monthly response. After all, congregations do not spend money evenly from month to month. They don't even receive it in equal monthly amounts. Offerings come in spurts, as you well know, high at Christmas and Easter with the low ebb in the summer. To compare actual income and expenses with an annual budget evenly divided by twelve is not entirely realistic, although that's better than nothing and it is easy to calculate.

It is very easy to look at a congregational financial statement in April, for example, see that more money has come in than has gone out and quickly assume that things are going great. Maybe they are, but maybe they are not.

Offerings during the first four months of a calendar year can be significantly more, proportionately, than offerings during the next eight months. To assume that a cash surplus then will mushroom into a year-end surplus three times as large is naive thinking. But it may be a reasonable expectation if the annual budget divided by twelve is the comparative tool. For example:

	Annual Budget	4 Months Budget	4 Months Actual
Offerings	$ 30,000	$ 10,000	$ 10,000
Disbursements	(30,000)	(10,000)	(9,000)
Excess of offerings over disbursements	$ -0-	$ -0-	$ 1,000

It is doubtful that the year-end surplus of $1,000 will be three times the surplus of the first four months in this example. Yet, this kind of report suggests that possibility. Instead, the four months' budget should be analyzed for timing of income and expense and not automatically determined as 1/3 of the annual budget. Thus:

	Annual Budget	Jan	Feb	Mar	Apr	4 Mos. Budget	4 Mos. Actual
Offerings	30,000	2,500	2,000	3,000	3,500	11,000	10,000
Disbursements	30,000	3,000	2,000	3,000	2,000	10,000	9,000
Difference	-0-	(500)	-0-	-0-	1,500	1,000	1,000

An anticipated budget surplus at the end of four months *was* realized, but year-end spending is still expected to be equal to offerings. No surplus is anticipated. It is clear that a careful analysis of the budget by months will give a clearer

WORKSHEET FOR ESTIMATING MONTHLY BUDGETS

Offerings	2,500	2,000	3,000	3,500	3,000	2,000	1,500	1,500	2,000	2,500	3,000	3,500	30,000
Expenses:													
Variable*	1,200	200	1,200	200	200	700	700	700	1,200	700	700	700	8,400
Regular	1,800	1,800	1,800	1,800	1,800	1,800	1,800	1,800	1,800	1,800	1,800	1,800	21,600
	3,000	2,000	3,000	2,000	2,000	2,500	2,500	2,500	3,000	2,500	2,500	2,500	30,000
Net	(500)	-0-	-0-	1,500	1,000	(500)	(1,000)	(1,000)	(1,000)	-0-	500	1,000	-0-

*Includes quarterly insurance payments, winter heat and summer cooling utility bills, promotional programs, fall educational supplies, etc.

Figure 9.1

picture of how the actual experience compares with the budget allocated by months.

It is not always easy to break an annual budget into monthly increments. There are several ways, however, in which a close estimate can be made.

Cash flow: For example, a simplified cash flow chart can be developed using last year's experience to plot when money will most likely be received and spent. Insurance premiums, for instance, are normally paid annually. The month of payment, therefore, will show an unusually large jump. Utility costs vary through the year, postage may be lower in summer months if activity drops off then. A special promotional effort in the fall could raise costs in those months. Figure 9.1 shows such a worksheet for estimated monthly budgets if you prefer not to take 1/12 each month.

When a monthly budget is regularly compared with actual offerings and expenditures for those months, deviations to the plan can be easily noted and action quickly taken. And that's what a budget is really for. Effective utilization of a congregation's resources requires careful analysis of just what is going on each month. An analysis makes it possible to anticipate future action on the basis of past experience.

Worksheet format: The proposals for your congregational program may have all been carefully prepared and presented to the membership, but as indicated previously, it is now up to the Finance Committee, with the help of your treasurer, to put the actual budget together based on expected income and desired programs. Several methods can be used and you may already have a workable procedure.

If you plan to put your budget together by using the experience of the previous year, a worksheet of some sort will be required. Since you cannot wait until the year is over to put the next year's budget together on that basis, it is necessary to make some guesses of what you may spend the last few months of the current year. Figure 9.2 shows you how to do that.

Once the format is developed, your Finance Committee can fill in the columns. In the first column the actual income and expenses for the most recent months would be tabulated by the treasurer. If the budget is being put together in November, ten months of actual experience would be available. In the illustration eleven months of activity are shown since the budget is presumably being put together in December.

Then someone has to make a guess on what the income and expenses will probably be for the rest of the year. That guess goes in the second column. The third column is the total estimated income and expenses for the year. The current year's budget is listed in column four for comparative purposes.

The last three columns are used to make projections for next year's budget. With information at hand in the first four columns, the Finance Committee must now begin to make some decisions.

Column five should include the minimum program originally developed by the Planning Committee. This proposal is the very minimum activity which the congregation should be expected to continue without seriously disrupting or changing the existing program.

Column six should be the maximum, the venture program which the Finance Committee originally thought the congregation could achieve. If it did, fine. But in the illustration, the last column of income reports the congregation's responses and expected income from other sources. The expense budget in the last column cannot exceed anticipated income unless there is surplus cash remaining from a previous period or from other available sources.

According to the final recommended budget therefore, as illustrated, the congregation is expected to contribute about $27,000 through offering envelopes. These would be the result of pledges and the fund raising effort previously held.

Procedures for Using the Budget Worksheet (Figure 9.2)

1. A seven column worksheet should be set up with headings as noted, including appropriate year designations and account descriptions.

2. From the most recent financial statements, actual receipts and disbursements can be inserted in the first column. A nine or ten months report may be available rather than the eleven months report as illustrated.

3. Receipts and disbursements for the rest of the fiscal year need to be estimated. These should be estimated actual experience and not a proportion of the budget. Total the first two columns for the third column listing.

4. The current year's budget should be listed in the fourth column. A comparison between columns three and four will reveal how close the congregation may come to what it originally expected to receive and spend.

5. In column five estimates of next year's minimum required budget to carry on the work of the congregation may be listed. The appropriate committee or Church Council must make these estimates.

6. Column six may be used to list a program that is more than the base minimum required to continue functioning. This column will offer choices to those making the final decisions on the budget. Depending on congregational pledging commitments, the proposed budget suggests a greater stewardship commitment than the bare minimum.

7. In the last column the budget finally agreed upon and which may be presented to the congregation for adoption is listed.

Figure 9.2

A CHURCH BUDGET WORKSHEET FOR INCOME AND EXPENSES BASED ON PREVIOUS SPENDING EXPERIENCE

	This year Actual 11 mos.	This year Estimate 1 mo.	This year Total	This Year Budget	Next year budget Minimum	Next year budget Proposed	Next year budget Final
Income:							
Offering envelopes	20,750	3,000	23,750	25,000	26,500	30,200	27,000
Loose plate offerings	2,350	300	2,650	2,850	2,600	2,800	2,700
Church School offerings	180	20	200	250	200	250	250
Communion offerings	150	50	200	100	200	250	250
Special gifts	150	-0-	150	100	200	500	400
Advent offerings	-0-	150	150	200	200	200	300
Parking lot rentals	360	40	400	500	150	600	500
Investment income	1,300	200	1,500	1,000	1,500	1,700	1,500
Total income	25,240	3,760	29,000	30,000	31,850	36,500	32,900
Expenditures:							
Benevolences:							
The Church abroad	1,850	150	2,000	2,000	2,000	3,000	1,500
The Church nationally	3,200	300	3,500	3,500	3,500	4,000	4,000
The Church at home	-0-	500	500	500	500	1,000	500
	5,050	950	6,000	6,000	6,000	8,000	6,000

Figure 9.2 (cont'd.)

Ministry of the Word:							
Pastor's salary	11,000	1,000	12,000	12,000	12,600	13,200	13,000
Housing allowance	2,750	250	3,000	3,000	3,000	3,000	3,000
Social Security allowance	1,100	100	1,200	1,200	1,300	1,300	1,300
Pension plan contributions	880	80	960	1,000	1,000	1,050	1,050
Other benefits	50	10	60	100	100	100	-0-
	15,780	1,440	17,220	17,300	18,000	18,650	18,350
Administration:							
Secretary salaries	1,100	100	1,200	1,200	1,200	1,200	1,200
Supplies, postage	450	50	500	400	600	800	600
Car allowance	2,400	300	2,700	2,250	2,500	3,000	2,700
Property maintenance	200	50	250	300	500	1,000	1,000
Utilities and insurance	1,100	100	1,200	1,000	1,500	2,000	1,500
	5,250	600	5,850	5,150	6,300	8,000	7,000
Program:							
Christian education	100	-0-	100	125	150	300	150
Youth	-0-	-0-	-0-	50	50	100	50
Worship and music	50	-0-	50	75	50	100	50
Stewardship	-0-	-0-	-0-	50	50	50	50
Outreach	-0-	-0-	-0-	50	50	100	50
	150	-0-	150	350	350	650	350
Debt:							
Church building loan	1,100	100	1,200	1,200	1,200	1,200	1,200
Total	27,330	3,090	30,420	30,000	31,850	36,500	32,900

Figure 9.2 (cont'd.)

Based on past experience the $27,000 probably represents about 90% of that which was actually pledged. Reducing pledges in that way helps to make anticipated income more realistic, thus keeping expense budgeting more realistic, too.

All sources of income are listed. Total funds available are then budgeted to be spent in the manner listed. A careful review of the proposals prepared by the Planning Committee should be made before a final budget is recommended. After all, the purpose of those two or three meetings of congregational representatives was to spell out just what those members wanted their church to do. The final recommendations of a budget, therefore, must correspond to those desires within the limits of anticipated income.

Different Kinds of Budgets

The budgets used in the various illustrations in these chapters are generally *line item budgets*. Such budgets specify specific amounts for particular types of expenditures, such as for salaries, utilities, etc. But not all budgets are line item expense budgets.

Program budgets define costs according to specific programs. Thus an evangelism program's costs include more than just the cost of folders to distribute to prospective members. It includes a percentage of the costs of the pastor's salary, the secretary's salary and other costs, too. The Sunday Church School program costs are more than just textbooks and supplies. They include a percentage of the costs of the secretary's salary, the costs of equipment, coordination costs, etc. Figure 9.3 compares a line item budget with a simple program budget.

Zero-based budgets begin from "scratch." While most budgeting procedures take last year's costs and add a percentage increase to most items to arrive at anticipated costs for next year, zero-based budgets assume no previous cost or experience. Every budgeted item must be justified whether the program is a new one or a continuing one. Figure 9.4 shows a sample worksheet for zero-based budgeting calculations.

A *unified budget* puts all the congregation's receipts and disbursements into "one basket." Every source of funds and every allocation of those funds is placed in one comprehensive budget. It's a budget that clearly outlines the total resources of the congregation. No monies are hidden in some Sunday School class's private bank account. Total funds expended for the youth, the men's, and the women's groups is clearly listed as part of the total resources of the congregation.

The procedure is not used very often because many groups simply want to hang onto their own money. But those who understand the use of a unified budget realize each group still maintains control, but simply agrees to recognize that its activities are part of the total program of the church. Thus listing its receipts and disbursements as part of that total program is a responsible and reasonable way to indicate the one-ness of the congregation's program goals.

COMPARISON OF A LINE ITEM EXPENSE BUDGET AND A PROGRAM BUDGET

A Budget for Our Church		A Program for Mission in Our Church	
For Missions:		**Mission to Our World:**	
Abroad	$ 1,500	Abroad	$ 1,500
Nationally	4,000	Nationally	4,000
Locally	500	Locally	500
	$ 6,000		$ 6,000
For Pastoral Ministry:		**Mission to Our Community:**	
Salary	$13,000	Evangelism (Visitation	
Pension	1,050	and work with non-	
Social Security All.	1,300	members)	$ 3,277
Parsonage allowance	3,000	Inter-Church (Council	
	$18,350	of Churches, etc.)	701
For Program:		Social Concerns	
Christian education	$ 150	(Counseling non-	
Worship & music	50	members, etc.)	2,624
Stewardship	50		$ 6,602
Outreach	50	**Mission to our Congregation:**	
Youth	50	Worship	$ 5,874
	$ 350	Education	6,074
For Administration:		Pastoral care (Visita-	
Travel & auto	$ 2,700	tion and counseling	
Mortgage payments	1,200	with members)	4,550
Utilities & ins.	1,500	Building maintenance	2,600
Repairs & maintenance	1,000	Mortgage payments	1,200
Postage & supplies	600		$20,298
Secretary	1,200		
	$ 8,200		
Total budget	$32,900	**Total program**	$32,900

Calculations required to change from line item expense budget to program budget format—

1. Pastor's Compensation and Expense Requirements

Salary	$ 13,000
Pension plan contributions	1,050
Social Security allowance	1,300
Parsonage allowance	3,000
Automobile allowance	2,700
	$ 21,050

Figure 9.3

2. Pastor's Time Allocation

Sermon preparation	25%	$ 5,263
Congregational meetings and preparation	25%	5,263
Visitation and counseling of members	20%	4,210
Evangelism visitation	15%	3,157
Counseling nonmembers	5%	1,052
Outside Meetings	10%	2,105
	100%	$21,050

3. Worship

Pastor's sermon preparation	25%	$ 5,264
Music supplies		50
Secretary's time	30%	360
Office supplies		200
		$ 5,874

4. Education

Pastor's preparation and meetings	25%	$ 5,263
Church Schools		150
Secretary's time	30%	360
Office supplies		200
Youth programs		50
Stewardship supplies		50
		$ 6,073

5. Pastoral Care

Pastoral visiting and counseling with members	20%	$ 4,210
Office supplies		100
Secretary's time	20%	240
		$ 4,550

6. Building Maintenance

Utilities & insurance		$ 1,500
Repairs & maintenance		1,000
Service & supplies		100
		$ 2,600

7. Evangelism

Pastor's time	15%	$ 3,157
Secretary's time	10%	120
		$ 3,277

Figure 9.3 (cont'd.)

8. Interchurch work		
Pastor's time	3⅓%	$ 701
9. Social Concerns		
Pastor's time counseling		
with nonmembers	5%	$ 1,052
Pastor's time at meet-		
ings	6⅔%	1,402
Outreach programs		50
Secretary's time	10%	120
		$ 2,624

Explanation of Line Expense Budget and Program Budget Compared (Figure 9.3)

1. The typical line expense budget is on the left, a program budget is on the right. Both budgets total the same dollars.

2. In the line expense budget, all costs are associated with some specific kind of expense. Thus, the pastor's compensation is listed as a total to be paid. Office supplies are listed as a total. Each item represents the costs for that particular item or service.

3. A program budget allocates those same costs to various programs. Thus, the pastor's time spent on various programs is estimated and the total compensation costs allocated accordingly.

4. Program costs are determined by allocating appropriate costs to each as shown in items 1 through 9. The total for each program is then summarized on the budget. Incurred costs are allocated on the same basis so that proper comparisons can be made between expected costs or programs and actual costs.

Figure 9.3 (cont'd.)

ZERO BASED PROGRAM BUDGET WORKSHEET

Programs	Justified Cost in Dollars or Time[1]	Proposed Budgets[2]		
		Minimum	Anticipated	Venture
Mission to our World:				
Abroad	$ 1,500	$ 750	$ 1,500	$ 1,800
Nationally	4,000	2,000	4,000	4,800
Locally	500	250	500	600
		$ 3,000	$ 6,000	$ 7,200

Figure 9.4

Mission to our Community:

Evangelism				
Pastor's time	15%	$ 2,842	$ 3,158	$ 3,654
Secretary's time	10%	-0-	120	240
Interchurch Activities				
Pastor's time	3⅓%	631	700	811
Social Concerns				
Pastor's time				
Counseling	5%	948	1,053	1,218
Meetings	6⅔%	1,263	1,403	1,624
Program needs	$ 50	30	50	100
Secretary's time	10%	-0-	120	240

Mission to our Congregation:

Worship				
Pastor's time	25%	$ 4,738	$ 5,263	$ 6,090
Music supplies	$ 50	$ 20	$ 50	$ 100
Secretary's time	30%	-0-	360	720
Office Supplies	$ 200	150	200	250
Education				
Pastor's time	25%	4,738	5,263	6,090
Secretary's time	30%	-0-	360	720
Church School supplies	$ 150	100	150	200
Office supplies		150	200	250
Youth programs	50	50	50	100
Stewardship supplies	50	-0-	50	80
Pastoral Care				
Pastor's time	20%	3,790	4,210	4,872
Office supplies	$ 100	20	100	150
Secretary's time	20%	-0-	240	480
Building Maintenance				
Utilities	$ 1,500	1,500	1,500	1,500
Repairs	1,000	400	1,000	2,000
Supplies	100	50	100	120
Mortgage payments	1,200	1,200	1,200	1,200
Total		$25,620	$32,900	$40,009

[1]As supported by proponents and/or committee.

[2]Final budget will be determined by response of members.

Compensation Proposals:

Secretary's salary	$ 1,200	$ -0-	$ 1,200	$ 2,400
Pastor's compensation				
and expense reimburse-				
ments—				
Auto allowance and				
other expenses	$ 2,700	$ 2,700	$ 2,700	$ 2,700

Figure 9.4 (cont'd.)

Supplemental benefits				
Pension plan	1,050	950	1,050	1,260
Social Security all.	1,300	1,300	1,300	1,300
Parsonage allowance	3,000	3,000	3,000	3,600
Salary	13,000	11,000	13,000	15,500
Total	$21,050	$18,950	$21,050	$24,360

Procedures for Developing a Zero-Based Budget (Figure 9.4)

1. A four column worksheet, as illustrated, can be set up. Columns headed as noted.

2. Since the illustration is also a program budget, the amounts in column one are either the actual costs for a specific item or a percentage of the total costs of a specific expense attributable to that particular program. Thus, the percentage of the pastor's time is estimated for each program. But all amounts in column one must be supported as necessary, regardless of prior year's experience.

3. A basic cost for the pastor's compensation and expenses reimbursement as well as for the secretary must be established.

4. Since this worksheet also suggests three alternative proposed budgets, depending on how the congregation eventually responds with its pledging, entries should be made in each column as determined to be appropriate by the committee or official Board. If response is sufficient to justify the Venture Budget, for example, then that may be the final proposal made to the congregation at its annual meeting.

Figure 9.4 (cont'd.)

Accounting procedures for such a program of budgeting do require some changes from typical arrangements. Other budgets do not normally affect accounting procedures, but with a unified budget it is necessary to set up procedures that do keep all funds separate yet provide a total picture as well.

For example, a unified budget system requires one church treasurer and one bank account. Each organization, however, will also designate a treasurer. The organization may collect its own money, deposit those funds in the church account, retain a copy of the deposit slip and send one copy to the church treasurer. Checks are written and distributed by the church treasurer upon voucher authorization request from the organization treasurer. Thus none of the funds collected by the organization or authorized for its use can be disbursed without the organization's treasurer requesting the payment.

Thus, the financial statements of the organization must agree at all times with those of the congregational treasurer. Control of cash is enhanced because only one responsible official has access to the bank account (or however many are authorized to sign checks). All funds are accounted for all the time. Even though organizations may come and go and treasurers may frequently change, a unified budget accounting system provides proper and appropriate systematic records. Figure 9.5.

COMPARISON OF A "TYPICAL" CHURCH BUDGET WITH A "UNIFIED" CHURCH BUDGET

	"Typical" Church Budget	Organizations and Funds	"Unified" Church Budget
Receipts:			
Envelope offerings	$27,000	$ 500	$27,500
Loose offerings	2,700		2,700
Church School offerings	250		250
Communion offerings	250		250
Special gifts	400	250	650
Memorial gifts	-0-	1,000	1,000
Advent offerings	300		300
Parking lot revenues	500		500
Investment income	1,500		1,500
Sales—bazaar	-0-	1,000	1,000
Catering revenues	-0-	1,500	1,500
Miscellaneous—other sales	-0-	150	150
Organ Fund gifts	-0-	4,750	4,750
	$32,900	$ 9,150	$42,050
Disbursements:			
For Mission			
Abroad	$ 1,500		$ 1,500
Nationally	4,000	$ 500	4,500
Locally	500		500
For Pastoral Ministry—			
Salary	13,000		13,000
Pension Plan	1,050		1,050
Social Security allowance	1,300		1,300
Parsonage allowance	3,000		3,000

Figure 9.5*

*Adapted from Church and Clergy Finance, Vol. 8, No. 14 ("The Unified Budget," by Manfred Holck, Jr.), published by Ministers Life Resources, Minneapolis, MN, used with permission.

For Program—

Christian education	150	200	350
Worship and music	50	1,450	1,500
Stewardship education	50		50
Outreach programs	50		50
Youth activities	50	150	200
Scholarships	-0-	500	500
To Organ Fund	-0-	5,000	5,000

For Administration—

Travel and auto allowance	2,700		2,700
Mortgage payments	1,200		1,200
Utilities and insurance	1,500		1,500
Repairs and maintenance	1,000	200	1,200
Postage, supplies	600		600
Secretary salary	1,200		1,200
Food service costs	-0-	1,000	1,000
Miscellaneous	-0-	150	150
Total Budget	$32,900	$ 9,150	$42,050

Organization and Fund Budgets

Women's Group—

Receipts:

Offerings	$ 500
Other gifts	250
Sale items	1,000
Catering committee	1,500
	$ 3,250

Disbursements:

National headquarters dues	$ 500
Nursery care costs	200
Window cleaning church nave	200
Food and supplies	1,000
Gift to Church for banners	500
Scholarships	500
Pastor's vestments	200
Miscellaneous	150
	$ 3,250

Youth Group—

Receipts:

From the Church budget	$ 50
Car wash donations	100
Walk-a-thon donations	50
	$ 200

Figure 9.5 (cont'd.)

Disbursements:
College Day trip	$ 100
Canoe trip	75
Supplies	25
	$ 200

Memorial Fund—
Receipts:
Offerings and gifts	$ 1,000

Disbursements:
Candles and altar furnishings	$ 500
Vestments and new paraments	250
To Organ Fund	250
	$ 1,000

Organ Fund—
Receipts:
Gifts and offerings	$ 4,750
From Memorial Fund	250
	$ 5,000

Disbursements:
To savings account	$ 5,000

Note: Total receipts and disbursements are not identical for both budgets because certain transfers between funds are not reflected in the "Unified" Budget.

Total Receipts: Budget	$32,900	$42,050
Organizations	9,450	-0-
	$42,350	$42,050
Total Disbursements: Budget	$32,900	$42,050
Organizations	9,450	-0-
	$42,350	$42,050

Procedures for Developing and Using a Unified Budget (Figure 9.5)

1. The typical congregational budget is shown in column one. In column two are budgets for each of the congregation's organizations. Column three is a unified budget.

2. The unified budget combines the congregational budget with all of the other organizational budgets into one comprehensive churchwide budget. This provides the congregation with a more realistic picture of total congregational resources and programs.

Figure 9.5 (cont'd.)

3. In the illustration, the unified budget is not the same total as the total of the typical budget plus all the organizational budgets. Due to transfers between funds, the total program of the congregation is not the sum of all those programs plus the congregational budget.

4. Anticipated receipts and disbursements of each organization are combined with the congregation's expected program to arrive at the total unified budget. Each group still retains the same resources as before. But as subsequent budgets are developed, the Church Council may wish to allocate more funds to certain organizations, say the youth, irrespective of how much the youth can raise on their own from car washes and other activites.

Individual organizational programs thus are not dependent on the funds which each on its own can raise in competition with all of the other organizations in the congregation. Besides, members can contribute to the total program of the congregation rather than dividing their giving between organizations. Gifts are given to the work of the church, not to specific groups with the most aggressive fund raising techniques.

Figure 9.5 (cont'd.)

A *capital budget* outlines the costs for a specific building or renovation project cost. Such budgets list: (1) all anticipated resources available for the project and (2) all costs estimated to be incurred for completing the project. Revenues would include all anticipated contributions and/or pledges, mortgage proceeds, earned interest, special gifts, and all money anticipated for use in the project. Every cost is listed as well, including all construction costs, interest on construction loans, fees, etc.—everything required to finish the project. See Figure 9.6 for an example. A capital budget is developed for the life of the construction phase of the project.

CAPITAL SPENDING BUDGET

Sources of Funds

Commitments from members		
Three year pledges[1]	$300,000	
less 10% uncollectable	30,000	$270,000
Interest income		
Cash on hand prior to debt payments[2]		
First year average investment	$ 3,000	
Second year average investment	7,500	10,500
Sale of old church building and land		200,000
Interest income on sale proceeds		15,000

Figure 9.6

First mortgage bank loan, 10 yrs, 9%	300,000
Special memorial gifts for windows	10,000
New organ fund accumulations to date	50,000
	$855,500
Current operating fund budget (if additional gifts do not materialize)	100,000
	$955,500

Allocation of Funds

New church building site	$100,000
Building construction contract	620,000
Landscaping	4,500
Architect fees	50,000
Legal fees and permits	1,000
Furnishings and furniture	100,000
Windows—special	10,000
Organ	50,000
Parking lot and lights construction contract	10,000
Construction loan interest	10,000
	$955,500

[1] Additional three year pledge commitment at end of first three year program, $300,000 less 10%; four year clean-up pledge commitment program for $200,000 less 10%

[2] Construction completed 18 months after pledges begin.

Procedures for Developing
A Capital Spending Budget (Figure 9.6)

1. The purpose of this budget is to list available resources and proposed disbursements for a specific capital improvements project.

2. All available resources should be listed:
   a. Anticipated contributions for a fund-raising activity.
   b. Estimated interest income on contributions until they are required for the project.
   c. Other sources of funds, such as proceeds from the sale of land, bequests, special gifts, grants, plus the interest that may be earned on those funds until used for the project.
   d. Mortgage or other loan proceeds.
   e. Any anticipated "subsidy" from the current operating budget.

3. The proposed allocation of these resources must then be budgeted, the total of the allocation not exceeding the available resources. List all expected costs, including interest on construction costs, all fees, expenses, contracts, furnishings, etc.

Figure 9.6 (cont'd.)

A *debt retirement budget* lists all resources and uses of funds required to pay off indebtedness. Such a budget should be developed annually for the life of a specific loan, carefully describing precisely how each debt will be paid and the sources of funds to meet those commitments. See Figure 9.7.

DEBT RETIREMENT BUDGET (CASH FLOW PROJECTED)

		Years after construction completed	
		1	2
	Uses of Funds		
1	Project costs	$ 955,500	
2	Amortization of loans:		
3	First mortgage principal	30,000	$ 30,000
4	First mortgage interest, 9%	27,000	24,300
5	Interim loan principal[1]	-0-	19,700
6	Interim loan interest, 10%	30,000	30,000
7		$1,042,500	$104,000
8	*Sources of Funds*		
9	Three year member commitments	$ 135,000	$ 90,000
10	Three year member commitments additional	-0-	
11	Four year clean-up member commitments	-0-	
12	Interest earned	10,500	
13	Sale of land	200,000	
14	Interest earned on land sale funds	15,000	
15	First mortgage proceeds	300,000	
16	Memorial gifts	6,000	4,000
17	Organ Fund	50,000	
18	Operating budget	-0-	10,000
19	Interim loan	326,000	
20		$1,042,500	$104,000

[1]Converted to second mortgage end of fourth year, due in full in six years.

	3	4	5	6	7	8	9	10
1								
2								
3	$ 30,000	$ 30,000	$ 30,000	$30,000	$30,000	$30,000	$30,000	$30,000
4	21,600	18,900	16,200	13,500	10,800	8,100	7,000	4,200
5	25,400	34,900	62,200	28,400	33,200	39,900	42,500	39,800
6	28,000	26,200	21,600	18,100	16,000	12,000	10,500	6,000
7	$105,000	$110,000	$130,000	$90,000	$90,000	$90,000	$90,000	$80,000
8								

Figure 9.7

	9	$ 45,000							
	10	45,000	$ 90,000	$ 90,000	$45,000	$45,000	$45,000	$45,000	$45,000
	11								
	12								
	13								
	14								
	15								
	16								
	17								
	18	15,000	20,000	40,000	45,000	45,000	45,000	45,000	35,000
	19								
	20	$105,000	$110,000	$130,000	$90,000	$90,000	$90,000	$90,000	$80,000

Procedures for Developing and Using
A Debt Retirement Budget (Figure 9.7)

1. The purpose of a debt retirement budget is to anticipate cash requirements and sources of funds for paying off any loan commitments for capital projects or other projects requiring extensive financing.

2. After completion of the project, resources and costs for each year of the anticipated life of all loans should be listed.

3. In the first year, the cost of the project is listed and all available funds are listed, too. This may be in part a repeat of the capital spending budget. The listing must also include any required payments on mortgages or loans in that first year.

4. In subsequent years, interest and principal on all loans should be listed together with the source of funds to meet those commitments. In the example it is expected that the current operating budget and a special fund-raising activity will provide all funds for debt retirement.

5. If a sinking fund (a fund into which deposits are regularly made and from which payments are made on indebtedness as required) is required for debt retirement, those deposits would be a periodic required use of funds, the source to be determined by the congregation.

Figure 9.7 (cont'd.)

Chapter Ten

Using the Church Budget: Financial Reporting with a Church Budget: Developing a Master Church Budget Plan

Putting a final budget together and getting it approved is, obviously, not the end of the budget. Now it must be used for all those reasons that budgets are made: setting policy, then planning, implementing, and controlling the program which the congregation has approved.

Once goals have been set, a program planned, and the budget approved, it can be implemented. Spending begins for those programs and continues up to the limits approved by the congregation. The budget is now used to make certain that funds are spent for the programs approved and that funds in excess of the budget are not paid out unless approved by the proper authorities.

Timely monthly or quarterly financial statements, of course, are required if that control is to be exercised by the official Board and spending patterns changed if necessary. A report that is a month late will be ineffective in trying to cut costs for the month already past. That time lag of more than a month will have created new demands. Timely reports are essential if the budget is to be used as a controlling device and corrective action taken. The budget must be compared with the actual results of operations as soon after the end of each period as possible; otherwise, your congregational leaders may as well forget about having a budget in the first place.

Figure 10.1 shows the use of a budget for comparison with actual operating results for a reporting period. The financial statement shows the budget for the same period of time as the statement. An annual budget isn't much help in comparison to six months of experience. The six months' budget needs to be shown.

USING THE BUDGET WITH PERIODIC FINANCIAL REPORTS

Christ Lutheran Church
Statement of Receipts and Disbursements
With Comparisons to Budget
For the Six Months Ending June 30, 19___

This Month				Six Months to Date		
Actual	Budget	Deviation		Actual	Budget	Deviation
			Receipts:			
$ 1300	$ 1500	$ (200)	Envelope offerings	$ 12000	$ 13500	$ (1500)
175	150	25	Loose plate offerings	1300	1350	(50)
-0-	-0-	-0-	Church School	130	125	5
25	15	10	Communion offerings	100	125	(25)
-0-	-0-	-0-	Special gifts	100	200	(100)
-0-	-0-	-0-	Advent offerings	-0-	-0-	-0-
-0-	42	(42)	Parking lot revenues	210	252	(42)
-0-	-0-	-0-	Investment income	750	750	-0-
$ 1500	$ 1707	$ (207)		$ 14590	$ 16302	$ (1712)
			Disbursements:			
			For Missions—			
$ -0-	$ 125	$ 125	Abroad	$ 750	$ 750	$ -0-
200	333	133	Nationally	1000	2000	1000
-0-	42	42	Locally	-0-	250	250
			For Pastoral Ministry—			
1083	1083	-0-	Pastor's salary	6500	6498	(2)
250	250	-0-	Housing allowance	1500	1500	-0-
325	325	-0-	Social Security allow.	650	650	-0-
88	88	-0-	Pension plan	528	528	-0-
			For Program—			
-0-	-0-	-0-	Christian education	10	20	10
5	-0-	(5)	Youth	10	25	15
5	-0-	(5)	Worship & music	10	15	5
-0-	-0-	-0-	Stewardship	-0-	-0-	-0-
-0-	-0-	-0-	Outreach	-0-	25	25

Figure 10.1

			For Administration—			
100	100	-0-	Secretary salary	600	600	-0-
20	40	20	Supplies, postage	300	310	10
175	150	(25)	Travel and auto allow.	1200	1350	150
-0-	83	83	Repairs & maintenance	100	498	398
100	120	20	Utilities & insurance	800	760	(40)
100	100	-0-	Mortgage payments	600	600	-0-
$ 2451	$ 2839	$ 388		$ 14558	$ 16379	$ 1821
$ (951)			Net cash for the period	$ 32		

How to Use the Periodic Financial Statement (Figure 10. 1)

1. A six column financial statement format may be developed with appropriate headings. The first three columns compare activity for the current month between budgeted and actual receipts and disbursements. The last three columns do the same comparison for the year to date. The annual budget is not shown, only the current month's proportion and the year to date.

2. The importance of this statement is not just to list the facts and see how the totals compare, but to analyze each line to see how individual receipts and disbursements compare with what was estimated. Serious variances need to be analyzed carefully and appropriate action taken when necessary.

For example, offerings from envelopes are below what had been estimated by more than 10%. At that rate, offerings could drop off by a large dollar amount by year end. Corrective action should be taken: a letter to the membership, special appeals, reductions in proposed costs. Fortunately, expenses have been kept down so that the year to date receipts are still more than disbursements even though both are less than budgeted.

Figure 10. 1 (cont'd.)

Comparison with last year's actual experience for the same period of time may also be helpful, although too many figures and columns can detract from the readability of the statement. The purpose of the statement is to compare this year's results with what has been budgeted so that deviations can be corrected as required. Last year's record helps readers to see just how this year's experience compares, but the budget is a more critical comparison.

A financial statement can reveal a tremendous amount of important information about the congregation's program and progress. For example, the congregation in Figure 10.1 has obvious problems that need some attention if the congregation's expected income is going to cover budgeted expenses. While the use of a variable budget such as is shown in Figure 10.2 offers a better comparison for expected costs for the six months, many congregations simply divide the annual budget by twelve, which was done in this example. That is much easier to do than estimating what portion of the total annual budget may be spent each month.

An analysis of the financial statement and its comparison with the budget reveals the following items of concern:

1. Income for the six months, as well as for the month, is considerably below that which was expected by this time. The principal problem seems to be the failure of the membership to keep up pledge commitments made for the six months. Even though those commitments are reduced by 10% in anticipation of some attrition, it appears now that only 80% of the pledged amount will be contributed. Perhaps the official Board needs to take some action to reverse and correct the trend.

2. The reduction in income means that expenses must be curtailed as well. Some congregations might have used other monies (either borrowed from the bank or other funds) to meet expense commitments, but unless more cash is available, current offerings will limit how much can be spent. The congregation has received only $14,590 in six months (even though $16,302 had been anticipated by this time) and thus cannot spend more than that. $14,558 has been spent, but $16,379 had been budgeted to be spent. Expenses have been curtailed wisely because income is lower than expected. As in most situations, benevolence contributions and payments suffer because of that failure.

3. Other sources of income are likewise not up to expectations. Not much can be done about loose plate offerings, especially in the summer. Special gifts may need to be solicited to meet budget requirements. And there must be an empty parking space as well that is losing rental income.

4. The pastor has been paid in full and presumably other required expenses met. But benevolences, as mentioned, which are generally not a required payment, go unpaid. Little is provided for program improvement either. Thus, with reduced income the congregation is barely holding its own and then only by paying no more than is required to meet existing commitments. The situation is disconcerting and needs a good push from someone to get things moving again.

But a financial statement such as this, presented on a timely basis, offers the official Board an excellent opportunity to find out that a problem exists and to do something about it. With the right kind of action, offerings and program might just pick up steam again by the time fall rolls around.

The use of *written comments* to accompany financial statements can be helpful to an understanding of what is going on. Something similar to items one to four above might be listed. Explanations are important and can offer suggestions on how problems might be resolved.

PROJECTED CASH FLOW—RECEIPTS AND DISBURSEMENTS

Receipts	Jan	Feb	Mar	Apr	May	Jun	Jul	Aug	Sep	Oct	Nov	Dec	Total
Envelopes	2200	2300	2500	3000	2000	1500	1500	1500	2000	2500	2500	3500	27000
Loose off.	220	230	250	300	200	150	150	150	200	250	250	350	2700
Church Sch.	25	25	25	25	25	-0-	-0-	-0-	30	30	30	35	250
Communion	20	20	30	25	15	15	15	15	15	30	20	30	250
Special	50	50	50	50	-0-	-0-	-0-	-0-	50	50	50	50	400
Advent	-0-	-0-	-0-	-0-	-0-	-0-	-0-	-0-	-0-	-0-	-0-	300	300
Parking lot	42	42	42	42	42	42	42	42	41	41	41	41	500
Investments	375	-0-	-0-	375	-0-	-0-	375	-0-	-0-	375	-0-	-0-	1500
Monthly	2932	2667	2897	3817	2282	1707	2082	1707	2336	3276	2891	4306	32900

Expenditures	Jan	Feb	Mar	Apr	May	Jun	Jul	Aug	Sep	Oct	Nov	Dec	Total
Benevolences:													
Abroad	125	125	125	125	125	125	125	125	125	125	125	125	1500
Nationally	333	333	333	333	333	333	333	333	334	334	334	334	4000
Locally	42	42	42	42	42	42	42	42	41	41	41	41	500
Ministry of the Word:													
Pastor sal.	1083	1083	1083	1083	1083	1083	1083	1083	1084	1084	1084	1084	13000
Housing all.	250	250	250	250	250	250	250	250	250	250	250	250	3000
S.S. all.	-0-	-0-	-0-	325	-0-	325	-0-	-0-	325	0-	0-	325	1300
Pension	88	88	88	88	88	88	87	87	87	87	87	87	1050

Figure 10.2

Administration:													
Secretary	100	100	100	100	100	100	100	100	100	100	100	100	1200
Supp. postage	50	50	60	60	50	40	40	40	50	50	50	60	600
Car allow.	220	230	250	300	200	150	150	150	200	250	250	350	2700
Maintenance	83	83	83	83	83	83	83	83	84	84	84	84	1000
Util., ins.	140	130	125	125	120	120	110	110	125	125	130	140	1500
Program:													
Christian ed.	5	5	5	5	-0-	-0-	-0-	-0-	100	20	5	5	150
Youth	5	5	5	5	5	-0-	-0-	5	5	5	5	5	50
Worship	-0-	-0-	15	-0-	-0-	-0-	-0-	-0-	15	5	10	5	50
Stewardship	-0-	-0-	-0-	-0-	-0-	-0-	25	-0-	25	-0-	-0-	-0-	50
Outreach	5	5	5	5	5	-0-	-0-	5	5	5	5	5	50
Debt Retirement:													
Church bldg.	100	100	100	100	100	100	100	100	100	100	100	100	1200
Monthly	2629	2629	2669	3029	2584	2839	2528	2513	3055	2665	2660	3100	32900
Monthly Difference	303	38	228	788	(302)	(1132)	(446)	(806)	(719)	611	231	1206	-0-

Figure 10.2 (cont'd.)

118

Procedures for Developing and Using the Cash Flow Budget (Figure 10.2)

1. A cash flow budget for receipts and disbursements is an estimate of cash actually expected to be received and spent each month of the budget year. Total receipts and disbursements are still the same as the total budget. But neither total is simply divided by twelve to arrive at expected monthly amounts.

2. The budgets so developed can be a more realistic guide to congregational performance. Thus in months of expected high offerings—Easter and Christmas—the use of a cash forecast helps to keep the proper perspective regarding forthcoming low offering months. When offerings are high any surpluses are obviously going to be required in low offerings months. The cash projection shows that. Hope for covering cash deficits in low income months can be seen in the projections for better times ahead.

3. Furthermore, a cash projection of receipts helps to identify those months when larger than usual expenses or annual, one-time expenses can be scheduled. The annual insurance premium for example might best be paid in April rather than in mid-summer. Or in the months of high utility costs, say summer air conditioning, other costs could be postponed to months with higher anticipated cash resources.

Obviously the Board must now take such action as it deems necessary. Immediate action is important if any attempt is going to be made to correct the situation, and the Board must be prepared to take action. The budget is probably not going to be met, so alternative plans must be agreed upon about what to do.

There will be those who will complain bitterly that benevolences are not paid in full or that so little is going to program. Thus, some sort of policy must be developed on what commitments will be paid up to budgeted amounts with whatever additional income may be received. The information to make those decisions is at hand when reports of this type are available for Board consideration promptly. It is the Board's responsibility to see that money is received and spent as budgeted. Otherwise the Board is not fulfilling its responsibilities for the congregation and the budget is meaningless.

A Master Budget Plan

Aggressive congregations make it a point to plan ahead. Thus a one year budget offers information and controls over the current year but has no bearing or relationship to any years beyond. A master financial plan can be a useful tool to planning and to avoiding the unexpected.

While no one can correctly foresee the circumstances in future years that will affect a congregation's program and finances, the discipline of looking ahead, planning and anticipating is essential to realistic budgeting. Conditions can change rather quickly or more slowly, but either way, the congregation that has made plans for the next few years will be able to handle those changing situations much more realistically.

Any future plan, however, is at best only a guess about what will be. It must therefore be flexible and always subject to change. In fact, as such plans are updated each year, they will be changed. And the further out one goes, the less reliable those later estimates will be.

A one year budget is basic. A three year budget is helpful, a five year budget may be useful, but anything beyond that is really anybody's guess.

Setting up a master plan can be done in much the same way as the annual budget's preliminary program is developed. For example, a selected group of interested members can be assembled as often as necessary to draft a plan for, say, five years. Members must obviously be knowledgeable and somewhat influential in the life of the congregation. Based on their experience as to what has been and what they see may be the direction of the congregation, a plan can be developed.

As always, the congregation's objective must be determined. What do you want to accomplish? What is the mission of the congregation? What direction should it take? How should it witness to the community? What are reasonable growth goals? In short, just what should the congregation be doing during each of the next several years?

Once objectives have been agreed upon (and that is by far the most difficult task in long range planning), costs for those programs must be estimated. That also may be difficult, but the best estimate should be obtained, at least as good as can be determined, knowing the facts today. Next year's estimate of those costs may be far different than the ones made now. But the plan will be updated every year anyway. Objectives may be changed, costs will surely change, and a new year will be added too.

Next, after objectives are agreed upon and costs estimated, income must be measured to be certain all of those programs can be accomplished. Most likely those costs will far exceed any reasonable estimate of costs so far determined. Nevertheless, in an active, aggressive congregation, more income should be available each successive year. The combination of membership growth and improved levels of giving by families should bring significant income growth.

Now not every congregation is going to grow within the next few years. Some may, in fact, for very good reasons anticipate severe setbacks. A declining budget may very well be the master plan for some. But whatever projection you anticipate for growth in dollars, it must somehow match or exceed those expenses required to meet objectives of the plan.

A more intensive stewardship effort may be necessary to reach those goals. A change in emphasis of some kind may be required. Alternate means for raising more dollars must be explored, even professional fund raising help may be needed. But a plan for increasing the income needed to meet the costs required to accomplish the objectives must also be developed.

Figure 10.3 shows an example of how a master plan may look. Notice that it is not in the same familiar format of the annual budget. The plan is intended to show objectives or goals to be accomplished, rather than specific line item costs to be achieved. Estimated costs for achieving those goals are then matched to the sources of income expected to accomplish that program.

Frequent revisions, constant updating, and periodic review of goal achievement is necessary if the master plan is to be an effective planning or management tool.

FIVE YEAR MASTER BUDGET PLAN

Christ Church
Five Year Master Budget Plan
19X1-19X5

Objective	Goal	Proposed Budgets				
		19X1	19X2	19X3	19X4	19X5
I. In Mission to our World: To increase our congregation's share of its total resources for use by others beyond our congregation to 25% of total budget by 19X5.	1. Abroad	800	800	800	1000	1000
	2. Nationally	5000	7000	9000	13500	19000
	3. Locally	200	200	200	500	880
		6000	8000	10000	15000	20880
II. In Mission to our Community: A. Evangelism: To secure greater participation by members in visitation and work with nonmembers.	1. To involve at least five new persons in the work annually. 2. To add twenty new members annually to the roll.					
	Total	3277	3309	3340	3370	3400

Figure 10.3

Proposed Budgets

Objective	Goal	19X1	19X2	19X3	19X4	19X5
B. Inter-church: To involve the congregation in non-congregational religious organizations.	1. To increase support of the Council of Churches by 2% per year.					
	2. To share in ministry to migrants by supporting one new person each summer.					
	Total	701	710	750	800	820
C. Social Concerns: To share with those in need the concerns and resources of our congregation.	1. To visit shut-ins, the sick, regularly.					
	2. To counsel nonmembers as needed.					
	3. To assist in welfare programs for the elderly.					
	Total	2624	2690	2720	2750	2800
III. In Mission to Our Congregation: A. To generate enthusiasm for and participation in the worship and music program.	1. To increase the Senior Choir to twenty persons.					
	2. To establish a children's choir.					
	3. To provide worship supplement materials.					
	4. To acquire a new organ within five years.					
	Total	5874	5925	5885	20900	30000

Figure 10.3 (cont'd.)

123

Objective	Goal	Proposed Budgets				
		19X1	19X2	19X3	19X4	19X5
B. To provide an atmosphere for Christian learning for all members.	1. To secure a part-time director by 19X4. 2. To increase Sunday School attendance by 10% each year. 3. To improve facilities and programs for Junior Highs. 4. To provide an annual teacher education training program.					
	Total	6074	6134	6190	9200	9300
C. To develop a program of concern for member's needs.	1. To plan and implement two EMV's annually. 2. To free pastor from administrative tasks. 3. To involve at least two lay leaders monthly in visitations to members.					
	Total					
D. To maintain the property and equipment of the church building						
	Total	4550	4600	4700	4750	4900

Figure 10.3 (cont'd.)

Objective	Goal	Proposed Budgets 19X1	19X2	19X3	19X4	19X5
	1. To prepare and update an inventory of all equipment.					
	2. To prepare a preventative maintenance program.					
	3. To replace the roof by 19X3.					
	4. To review insurance coverage annually.					
	Total	2600	2800	12920	13000	5420
E. To provide for regular debt retirement program.	1. To pay off mortgage by 19X6.					
	2. To encourage pre-payments and additional gifts.					
	Total	1200	2400	3600	4800	6000
Total proposed budgets		$32900	$36568	$50105	$74570	$83520

Figure 10.3 (cont'd.)

Part Three

Church Accounting Techniques:
Selecting the Best Procedure
For Achieving the Most Effective
Record Keeping System

Chapter Eleven

Accounting for Income:
A Responsibility and Trust
To Every Donor,
A Stewardship to the Congregation

The primary source of income for almost every congregation is the Sunday morning offering. While some congregations do have other sources of income, sometimes in substantial amounts, the regular weekly offering is by far the most significant source of funds. Accounting for that income as well as for the other income from whatever source becomes an important and crucial responsibility for your congregational treasurer.

That primary source of funds which support the ongoing program of your congregation may in fact not all be received during worship services. Offerings do come in through the week by mail. And not every one gives weekly either, thus substantial gifts might be received even on a quarterly or annual basis. But offerings are received, and the gifts received to support the program and activities of the congregation are by far the largest source of revenue for most congregations.

In addition to this source, many congregations have income from investments, either securities or savings accounts, or rental properties, or something else. The income so generated may or may not be restricted, but it certainly must be accounted for. For congregations with substantial endowments, investment income can be a significant source of revenue.

Congregations which have unrelated business activity must also account for the sales revenue generated by those activities. Even bake sales, bazaars, and garage sales generate income that must be carefully collected, deposited, recorded and reported.

It is obvious that all those sources of income are important. Thus, proper procedures should be established to be certain that the funds are finally used for the purposes given or designated.

Control Over Income

In a later chapter more will be said about the concept of internal control and how it relates to the accounting functions of congregations. It is sufficient here to indicate that internal control is simply the creation of a system of procedures that will control the flow of money within an organization in such a way that it cannot easily, if at all, be misappropriated or diverted to other uses.

In the case of cash, sufficient control must be created so that there is a record of all cash received and an assurance that it was all deposited properly in the bank account.

That control is particularly difficult for congregations since so much of the income comes through the weekly offering rather than in the sale of goods and services. There are no records possible to verify the receipt of a specified offering. Not until the money is counted is there any notion of how much money has been or should have been placed in the offering plates.

Thus, a duplicate, prenumbered and controlled receipt cannot be given, normally, at the time money is first received by a congregation. To do so, if it were possible, would indeed provide the same record which a business requires of cash actually received. Total receipts could then be compared with total cash received. Any deviation would cause concern.

But congregations receive cash without the benefit of a careful check on how much should have been paid in. Thus, it is critical that two people are always involved with the congregation's cash once it has been placed in the offering plate and until it is safely deposited. While misappropriation is always a risk if only one person has access to cash, there is also the risk that someone will *think* cash has been misappropriated. To avoid either situation, at least two people should always be around the offering plates when there is cash in them. It avoids the risk of loss as well as the accusation that there was a loss.

Many members do make their gifts by using checks. It is, in fact, the sensible way to give money. Not only does it provide the giver with evidence of the gift, but a check is more difficult to misappropriate than cash. Nevertheless, many members do contribute cash, sometimes in large sums; thus, controls for such giving must be implemented.

Careful control over the receipt of checks, however, is still important. When received, those checks should be promptly and correctly endorsed. That avoids the risk of someone else endorsing the check and fraudulently attempting to cash it. A proper endorsement will read, "Pay to the order of the First National Bank, Minneapolis, Minnesota, for deposit only to the account of All Saints Church —Account Number 11-54321."

All cash and all checks should, of course, be deposited promptly, intact, in the bank. No part of the offering should be used to pay bills or otherwise diverted to some other use. What is received should be deposited. Payments also need to be controlled and recorded, as will be noted in the next chapter. Thus, appropriate procedures must be followed if such items are to be properly reported to the membership. A record of total receipts and total expenses is possible only if such procedures are followed.

Furthermore, your congregational treasurer should not be involved in any way in the receipt or counting or depositing function of any cash. Anyone who has access to the record keeping process should not be permitted access to cash. The chance of misappropriation is much greater when those in charge of record keeping are also responsible for counting the cash.

Of course, the treasurer must know the total amount deposited and must have access to counting reports, but if adequate control over cash is to be maintained, someone else must count the money.

How to Count the Sunday Offering*

Every congregation has developed some kind of a system for taking care of this Sunday morning activity, from the most informal (maybe the pastor does it!) to the most elaborate. Most of those procedures, however, are probably in need of considerable improvement. Too often proper controls are lacking, opportunity for misappropriation is obvious (and it happens, even in the church), and a congregation's trust in those persons "who have always counted the money" is taken advantage of.

The procedure for counting the Sunday offering, the timing of the count, recording the results, and getting the money to the bank are all critical elements in the process. Proper internal control procedures will assure the membership that money given will be money used for the purposes intended.

So, to begin with, the offering should be counted immediately following the services. If that seems impossible or impractical (it does interfere with Sunday dinner), then the entire offering can be placed in a bank bag and immediately placed in the night depository of the bank. Counting can wait until later in the week. But the ideal time is Sunday morning.

As previously noted, two or more persons (always at least two people) should be assigned the counting task each week. Some continuity in personnel will facilitate the actual counting process, but alternating counters is a good internal control procedure. It reduces the chances for misappropriation.

Both persons remove the offering from the sanctuary and immediately take it

---

*Adapted from *Church and Clergy Finance*, Vol. 6, No. 13 ("How to Count the Sunday Morning Offering," by Manfred Holck, Jr.), published by Ministers Life Resources, Minneapolis, MN, used with permission.

to a counting room. This will be a safe, secure, locked room, where the count can be made without interference and without the chance of a forced entry by some intruder. Security is important. A quiet place expedites an efficient and quicker count.

Those persons will then sort coins, bills, checks and offering envelopes. Loose offerings are counted first and tallied on the count sheet. Envelopes are then opened, amounts enclosed verified and marked on each envelope, with the total coins, bills and checks then totaled for agreement with the amounts marked thereon.

Notations about special gifts are made on the count sheet. A deposit slip of all monies is prepared. The total deposit must be equal to the coins, bills, and checks noted on the count sheet. Totals of envelopes, special gifts, and the loose offerings must also equal the total deposit.

The deposit is taken (by two people) to the bank's night depository immediately after the count is completed.

The deposit slip and the count sheet are prepared in triplicate. Totals of both must be equal. Distribution of copies goes this way:

Count sheet

Original to the treasurer to explain the distribution of the deposit.

First copy to the financial secretary to be attached to a copy of the deposit slip for verification and recording of all offerings received and deposits made.

Second copy to the assistant financial secretary for verifying posting of total member contributions to individual record sheets.

Deposit slip

Original to the bank and eventually returned to the treasurer with the bank statement.

First copy to the treasurer so the deposit can be properly noted in the checkbook and cash receipts journal.

Second copy to the financial secretary for attachment to the count sheet verifying that funds received are deposited.

If the funds are counted later in the week because of the impracticality of doing so on Sunday, similar procedures may be followed. At least two designated persons will remove the deposit bag from the bank night depository to sort and count the funds right there. Count sheets and deposit slips are made up on the bank's premises. Once placed in the night depository, the offering money never leaves the bank building.

In addition to the two or more persons assigned responsibility for receiving, counting, and depositing the offerings, other individuals, as noted, are involved in the process. The church treasurer never has access to the offering monies (separation of duties between spending and receiving is critical) but must know the amounts for entry into the cash receipts journal and the check book.

The financial secretary keeps accurate record of all monies received, but has no access to the checkbook and can thus spend nothing (again, separation of duties between spending and receiving cash). A week by week tally of all the offerings and their purpose is easily maintained from the weekly count sheet. A report by the financial secretary of all offerings must agree with deposits noted by the treasurer.

An assistant financial secretary records member contributions to their individual contributions record sheets. Separation of functions requires that those who record contributions to member's individual record sheets may not have access to the receipt or payment of any cash. Members' envelopes, properly marked on the outside by the counting tellers, provide the data for entries. Total of all envelopes is verified on the count sheet.

Tellers assigned to count the offering should not be the treasurer, the financial secretary, or the assistant financial secretary. Internal control procedures require the strict separation of cash disbursements, receipts, and recording of member contributions records.

That, of course, would be the ideal system and one you might want to strive for in your congregation. Chances are you have some variation on that plan. But if you really want to maintain the control you should, this is the way things ought to be arranged.

A carefully outlined procedure, in writing, will also facilitate some continuity in the counting process. Those instructions should be kept as simple as possible, but complete. Too much detail or explanation may only encourage noncompliance or unwanted variation.

Perhaps you'll need a special committee or person assigned to the tasks of coordinating this process. Someone must make sure that the Sunday morning offering will be counted right, recorded, deposited, and accurately accounted for to the membership.

COUNT SHEET—SUNDAY MORNING OFFERING   Date_____

	Coins	Bills	Checks	Total	
Benevolences					
Loose	___	___	___	___	
Envelopes	___	___	___	___	___
Current					
Loose	___	___	___	___	
Envelopes	___	___	___	___	___
Building Fund					
Loose	___	___	___	___	
Envelopes	___	___	___	___	___

Figure 11.1

Special Offerings
   Loose   ____   ____   ____   ____
   Envelopes   ____   ____   ____   ____   ____
Total Deposit   ____   ____   ____   ____   ____

Counted by _____ Date _____
Counted by _____ Date _____

Figure 11.1 (cont'd.)

MONTHLY OFFERING COUNT SUMMARY REPORT   Date _____

	Week 1	Week 2	Week 3	Week 4	Week 5	Total
Benevolences						
Loose						
Envelopes						
Current						
Loose						
Envelopes						
Building Fund						
Loose						
Envelopes						
Special Off.						
Loose						
Envelopes						
Total Offerings						
Total Deposits						

Note: Total offerings and total deposits must be equal.

Prepared by   Date

Figure 11.2

Protecting and Maximizing Cash

The security of your congregation's cash and maximizing its use is equally important to proper control. Adequate protection through proper procedure will diminish the risk of loss through misappropriation, but equally important is the need to provide safekeeping for cash and to maximize the return on cash.

The obvious way to protect the congregation's cash is to place it on deposit in a bank account. Cash should never be left lying around the church building any longer than necessary. Prompt deposit eliminates the chances for theft or loss.

A checking account is generally a necessity for any congregation. And banks will eliminate service charges when minimum balances are carried so there is no cost. All of the bank services will then be available to the congregation. Normally, one cash account will be sufficient for a congregation even though there may be several funds involved. With a carefully kept set of financial records, one checking account will actually be less complicated and offer more flexibility to your congregational treasurer.

Advantages of one checking account

Of course, organizations may object, sometimes rather strenuously, but the advantages of one account for the congregation are impressive.

(1) One account eliminates the possibility of service charges on several different smaller accounts. A minimum balance in one account will involve less cash tied up in non-interest bearing accounts than will many accounts, all with minimum balances.

(2) The transfer of cash between funds is relatively simple even with only one cash account. Only a journal entry is required. Otherwise, with separate accounts, it would be necessary to write a check on one account and deposit it in the other fund. One bank account does require a careful reconciliation periodically of all fund cash balances.

(3) Your congregation has much better control over the use of all contributions, and thus, all cash funds, when only one bank account is used. Too often in congregations with a dozen or more checking accounts, some accounts simply get lost. Organizations come and go, so do treasurers, and sometimes funds simply disappear because no one knows about them or the people originally involved no longer are available or the organization simply disbands or more likely fades out of existence. A common account for all cash requires an appropriate accounting of all cash.

(4) Payments can be more timely and more accurately made with only one account. Requests by any organization for payment of invoices is easily done with a voucher form. Properly authorized vouchers are sufficient for payment of the request by the treasurer. Deposits may be made by anyone or any organization, but duplicate deposit slips and a count sheet must be given to the church treasurer for recording to that fund.

(5) Fund balances and organization accounts will be more accurate because both treasurers (the congregational treasurer and the organizational treasurer) must reconcile their respective fund balances periodically. And without any loss of proprietary interests over individual checking accounts, a single church bank account offers the opportunity for more accurate record keeping and reporting. It's a stewardship responsibility church leaders need to be aware of.

Figure 11.3 shows how various funds and organizations in a congregation can pool their cash without loss of control yet with the assurance of better reporting and stewardship.

(6) One bank account and the totals shown on a report, such as in Figure 11.3, accurately reveal the financial situation of the total congregation. After all, even the organizations are part of the total work of the church. And it should be clear to the women and the Sunday School and to others that their groups are part of the total program of the church, not a competitive organization or an isolated independent unit.

Christ Church
Statement of Revenues, Disbursements and Transfers
Twelve Months Ending December 31, 19X2

	Congregation	Sunday School	Bldg. Fund	Women	Youth	Total
Income:						
Offerings	20000	1000	10000	500	50	31550
Loans			10000			10000
Investment income	2000		500	10		2510
	22000	1000	20500	510	50	44060
Disbursements:						
Salaries	10000					10000
Benevolences	5000			200		5200
Debt payments			4000			4000
Administration exp	5000	200				5200
Programs	1500	900		100	150	2650
Maintenance			15000			15000
	21500	1100	19000	300	150	42050
Excess of income over disbursements	500	(100)	1500	210	(100)	2010
Transfers	(250)	200		(100)	150	-0-
Cash balance beginning	300	50	2000	400	-0-	2750
Cash balance ending	550	150	3500	510	50	4760

NOTE: $100 was transferred by the Women for the congregation's program. The congregation's program transferred $200 to the Sunday School and $150 to the Youth in partial support of those activities.

Figure 11.3: An example of how cash balances in all funds and organizations can be properly accounted for with only one checking account

Reconciliation of Cash Balances to Bank Accounts

	Congre-gation	Sunday School	Bldg. Fund	Women	Youth	Total
Savings account						
Beginning balance	200		2000	200		2400
Additions	100		20500	200		20800
Removals			(19000)			(19000)
Ending balance	300		3500	400		4200
Checking account						
Beginning balance	100	50		200		350
Additions	22000	1200		510	200	23910
Removals	(21850)	(1100)		(600)	(150)	(23700)
Ending balance	250	150		110	50	560
Total cash balances	550	150	3500	510	50	4760

NOTE: Balances in the savings accounts and checking accounts are considered all in the same fund balance total. Deposits to savings accounts are made by check, thus all income goes into the checking account and removals from the checking accounts will include disbursements, transfers, and deposits to the savings accounts.

Figure 11.3 (cont'd.)

(7) Furthermore, the total funds of the congregation should be available for the work of the church. The trustees should not have to depend on the women to support the program of the congregation, but should see that their efforts together are the program. Likewise, the youth group should not feel compelled to raise their own money for their own projects. Their offerings and their expenses are part of the total program of the congregation. Each group complements the other and all need to cooperate. One bank account helps to create that attitude and to generate a sense of cooperation and sharing that must exist within the church.

Using a savings-checking account

In some states you may be able to eliminate a service charge altogether and earn interest, besides, by using a so-called NOW account. That's virtually the same thing as a checking account that earns interest. At least you do earn interest and can withdraw your funds when you need them. Ask at your local bank about the possibilities.

If that arrangement is not possible, you can still deposit the Sunday morning offerings into a daily interest savings account and then withdraw the funds whenever you need them. You may even be able to work out an agreement to have funds transferred between your savings account and your checking account just by telephone. Thus, your congregation's temporarily idle cash can earn interest. By scheduling your bill paying days at specific regular intervals, you can easily maximize your cash flow and earn extra dollars for your congregation.

Individual Contribution Records

Accounting for income involves more than just making sure all the offerings are received and put in the bank. It's more than making sure that the church is earning all it can on its idle cash and endowment monies. It's more than counting the Sunday morning offering.

One of the more important functions is that of recording individual contributions. In large congregations that task can be enormous. Even in smaller congregations it is not a small task. But in either instance it is certainly an important task, one to be done accurately and with all the necessary controls applied to be certain all contributions are properly recorded.

The general concept of internal control that requires the separation of duties among those who handle cash, applies equally to the responsibilities of recording contributions from individuals. The person responsible for this task must not handle offerings, write checks, or in any other way be involved in cash management. To mingle those responsibilities increases the opportunities for misappropriation of cash.

Every congregation will initiate its own procedures, but the principles outlined here and the forms suggested offer ideas for developing an individual system.

Generally, the source of information for recording an individual's contribution is the weekly offering envelope, properly marked and coded. Notations of personal checks not included in envelopes or offerings (given in other ways) must be reported so that proper credit can be given.

A copy of a form similar to that in Figure 11.2 will be given to the person responsible for recording individual contributions. The totals on that form will support the empty but properly coded envelopes also given to this secretary. Obviously, an adding machine tape of the envelopes should match the amounts recorded on the form.

The offering envelopes are then placed in numerical order and amounts posted to the proper accounts. After posting, a trial balance tape should be run from the individual members' ledger accounts to determine that all amounts have been posted. The total of that tape must correspond to the total of the tape attached to the envelopes and that shown on the counting report. This tape of contributions recorded is important to verify that all contributions have been properly posted.

Such a tape, however, does not verify that the posting was made to the correct account, only that it was made.

But confirmation to the member will signal any discrepancies. An inaccurate posting will involve two inaccurate accounts, both of which may well be called to the attention of the secretary by the donors affected.

Figure 11.4 suggests a format for recording individual contributions in a smaller congregation. Larger congregations may wish to use some variation of a

Name_____ No. _____

Address_____

Phone_____

Year	S u n	First Quarter			Second Quarter			Third Quarter			Fourth Quarter		
Pledged Given		Jan.	Feb.	Mar.	April	May	June	July	Aug.	Sept.	Oct.	Nov.	Dec.
Current Pledge/wk.	1												
$_____ Given:/qrt.	2												
1_____	3												
2_____	4												
3_____													
4_____	5												
T_____	T												
Benevolence Pledge/wk.	1												
$_____ Given:/qrt.	2												
1_____	3												
2_____	4												
3_____													
4_____	5												
T_____	T												
Building Fund Pledge/wk.	1												
$_____ Given:/qrt.	2												
1_____	3												
2_____	4												
3_____													
4_____	5												
T_____	T												
Special Offerings Given:/qrt.	1												
	2												
1_____	3												
2_____	4												
3_____													
4_____	5												
T_____	T												

Individual Contributor's Record

Figure 11.4

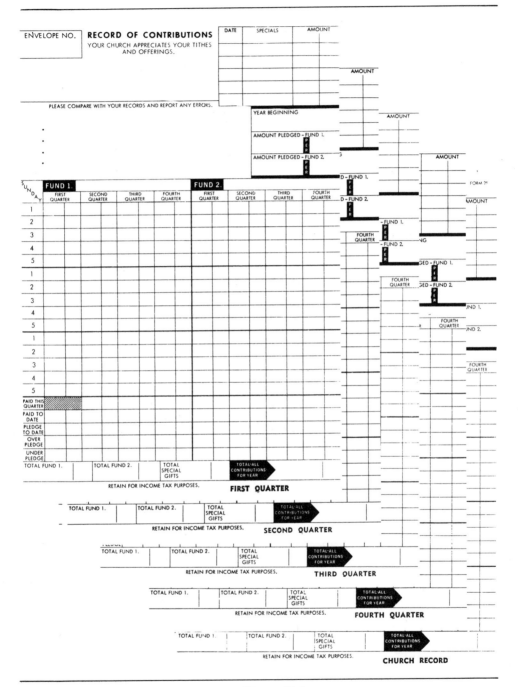

Figure 11.5

five part carbon record, as shown in Figure 11.5. Such a record provides a quarterly report to the members without additional posting. The final quarterly report (fourth carbon) may show contributions for each Sunday of the year. A final, fifth carbon is the congregation's record of that member's giving.

Computer type records are also frequently used to record individual contributions. These vary from a simple listing to elaborately detailed analyses. Such reports are generally kept on a monthly basis and congregations may mail Sunday envelopes to the company handling the procedure. In fact, the most popular use of the computer is probably for this purpose. Selected firms that offer such services are listed on page 218.

Responsibility for recording the members' gifts usually rests with the church secretary and that may be appropriate. The treasurer will handle disbursements, the financial secretary will be responsible for offerings, and another designated person, such as the church secretary or an assistant financial secretary or a recording financial secretary will handle member's contributions. Clear lines of responsibility, however, must be described and assiduously adhered to.

A Typical Cash Receipts Journal

While the checkbook will indeed record all deposits and cash receipts, that document by itself is cumbersome to use in developing a financial report of where the congregation's money has come from. Thus, a cash receipts journal is appropriate and is one of the various journals always found in any accounting system.

The cash receipts journal summarizes the organization's income. A typical format would be arranged something like Figure 11.6.

Typical Cash Receipts Journal Format

Date	Payor	Cash Dr.	Offerings Cr.	Accounts Receivable Cr.	Other Income Cr.

Figure 11.6

Since it is usually impractical for a congregation to list every person by name who made a contribution, the total of each deposit made is generally the only information recorded in the cash amount column of the cash receipts journal. The payor column is left blank. But the distribution of that deposit is important to record the various intended uses of that money. That information should be available from the offering count sheet and must be noted on the cash receipts journal in the appropriate column. If an accurate report is to be made on where the congregation's funds have come from, analysis of each deposit is important.

The total of the column showing the amount of the cash deposited must be equal to the sum of all the other columns. It must also equal the total deposits added to the checkbook for the period.

In the typical bookkeeping system, the totals of all columns are then posted (transferred) to the appropriate account ledger sheet. The several systems illustrated in the next few chapters show how this is to be done in each system.

Chapter Twelve

Accounting for Disbursements: Using Generally Accepted Accounting Principles to Control Spending

It is not easy to spend the church's money! Well, it may be easy enough to write checks and deplete the bank account and overdraw the budget, but spending a congregation's money carries with it such a prominent responsibility that it is really not that easy.

Congregational officials have a stewardship responsibility and a command from the congregation to spend that money only in certain ways for certain purposes. The congregation has adopted a budget that sets the parameters of spending. The members, individually, have pledged their support expecting their contributions to be used in the way so agreed when the budget was adopted.

Thus, those church leaders may spend the congregation's money only for those purposes so approved. They may not deviate. And while that may not be too difficult to follow, when offerings fail to reach commitment promised or the spending approved, those officers do have a difficult time deciding how the money should be spent.

Proper and appropriate controls, therefore, are just as important for spending the congregation's money as they are for recording the congregation's income. Approved procedures and authorized controls make the task of spending that money—and keeping track of that spending—much easier. Even the proper financial records are essential for the officers to know how much is left to spend.

Thus, this chapter describes those accounting principles best used in order to control spending. At the outset, however, let it be said that such principles and procedures are not intended to limit spending, rather to control it through proper procedures and records. The budget as adopted places the limit on spending. Accounting procedures provide the means whereby that spending can be controlled intelligently and in the best interests of the members who have given their money to support their church.

Authorization for Spending

There should be no money spent without proper prior approval. Which means, of course, that even committing the congregation to a future payment must be approved. It doesn't make much sense for the treasurer to present a long list of bills to the official Board asking for approval to pay. If the bills are due, if the congregation has committed itself to paying for goods and services received, then there is not much point in going through the exercise of approving bills. They were approved before they were incurred.

Once again, the budget is critical. As approved, it sets the limit. Committees interested in spending their allotment may get permission from the Board by outlining a proposal within the limits of their budgeted amounts. Once approved, that is authority for spending. Upon certification by the person purchasing those goods and services that, in fact, they have been received, the treasurer pays the bill.

The appropriate vehicle for that procedure is usually some type of voucher form, such as that shown in Figure 12. 1

Sample Authorization for Payment Voucher

```
                                                    Date_____

Please pay to: _____

$_____ Account #_____ Program _____

Organization _____ Committee _____

for _____

As approved by the Official Board on _____ or as

listed on the church budget under item _____.

Requested by: _____

Approved for payment by: _____

Date paid _____ Check #_____ Cleared _____
```

Figure 12. 1

Every check disbursed should be supported by a voucher form, approved by the appropriate person. Such supporting documentation verifies that the check was properly written and that the funds of the congregation have been used as originally intended. Any deviation then is the joint responsibility of the treasurer and those who presented and approved the voucher for payment.

So, for example, when the worship committee buys music, it is not enough to present a copy of the invoice or the receipt or the statement to the treasurer asking that the bill be paid or the purchases reimbursed. A voucher request must be submitted, also.

Or where the congregation has only one checking account (a unified budget) and each organization must request funds from the church treasurer, a voucher form must be completed to remove money from that organization's account. When the women have a convention to attend, for example, registration fees must be paid by the church treasurer upon voucher request by the organization's treasurer, which is a reasonable control procedure.

Or when the treasurer pays the monthly heating bill, a voucher form is completed with all the necessary information attached, the check written and mailed. That cost has been authorized by the budget, is an ongoing contract with the utility company and needs no further authorization or approval. But a voucher form describes the payment in full and provides the necessary documentation.

Upon audit of the congregation's financial records, an examination of selected vouchers and corresponding checks will verify the appropriateness of any disbursements. The proper use of a voucher system to request spending and control disbursements can take more time and effort than simply writing out a check. But it offers the required control which any official Board should insist upon.

Responsibilities of the Treasurer

Every congregation must have a treasurer. Generally, that person is a volunteer, elected by the congregation or the official Board to oversee the financial accounting responsibility of that Board for monies received. A church treasurer may be assigned only supervisory responsibility with a paid staff doing all the work. Or the treasurer may, in fact, be the bookkeeper, too.

Generally, a church treasurer should have some knowledge of accounting or at least bookkeeping. At least that helps. The purpose of this book is to offer assistance to that person, especially where such financial record keeping ability is at a minimum.

The treasurer may report directly to the official Board, the congregation, or to a Finance Committee. If a Finance Committee is generally responsible for the fiscal affairs of the congregation, then the treasurer is assigned responsibility for spending, the financial secretary for income. But the books of account, the journals and ledgers would be maintained by the treasurer. Financial reports and all other fiscally related reports would be prepared by the treasurer.

The treasurer would maintain the checkbook and be one of the two persons who signs all checks. The treasurer may also be involved in the preparation of the annual church budget.

Again, it is important that the principle of separation of duties be adhered to quite strictly with respect to the treasurer's assigned responsibility. Those who sign checks should not count money or record individual contributions. The record of deposits must be given to the treasurer, but the treasurer must not have access to the cash prior to its deposit in the bank. The same person may not receive, record, and spend the church's money.

A Checking Account

A congregation should have a checking account. It's the only way to achieve effective control over cash. And except for the very smallest, rural congregation, almost every congregation will have a checking account. In fact, some may have several accounts, as noted in a previous chapter. But one is enough.

The way in which a checking account offers control over cash is in the permanent record which each check offers and in the safety afforded by keeping the cash in the bank. As checks are written they eventually come back to the church as evidence of payment of a debt. Paying cash offers no such record. Writing checks also helps to keep the people who count the cash separate from those who spend it. Without a checking account, those same people would be involved. So, all bills are paid by check, nothing is paid by cash except from a petty cash fund as described later.

A checking account will include appropriate business checks. That means checks printed with the name of the congregation and its address. Checks will be numbered consecutively and every check properly accounted for. Two signatures will be required, again for better control. That way one person cannot run off with all the money. Two people must approve how the money is spent.

Obviously, it defeats the purpose of control if one of those approved check signers signs a bunch of blank checks in advance. There is no control in that, even though it is more convenient. To make sure both signers are around when a check needs to be signed, more than two people could be authorized to sign, so that two of any three or four persons so designated would be acceptable. The pastor should not be one of those persons.

Blank checks should always be kept under proper control of the treasurer.

The Bank Reconciliation

Every bank statement should be reconciled regularly with the financial records of the church. Discrepancies should be noted and corrected promptly. Even with the use of computers, one cannot assume that bank statements are correct. Banks do make mistakes. But, beyond that, it is important that any error in the congregation's records be noted and corrected as soon as possible. Besides, banks often make charges to an account or give credit. These items need to be noted properly on the congregation's records.

Since the treasurer writes the checks and the financial secretary makes the deposits to the bank account, neither should receive the bank statement nor prepare the bank reconciliation. Once again, the separation of the responsibility of receiving, spending, and recording cash must be considered. If the person who writes the checks receives the bank statements, too, improperly written checks can be removed and discarded with necessary journal entries made without arousing the suspicion of anyone. Eventually, that activity might be discovered, but it may be too late. The point is, that by having someone else receive the statement and make the reconciliation, such misappropriation cannot occur so easily. A member of the Finance Committee might be designated to handle this matter.

A typical bank reconciliation procedure would go something like this:

(1) Sort the cancelled checks by number. Compare these checks with the listing of outstanding checks from the previous month and with those checks written for the current month. Make a list of all checks written which have not been returned by the bank. These are the outstanding checks for the current month.

(2) Compare all deposit slips received from the financial secretary with the deposits noted on the bank statement. Deposits not yet recorded on the bank statement are deposits in transit. List them. Any missing deposit slips should be traced immediately.

(3) Note any charge slips or additions to the account recorded by the bank.

(4) Use the form illustrated to reconcile the balances. Add deposits in transit and deduct outstanding checks from the balance of the bank account as shown on the bank statement. Deduct any charges, add any credits to the cash balance shown on the checkbook stubs. When the adjusted balances of the bank statement and the checkbook agree, the bank statement has been reconciled to the congregation's records. Be sure that any charges and credits noted by the bank are reflected not only on the checkbook but also on the journals of the church.

Use the format shown in Figure 12.2

Bank Charges and Credits

Bank statements often include additional charges and credits not previously recorded on the congregation's records. However, when a bank sends through a debit charge to your bank account, you must deduct that amount from your balance. When the bank credits your account, you must add to your cash balance. Which, as noted, is just the opposite of the way the journal entry would appear on the congregation's records. As you know, the cash account of the congregation is increased by a debit and decreased by a credit entry.

Bank Reconciliation Format Worksheet

Congregation's Records   Bank's Records

Check Book balance	_____	Bank Statement balance	_____
Add bank credits	_____	Add deposits in transit	_____
Deduct bank charges	_____	Deduct outstanding checks	_____
Adjusted balance	_____	Adjusted balance	_____

(The adjusted balances must be equal for reconciliation to be in balance.)
The following Journal Entry, if any, is required on the cash disbursements journal:

_____

_____

_____

Figure 12.2

It happens this way because on the bank's records your account is a liability for the bank. Thus, it has a credit balance for your account. Whenever you deposit money in the bank, then the bank owes that money to you. Thus, whenever the bank reduces your account on their records because of a service charge or something else, it must debit your account and so advise you. On your record, you must credit cash to reduce the amount in the bank. Similarly, when the bank adds a deposit to your account, it credits your account, but on your records, you must debit your cash balance to add to it.

Communications from banks can often be confusing, but understanding the transactions this way should be helpful.

Continuity

It is the very nature of the congregational organization structure that the position of treasurer will change frequently. Either the constitution will require a periodic change, or the treasurer will move or resign, or an election will put someone else in the position. It is probably a good idea to change personnel from time to time simply to give new people an opportunity to work at that job. It is also a good method of internal control. Changes in personnel tend to reduce the potential for misappropriation. The same person handling the same cash function for decades could get by without detection of an error for a long time. The matter of controls is as important in congregations as in business. Changing personnel from time to time is one effective method of control.

But changing the officers creates problems in continuity of record keeping. Many new treasurers will insist that the previous procedures are inadequate or inaccurate and will, therefore, recommend changes, perhaps even implementing them without prior approval. Changes may well be needed in a system but there is danger in changing the system every time a new treasurer is appointed. The lack of continuity in the recording and reporting process can be confusing.

One of the functions of accounting is to report accurately and consistently the financial transactions of an organization. The accuracy of recording will not suffer through a change in systems, but consistency may. And that may create some confusion. If the pastor's transportation costs (car allowance), for example, have been calculated in a certain way and reported in one way for years, a change in the method of calculation and the reporting procedure could be confusing although the change may be quite appropriate.

Thus, if reimbursement to the pastor has been $150 a month and that payment has been consistently reported as part of compensation, it may be confusing, although it would be appropriate, to change the reimbursement to 18¢ a mile and report the payment as part of administration costs. Adequate explanation of such a change would be required. But many changes like that by a new treasurer may create reporting problems.

The point is that many treasurers with accounting experience will believe a better system for the congregation is required, as well it may be. If a change is needed, then by all means it should be made. And the purpose of this book is to offer alternative suggestions on just how those changes may be made.

New treasurers who are eager to change the system to a pet procedure of their own should proceed with caution. It may be better to live with the old system for a while and then gradually implement the new. With any change, of course, complete and detailed explanation should be required to justify the new procedure.

What is important, though, is that the transition between treasurers be smooth and uncomplicated and that the continuity of financial record keeping be maintained.

Petty Cash

Many congregations maintain a petty cash fund of one sort or another as a convenience to those persons required to make periodic small cash payments for goods and services or who request reimbursement for such items and for which a check may be impractical. The obvious example is postage due to the postman. An appropriate petty cash fund will provide the necessary small change quickly and easily. Or reimbursement to a teacher for crayons for a Sunday School class can be made quite easily and efficiently through a petty cash fund.

Such a fund is nothing more than the setting aside of a specific amount of cash to be replenished periodically as it is used. Control of the fund will be the specific responsibility of one individual who must at all times be prepared to account for the total cash or its use. The procedure for setting up such a fund may go something like this:

A petty cash treasurer will be designated. An appropriate lock box and security measures will be developed. Cash will be transferred and a regular accounting of funds procedure set up.

The church treasurer will write a check, payable to the bank, marked for "petty cash," in order to secure the cash funds needed. A fund of $50 is probably adequate. Since this disbursement is not yet an expense to the congregation, the $50 amount is charged (debited) to an asset account called "petty cash." A sum of $50 has merely been transferred from one cash account to another.

When requests for reimbursement are required or the postman comes in with a postage due amount, the petty cash treasurer will pay out the cash and fill in a petty cash voucher form to be signed by the payee. (See Figure 12.3).

PETTY CASH VOUCHER

Paid to _____

For _____

Amount $ _____ Date _____

Signed by payee _____

Signed by PC treasurer _____

Figure 12.3

Thus, at any time the total cash in the petty cash box plus the sum of all those petty cash vouchers must equal $50. When the cash is just about all used up, the petty cash treasurer will add up the vouchers, make a listing of the types of expense paid for, and request, by voucher, reimbursement from the church treasurer. A check will be prepared, made payable to the bank and marked for petty cash and cashed by the petty cash treasurer. The cash will be placed in the petty cash box. The petty cash fund is now replenished. And so the procedure is repeated as needed.

The appropriate journal entries for these transactions would be these:

	Debit	Credit
Petty Cash Fund	$50	$
Cash in Bank		50
To set up new petty cash fund		

Supplies Expense	12	
Postage	5	
Bulletins	10	
Cash in Bank		27

To replenish petty cash fund per petty cash voucher receipts

Cash in Bank	20	
Petty Cash Fund		20

To reduce the petty cash fund to $30

Cash in bank	30	
Petty Cash Fund		30

To discontinue the petty cash fund

A Typical Cash Disbursements Journal

The purpose of the cash disbursements journal, a feature of any accounting system, is to provide a convenient procedure for tabulating all of the checks written by the treasurer. Generally, a checkbook by itself is simply inadequate to allocate properly all disbursements to the proper accounts. While the checkbook will always record the appropriate cash balance and be in agreement with the differences between the totals of the cash receipts and cash disbursements journal, it cannot easily by itself provide necessary information to the membership on fund receipt and allocation.

The cash disbursements journal uses a columnar format such as that in Figure 12.4

Typical Cash Disbursements Journal

Date	Payee	Ck. #	Cash Cr.	Salaries Dr.	Supplies Dr.	Postage Dr.	Etc. Dr.

Figure 12.4

All checks written are recorded in the journal with the appropriate information noted. Thus, the total of the cash column is cash spent and is a reduction of the cash asset account. The amount of that check is then entered again in the appropriate payment column either as an expense, an addition to the assets, a reduction of liabilities or a change in some fund balance. At the end of the period the total of the cash column must equal the sum of the totals of all the other columns.

Depending on the accounting system used, but typical to most bookkeeping systems, the totals of each column are then copied (posted) onto the appropriate ledger card for that account.

When the financial statement is prepared, the balances in those various accounts (representing net amounts from the cash disbursements journal and perhaps other journals as well) are listed.

Recall that the purpose of the entire accounting function is to report to interested persons precisely how the organization's money has been used and the balances that still remain. The cash disbursements journal is one procedure that helps to make that reporting less complicated and more accurate.

Appropriate formats for suggested cash disbursements journals are noted in the several chapters describing specific accounting systems.

Chapter Thirteen

Fund Accounting:
A Basic System for
Church Financial Record Keeping

The value of the services which your congregation provides to its membership and the community it serves cannot be quantitatively measured in the financial statements of the annual report. It can be measured only in terms of the human needs, public good, and the faith of the membership.

Unlike a business operation where the financial statements purport to show the value of the services rendered and their profitability to the owners, the fundamental purpose of your congregation's financial statement is to show how available resources have been acquired and used to accomplish goals and achieve objectives. There is no profit, but there is a tremendous amount of value associated with services voluntarily given and shared but not financially measurable.

Thus, your congregation's financial statements should reflect as accurately as possible the total financial resources available to carry out all of your programs to which you are committed, as well as how those resources were used. It cannot show the other nonfinancial values.

Not all of your congregational financial resources, however, are available to carry out the total program of the church. Restrictions have been placed on gifts by donors, for whatever reason, limiting the use of those resources to specific rather than general projects. Bequests are given restricting the principal and not the income; for example, memorials are given for flowers, gifts for candelabras, and fund are solicited for specific projects through sales and bazaars.

In a situation where resources are limited either directly or indirectly, not all of the congregation's resources may be available for general use. Separate systems of account must be maintained to keep account of those restricted funds, to be certain they are used for the purposes intended. Separate accounts or funds give recognition to those restrictions.

For this reason, congregations may find that the use of a fund accounting system will make record keeping less complicated and financial reporting more meaningful than will the use of a conventional system.

Under the fund accounting concept, separate accounting entities or funds are created as needed. Each fund is in a sense a separate set of records with its own statement of operations, balance sheet, and application of funds report. Wherever it is necessary to segregate funds in order to make a fair presentation of the use of those resources available without restriction and of those for which restrictions have been imposed, separate funds may be used.

The most common funds used are fully explained in Chapter 4 and include General or Current Unrestricted Funds; Current Restricted Funds; Land, Building, Equipment or Plant Funds; Endowment Funds; and Quasi-Endowment or Board-Directed Funds. Other funds could include custodial funds, so designated when assets are received by a congregation to be used and disbursed only upon the instruction of another organization or person, or loan or annuity funds when applicable.

Financial statements in a fund accounting system must show the unrestricted and restricted funds separately. For each fund there should be a statement of revenues, disbursements and transfers, and changes in fund balance to reflect the activity within each fund. A statement of the functional operating expenses used in support of the total program may be shown. Balance sheets would be included for each fund also.

In the following illustration one month's activities for the congregation are shown, including the original entries into the cash receipts and cash disbursements journals, trial balance and general ledger accounts (after posting of all entries and closing entries) and appropriate financial statements for each fund.

Accounting Procedure Used

1. All cash receipts are entered into the appropriate cash receipts journals for each fund, totaled, and balanced across.

2. All cash disbursements (checks written) are listed by fund in the cash disbursements journal, totaled, and balanced across.

3. Closing entries are shown in the general journal and are appropriate at the end of the period. In order to illustrate the correlation of ending fund balances shown in the financial statements with those shown in the general ledger, closing entries for the period are made. Financial statements, however, reflect only one month's activity rather than year to date. Ending fund balances, of course, would be the same in either instance.

4. Account totals from the cash receipts journal and the cash disbursements journal are then posted to the general ledger for each account for each fund. To simplify the illustration, posting has been done to a month-beginning trial balance with debits and credits shown in the middle two columns. A final month end trial balance would normally be taken from the general ledger account balances, but is in the format shown instead for purposes of illustration.

5. Statements of revenues, disbursements, and transfers and a balance sheet have been prepared for each fund from the general ledger trial balance.

6. A summary of all journal entries required for all transactions for each fund is listed for further explanation.

Transactions for the Month

General Fund:

1. Contributions from offerings, envelopes, and other sources was $5,000.

2. Investment income from the endowment fund was $600. This income is unrestricted as to use, therefore it comes directly to the General Fund and appears nowhere in the Endowment Fund.

3. Expenses were made as follows: Salaries, $2,000; Administration costs, $3,000; Maintenance expenses, $100; Depreciation, $500; and other costs, $500. Since depreciation costs are being funded, the $500 cash is transferred to the Plant Fund.

4. In addition $1,000 of the General Fund was transferred to the restricted Scholarship Fund.

Restricted Fund:

1. Contributions received by the Altar Fund for the month were $500.

2. Endowment Fund income restricted for scholarship purposes was $2,000, and for the pastor's Discretionary Fund was $300.

3. Disbursements were made from the Scholarship Fund for $800 to pay for the scholarship owing at the first of the month; from the Altar Fund for $200 for flowers; and from the pastor's Discretionary Fund for $100.

4. In addition, $1,000 was received from the General Fund for scholarship purposes.

Plant Fund:

1. Building Fund contributions were $1,000, and $150 was received from Plant Fund replacement investments.

2. New equipment costing $900 was purchased. A $2,000 mortgage payment was made plus $500 interest.

3. $500 was received from the General Fund for depreciation funding.

Endowment Funds:

1. Gifts and bequests, the principal of which is restricted to Endowment Fund purposes, were received for $10,000.

2. Endowment Fund income restricted to Endowment Fund purposes was received from investments, $2,000. (Endowment Fund income not restricted is recorded in the General Fund.)

3. Securities that cost $4,000 were sold for $5,000.

4. Securities were purchased for $9,000; administrative expenses were $200.

Quasi-Endowment Funds: (Board-Designated Funds)

1. Special unrestricted gifts of $4,000 were received and placed in the Quasi-Endowment Fund by Board action.

2. Income from Quasi-Endowment Funds was $100.

3. Funds were used for a $5,000 neighborhood project grant; administrative costs were $50.

Chart of Accounts

Fund Groups

    100 General Funds
    200 Restricted Funds
    300 Plant Funds
    400 Endowment Funds
    500 Quasi-Endowment (Board-
        Designated) Funds

Assets

    01 Cash
    02 Pledges receivable
    03 Investments
    10 Land, buildings, equipment
    11 Reserve for depreciation

Liabilities

    30 Accounts payable
    35 Mortgages payable

Interfund Receivables/Payables

41 General Fund
42 Restricted Funds
43 Plant Funds
44 Endowment Funds
45 Quasi-Endowment Funds

Fund Balances:

46 Unrestricted
47 Restricted special funds
48 Restricted special funds
49 Restricted special funds
50 Restricted special funds

Income

51 Contributions
52 Investment income
53 Realized gain or loss
54 Grants
55 Other income
56 Gifts and bequests

Expenses

60 Salaries
61 Administration
62 Maintenance
63 Depreciation
64 Other costs
65 Interest
66 Scholarships

Examples: General Fund cash 101   Plant Fund cash 301
            Endowment Fund investment income 452
            Plant Fund investment income 352

Cash Receipts Journal

General Fund		101	151	152	155
Explntn	Date	Bank	Cont.	Inc.	Other
	7-31	5,000	5,000		
	7-31	600		600	
		5,600	5,000	600	

Restricted Funds Explntn	Date	201 Bank	Fund	251 Cont.	252 Inc.	255 Other
	7-20	500	Altar	500		
	7-22	2,300	Disc.		300	
			Sch.		2,000	
	7-24	1,000	Sch.			1,000 Transfer
		3,800		500	2,300	1,000

Plant Fund Explntn	Date	301 Bank	351 Cont.	352 Inc.	355 Other
	7-15	1,000	1,000		
	7-16	150		150	
	7-31	500			500 Depreciation
		1,650	1,000	150	500

Endowment Funds Explntn	Date	401 Bank	456 Gifts	452 Inc.	455 Other
	7-10	10,000	10,000		
	7-15	2,000		2,000	
	7-21	5,000			5,000 Sale of Securities
		17,000	10,000	2,000	5,000

Quasi-Endowment Explntn	Date	501 Bank	556 Gifts	552 Inc.	555 Other
	7-31	4,000	4,000		
	7-31	100		100	
		4,100	4,000	100	

Cash Disbursements Journal

General Fund Payee	Date	Ck. #	101 Bank	160 Sal.	161 Adm.	162 Mntc.	163 Dep.	164 Other
J. Jones	7-20	7451	2,000	2,000				
S. Supplies	7-20	7452	1,000		1,000			
Heating	7-21	7453	100			100		
Insurance	7-23	7454	1,500		1,500			
C. Store	7-24	7455	500		500			
Plant Fnd	7-25	7456	500				500	
P. Store	7-27	7457	500					500
Sch. Fnd	7-31	7458	1,000					1,000
			7,100	2,000	3,000	100	500	1,500

Restricted Funds Payee	Date	Ck. #	201 Bank	247 Sch.F	248 Alt.F	249 Dis.F	250 Other
B. Florist	7-4	221	50		50		

Payee	Date	Ck. #	Bank			
B. Florist	7-11	222	50		50	
B. Florist	7-18	223	50		50	
Rev. Hock	7-19	224	100			100
B. Florist	7-25	225	50		50	
C. Gray	7-31	226	800	800		
			1,100	800	200	100

Plant Funds			301	310	335	365	364
Payee	Date	Ck. #	Bank	Eqmt	Mort.	Int.	Other
A-V, Inc.	7-30	45	900	900			
1st Bk	7-31	46	2,000		2,000		
1st Bk	7-31	47	500			500	
			3,400	900	2,000	500	

Endowment Funds			401	403	461	464
Payee	Date	Ck. #	Bank	Sec.	Adm.	Other
Merrill L.	7-20	109	4,000	4,000		
Supplies	7-21	110	200		200	
Pifer	7-31	111	5,000	5,000		
			9,200	9,000	200	

Quasi-Endowment Fund			501	561	564	
Payee	Date	Ck. #	Bank	Adm.	Other	
Supplies	7-10	21	50	50		
Nghbrhd	7-15	22	2,500		2,500	Project grant
Nghbrhd	7-31	23	2,500		2,500	Project grant
			5,050	50	5,000	

General Journal (Closing Entries)

1

July 31

151	Contributions	30,000	
152	Investment income	4,200	
146	General Fund Balance	13,300	
160	Salaries		12,000
161	Administration		17,000
162	Maintenance		2,500
163	Depreciation		3,500
164	Other		6,500
166	Transfers		6,000

To close revenues, disbursements and transfers accounts to General Fund Balance account.

2

July 31

351	Contributions	7,000	
352	Investment income	1,050	
365	Interest expense		3,500
346	Plant Fund Balance		4,550

To close revenues, disbursements and transfers accounts to Plant Fund Balance account.

3

July 31

456	Gifts	10,000	
452	Investment income	14,000	
453	Gain on sale of securities	1,000	
464	Expenses		1,400
446	Endowment Fund Bal.		23,600

To close revenues, disbursements and transfers accounts to Endowment Fund Balance account.

4

July 31

556	Gifts	4,000	
552	Investment income	700	
546	Quasi-Endowment Fund Balance	650	
554	Grants paid		5,000
564	Expenses		350

To close revenues, disbursements and transfers accounts to Quasi-Endowment Fund Balance account.

General Ledger

General Fund Accounts

		Bal. 7-1 Dr. (Cr.)	Transactions Dr.	Cr.	Bal. Dr. (Cr.)	Closing Entries Dr.	Cr.	Bal. 7-31 Dr. (Cr.)
101	Cash	3,000	5,600	7,100	1,500			1,500
102	Pledges rec.	1,000			1,000			1,000
146	Fund Bal.	(15,800)			(15,800)	13,300		(2,500)
151	Contrib.	(25,000)		5,000	(30,000)	30,000		-0-
152	Inv. inc.	(3,600)		600	(4,200)	4,200		-0-
160	Salaries	10,000	2,000		12,000		12,000	-0-
161	Administ.	14,000	3,000		17,000		17,000	-0-

162	Maintenance	2,400	100		2,500		2,500	-0-
163	Deprectn.	3,000	500		3,500		3,500	-0-
164	Other costs	6,000	500		6,500		6,500	-0-
166	Transfers	5,000	1,000		6,000		6,000	-0-
		-0-	12,700	12,700	-0-	47,500	47,500	-0-

Restricted Fund Accounts

201	Cash	7,400	3,800	1,100	10,100			10,100
231	Accounts pay	(800)	800		-0-			-0-
247	Scholrshp Fund	(4,200)		3,000	(7,200)			(7,200)
248	Altar Fund	(400)	200	500	(700)			(700)
249	Discrtnry Fund	(2,000)	100	300	(2,200)			(2,200)
		-0-	4,900	4,900	-0-			-0-

Plant Fund Accounts

301	Cash	2,000	1,650	3,400	250			250
302	Pledges rec.	3,000			3,000			3,000
303	Investmnts	195,000			195,000			195,000
310	Land, bldg.	950,000	900		950,900			950,900
311	Res. dep.	(350,000)		500	(350,500)			(350,500)
335	Mortg. Pay	(100,000)	2,000		(98,000)			(98,000)
346	Fund Bal.	(696,100)			(696,100)		4,550	(700,650)
351	Contrbtns.	(6,000)		1,000	(7,000)	7,000		-0-
352	Inv. inc.	(900)		150	(1,050)	1,050		-0-
365	Int. exp.	3,000	500		3,500		3,500	-0-
		-0-	5,050	5,050	-0-	8,050	8,050	-0-

Endowment Fund Accounts

401	Cash	2,800	17,000	9,200	10,600			10,600
403	Securities	60,000	9,000	4,000	65,000			65,000
446	Fund Bal.	(52,000)			(52,000)		23,600	(75,600)
456	Gifts	-0-		10,000	(10,000)	10,000		-0-
452	Inv. inc.	(12,000)		2,000	(14,000)	14,000		-0-
464	Expenses	1,200	200		1,400		1,400	-0-
453	Gain	-0-		1,000	(1,000)	1,000		-0-
		-0-	26,200	26,200	-0-	25,000	25,000	-0-

Quasi-Endowment Funds

501	Cash	1,000	4,100	5,050	50			50
503	Securities	12,000			12,000			12,000
546	Fund Bal	(12,700)			(12,700)	650		(12,050)
556	Gifts	-0-		4,000	(4,000)	4,000		-0-
552	Inv. inc.	(600)		100	(700)	700		-0-
554	Grants	-0-	5,000		5,000		5,000	-0-
564	Expenses	300	50		350		350	-0-
		-0-	9,150	9,150	-0-	5,350	5,350	-0-

Financial Statements

Statements of Revenues, Disbursements and Transfers
Twelve Months Ending July 31, 19X2

General Fund:	Monthly Budget	This Mo Actual	Year to Date Actual
Revenues: Contributions	$5,500	$ 5,000	$ 30,000
Inv. inc. from End. Fund	500	600	4,200
	$6,000	$ 5,600	$ 34,200
Disbursements:			
Salaries	$2,000	$ 2,000	$ 12,000
Administration	2,500	3,000	17,000
Maintenance	400	100	2,500
Depreciation	500	500	3,500
Other costs	500	500	6,500
	$5,900	$ 6,100	$ 41,500
Excess of rev. over disb.	$ 100	$ (500)	$ (7,300)
Fund Balance beginning		4,000	15,800
Transfers to Scholarship Fund		(1,000)	(6,000)
Fund Balance ending, July 31		$ 2,500	$ 2,500

	Accounts Payable	Scholar-ship Fund	Altar Fund	Discre-tion Fund	Total
Restricted Funds					
Revenues:					
Contributns			$500		$ 500
Inv. inc.		$2,000		$ 300	2,300
		$2,000	$500	$ 300	$ 2,800
Disbursements:					
Altar flowers			$200		$ 200
Pastor's Dis. Fund				$ 100	100
Schlshp due	$ 800				800
	$ 800		$200	$ 100	$ 1,100
Excess of rev. over disb.	$(800)	$2,000	$300	$ 200	$ 1,700
Fund Bal. beg.	800	4,200	400	2,000	7,400
Transfers from other funds		1,000			1,000
Fund Bal. end	-0-	$7,200	$700	$2,200	$10,100

	Unex-pended	Expended	Total
Plant Funds:			
Revenues: Contributions	$ 1,000		$ 1,000
Investment income	150		150
	$ 1,150		$ 1,150

Disbursements:

New equipment	$ 900		$ 900
Mortgage—Principal	2,000		2,000
Interest	500		500
	$ 3,400		$ 3,400
Excess of revenues over disb.	(2,250)		(2,250)
Fund Balance beginning	200,000	$ 500,000	700,000
Reduction of liabilities		2,000	2,000
Additions to assets		900	900
Transfers from other funds (Dep.)	500	(500)	-0-
Fund Balance ending, July 31	$ 198,250	$ 502,400	$ 700,650

Endowment Funds	This Month	Year to Date
Revenues: Gifts & bequests	$ 10,000	$ 10,000
Investment income*	2,000	14,000
Gain on sale of investments	1,000	1,000
	$ 13,000	$ 25,000
Disbursements:		
Administrative expenses	$ 200	$ 1,400
	$ 200	$ 1,400
Excess of revenues over disbursements	$ 12,800	$ 23,600
Fund Balance beginning	62,800	52,000
Fund Balance end, July 31	$ 75,600	$ 75,600

*Income restricted for specific term to Endowment Fund.

Quasi-Endowment Funds		
Revenues: Special gifts—unrestricted	$ 4,000	$ 4,000
Investment income	100	700
	$ 4,100	$ 4,700
Disbursements:		
Administrative costs	$ 50	$ 350
Neighborhood Project Grant	5,000	5,000
	$ 5,050	$ 5,350
Excess of revenues over disbursements	$ (950)	$ (650)
Fund Balance beginning	13,000	12,700
Fund Balance ending, July 31	$ 12,050	$ 12,050

Balance Sheets

Twelve Months Ending July 31, 19X2

	7-31-19X1	7-31-19X2
General Fund		
Assets: Cash	$ 3,000	$ 1,500

Pledges receivable	1,000	1,000*
	$ 4,000	$ 2,500
Fund Balance	$ 4,000	$ 2,500

*Adjusted annually at year end.

Restricted Fund

Assets: Cash	$ 7,400	$ 10,100
Liabilities: Scholarship pay.	$ 800	$ -0-
Fund Balance: Scholarship	4,200	7,200
Altar	400	700
Discretionary	2,000	2,200
	$ 7,400	$ 10,100

Plant Fund

Assets: Cash	$ 2,000	$ 250
Pledges receivable	3,000	3,000*
Investmnts-Replacmnts	195,000	195,000
Land, bldgs. equip.	600,000	600,400**
	$800,000	$798,650
Liabilities: Mortgage payable	$100,000	$ 98,000
Fund Balance begin: Expended	500,000	502,400
Unexpended	200,000	198,250
	$800,000	$798,650

*Adjusted annually.

**Cost less depreciation.

Endowment Fund

Assets: Cash	$ 2,800	$10,600
Securities	60,000	65,000
	$62,800	$75,600
Fund Balance:	$62,800	$75,600

Quasi-Endowment Fund

Assets: Cash	$ 1,000	$ 50
Securities	12,000	12,000*
	$13,000	$12,050
Fund Balance	$13,000	$12,050

*Unrestricted gifts separately invested.

Chapter Fourteen

The One Fund Approach: An Alternative to Church Fund Accounting

A one fund type of typical double entry bookkeeping procedure is probably the most frequently used system in congregations. While a fund accounting approach offers the most informative type of reporting about sources and applications of funds, other systems are less difficult to use and can produce useful and reasonable reports.

In fact, the least complicated type of record keeping system is the checkbook system. No records are kept except the checkbook stubs. The checkbook is the book of original and final entry. A summary worksheet is required to analyze the checkbook entries and prepare meaningful reports.

For the smallest congregations with minimum activity, a checkbook system may suffice. But it is obvious that when many transactions are required, developing financial statements becomes extremely cumbersome if only the checkbook is available. It may work for your personal checking account and financial management, but your congregation's financial record keeping procedures do require something more extensive. Besides, a checkbook system is not a recognized or formal system of double entry bookkeeping.

A typical double entry bookkeeping system will include the use of the standard journals and ledgers: cash receipts journal, cash disbursements journal, and general ledger, the basic books of original and final entry for any accounting system. Financial reports will include a statement of revenues, disbursements, and transfers for the current operating fund, a summary statement of the changes in fund balances for separately designated funds, and a balance sheet.

In the illustration in this chapter transactions are listed for the month and entered in the appropriate journals. The journals are totaled and posted to the general ledger. In lieu of a general ledger, however, the illustration lists a beginning trial balance; entries are posted in the next two columns; another trial balance is taken; then closing entries are listed; and the final trial balance is calculated indicating the final balances in all accounts for the balance sheet.

All three financial statements are prepared directly from the information in the trial balances.

Included in this chapter also is a simplified procedure which assumes that the use of a general ledger or a balance sheet is not important or necessary. And in fact a very accurate set of financial records can be kept in a smaller congregation without the use of a general ledger, as is demonstrated. The validity of a balance sheet as a listing of pertinent and important information for a congregation is often a question anyway. Net worth has little meaning, really, for a congregation, and the value of assets is often seriously understated or not even known. A separate listing of debts, however, is always desirable.

The simplified system does offer necessary information about current operations and comparisons to budgeted amounts. It also retains control over the separation of the various funds. Month-end balances for various accounts are always available for updating in the next periodic reports.

Transactions for the Month—Cash Basis

1. Contributions were received as follows: $2000 on July 4, $2000 on July 11, $1500 on July 18, $1500 on July 25.

2. A special gift was received on July 12, $2000.

3. Investment income of $500 was received, July 31.

4. Contributions were received for the Scholarship Fund, $50; the Altar Fund, $100; and the Organ Fund, $200. The Organ Fund contribution was deposited directly to the savings account. All other revenues were deposited in the congregation's single checking account.

5. $1000 was transferred to the Scholarship Fund.

6. Salaries of $1000 were paid on July 15 and July 31.

7. Administrative costs were paid on July 15 for $50, on July 31 for $500, insurance premiums were $200 on July 15, and the pastor's car allowance of $250 was paid on July 31.

8. The July air conditioning bill was $100, and the roof was repaired for $400.

9. The monthly mortgage payment was paid, $1000, all for principal.

10. Supplies were purchased on July 31 from two different sources, one for $200, the other $100.

11. Altar flowers cost $50.

Chart of Accounts

Assets

      101 Cash—checking

      102 Cash—savings

    *103 Pledges receivable

      110 Furniture and fixtures

    *111 Reserve for depreciation

      120 Land, buildings

    *130 Prepaid expenses

Liabilities

      201 Mortgages payable

    *202 Accounts payable

Fund balances

      301 Equity—unrestricted

      302 Scholarship Fund

      303 Altar Fund

      304 Organ Fund

Income

      401 Contributions

      402 Gifts

      403 Investment income

Expenses

      501 Salaries

      502 Administrative expenses

      503 Maintenance

      504 Supplies

    *505 Depreciation

      506 Other

---

*Additional accounts used for accrual basis entries.

CASH RECEIPTS JOURNAL

Date	101 Bank	102 Bank	401 Cont.	402 Gifts	403 Inv.	302 Sch.	303 Altar	304 Organ
July 4	2050		2000			50		
July 11	2000		2000					
July 12	2000			2000				
July 18	1600		1500				100	
July 20	500				500			
July 25	1500		1500					
July 31		200						200
	9650	200	7000	2000	500	50	100	200

CASH DISBURSEMENTS JOURNAL

Payee	Date	Ck. #	101 Bank	501 Sal.	502 Adm.	503 Mntc.	201 Debt	504 Supp.	302 Sch.	303 Altar	506 Other
J. Jones	7-15	451	1000	1000							
S. Smith	7-15	452	50		50						
Insurance	7-15	453	200		200						
B. Repair	7-16	454	400			400					
H & AC	7-17	455	100			100					
1st Bnk	7-30	456	1000				1000				
J. Jones	7-31	457	1000	1000							
O. Hdw	7-31	458	200					200			
K. Boxes	7-31	459	100					100			
Solomon	7-31	460	500		500						
J. Jones	7-31	461	250		250						
Florist	7-31	462	50							50	
			4850	2000	1000	500	1000	300	-0-	50	-0-

GENERAL JOURNAL

Entry # 1

July 31

301	Transfers General Fund	1000	
302	Scholarship Fund		1000

To transfer unrestricted gifts to the Scholarship Fund.

General Ledger

		Trial Bal. Begin Dr. (Cr.)	Transactions Dr.	Transactions Cr.	Trial Bal. Dr. (Cr.)	Closing Entries Dr.	Closing Entries Cr.	Trial Bal. End Dr. (Cr.)
101	Cash—Ckg	950	9650	4850	5750			5750
102	Cash—Sav	1300	200		1500			1500
110	Furn & fix	100000			100000			100000
120	Land, bldgs	900000			900000			900000
201	Mrtg pay	(99000)	1000		(98000)			(98000)
301	Equity	(896650)	1000		(895650)		10500	(906150)
302	Scholarshp	(350)		1050	(1400)			(1400)
303	Altar F.	(150)	50	100	(200)			(200)
304	Organ Fund	(1300)		200	(1500)			(1500)
401	Contributns	(27000)		7000	(34000)	34000		-0-
402	Gifts	-0-		2000	(2000)	2000		-0-
403	Inv. inc.	(500)		500	(1000)	1000		-0-
501	Salaries	12000	2000		14000		14000	-0-
502	Adminstrtn	6000	1000		7000		7000	-0-
503	Maintenance	3000	500		3500		3500	-0-
504	Supplies	1700	300		2000		2000	-0-
		-0-	15700	15700	-0-	37000	37000	-0-

Closing Journal Entry
(If the fiscal year ends on July 31, it is necessary to close out all income and expense accounts in the Fund Balance. That procedure will generate a Fund Account Balance as shown on the balance sheet.)

GENERAL JOURNAL

Entry #2

July 31

401	Contributions	34000	
402	Gifts	2000	
403	Investment income	1000	
501	Salaries		14000
502	Administration		7000
503	Maintenance		3500
504	Supplies		2000
301	Fund Balance		10500

To close out revenues, disbursements and transfers accounts to Fund Balance account.

FINANCIAL STATEMENTS

Balance Sheet
As of July 31, 19X2

Assets:

Cash—Checking	$ 5750	
Savings	1500	$ 7250
Furniture and Fixtures		100000
Land, Building		900000
		$1007250

Liabilities

Mortgages payable		$ 98000

Equity

Fund Balance unrestricted	$895650	
Add current year increase	10500	
	$906150	
Scholarship Fund	1400	
Altar Fund	200	
Organ Fund	1500	909250
		$1007250

Statement of Revenues, Disbursements and Transfers
Twelve Months Ending July 31, 19X2

	This Month	Year to date	Budget to date
Cash balance, beginning	$ 450	$ 1650	
Revenues:			
Contributions	$7000	$34000	$35000
Special gifts	2000	2000	1000
Investment income	500	1000	800
	$9500	$37,000	$36800
Disbursements:			
Salaries	$2000	$14000	$14000
Administration	1000	7000	5000
Maintenance	500	3500	6000
Debt retirement	1000	7000	7000
Supplies	300	2000	2500
	$4800	$33500	$34500
Transfers:			
Scholarships	1000	1000	
	$5800	$34500	
Excess of revenues over disbursements	$3700	$ 2500	
Cash balance, ending, July 31	$4150	$ 4150	

Changes in Fund Balances—This Month

	Bal. Beg.	Revenues	Disbursements	Trsfs	Bal. End
301 General Fund	$ 450	$ 9500	$ 4800	$(1000)	$4150
302 Scholarship Fund	350	50		1000	1400
303 Altar Fund	150	100	50		200
304 Organ Fund	1300	200			1500
	$2250	$ 9850	$ 4850	-0-	$7250
101 Cash—checking	$ 950	$ 9650	$ 4850		$5750
102 Cash—savings	1300	200	-0-		1500
	$2250	$ 9850	$ 4850		$7250

Changes in Fund Balances—Year to Date

301 General Fund	$1650	$37000	$33500	$(1000)	$4150
302 Scholarship Fund	3200	200	3000	1000	1400
303 Altar Fund	500	200	500		200
304 Organ Fund	1000	500			1500
	$6350	$37900	$37000		$7250
101 Cash—checking	$5350	$37400	$37000		$5750
102 Cash—savings	1000	500			1500
	$6350	$37900	$37000		$7250

A Simplified System

If a balance sheet is not important and the general ledger can be eliminated, then, assuming the same facts as in the foregoing illustration:

CASH RECEIPTS JOURNAL

	Date	Bank	Cont.	Gifts	Inv. Inc.	Sch.	Altar	Organ
Bal. YTD		28050	27000		500	150	100	300
	7-4	2050	2000			50		
	7-11	2000	2000					
	7-12	2000		2000				
	7-18	1600	1500				100	
	7-20	500			500			
	7-25	1500	1500					
	7-31	200						200
This month		9850	7000	2000	500	50	100	200
Year to date		37900	34000	2000	1000	200	200	500

CASH DISBURSEMENTS JOURNAL

Payee	Date	Ck. #	Bank	Sal.	Adm.	Mntc	Debt	Supp	Sch	Altar
Bal. YTD			32150	12000	6000	3000	6000	1700	3000	450
J. Jones	7-15	451	1000	1000						
S. Smith	7-15	452	50		50					
Insurance	7-15	453	200		200					
Repair	7-16	454	400			400				
H & AC	7-17	455	100			100				
1st Bank	7-30	456	1000				1000			
J. Jones	7-31	457	1000	1000						
Hdw	7-31	458	200					200		
K. Boxes	7-31	459	100					100		
Solomon	7-31	460	500		500					
J. Jones	7-31	461	250		250					
Florist	7-31	462	50							50
This month			4850	2000	1000	500	1000	300	-0-	50
Year to date			37000	14000	7000	3500	7000	2000	3000	500

GENERAL JOURNAL

General Fund	1000	
Scholarships		1000

To transfer $1000 from the General Fund to the Scholarship Fund

FINANCIAL STATEMENTS

Statement of Revenues, Disbursements and Transfers
Twelve Months ending July 31, 19X2

	This Month	Year to Date	Budget to Date
Cash balance beginning*	$2250	$ 6350	
Revenues:			
Contributions	$7000	34000	$35000
Gifts	2000	2000	1000
Investment income	500	1000	800
General Fund total	$9500	$37000	$36800
Scholarship Fund	50	200	
Altar Fund	100	200	
Organ Fund	200	500	
	$9850	$37900	

*Same as end of last month or end of last year.

Disbursements:

Salaries	$2000	$14000	$14000
Administration	1000	7000	5000
Maintenance	500	3500	6000
Debt payments	1000	7000	7000
Supplies	300	2000	2500
General Fund total	$4800	$33500	$34500
Scholarship Fund	-0-	3000	
Altar Fund	50	500	
Organ Fund	-0-	-0-	
	$4850	$37000	
Excess of Revenues over			
Disbursements	$5000	$ 900	
Cash balance ending	$7250	$ 7250	

CHANGES IN FUND BALANCES

This Month	Bal. Begin	Revenues	Disbursments	Trsfrs	Bal. End
General Fund	$ 450	$ 9500	$ 4800	$(1000)	$4150
Scholarship Fund	350	50	-0-	1000	1400
Altar Fund	150	100	50	-0-	200
Organ Fund	1300	200	-0-	-0-	1500
	$2250	$ 9850	$ 4850	-0-	$7250
Checking account	$ 950	$ 9650	$ 4850		$5750
Savings account	1300	200	-0-		1500
	$2250	$ 9850	$ 4850		$7250
This Year to Date					
General Fund	$1650	$37000	$33500	$(1000)	$4150
Scholarship Fund	3200	200	3000	1000	1400
Altar Fund	500	200	500	-0-	200
Organ Fund	1000	500	-0-	-0-	1500
	$6350	$37900	$37000		$7250
Checking account	$5350	$37400	$37000		$5750
Savings account	1000	500	-0-		1500
	$6350	$37900	$37000		$7250

Note: All financial statement information is taken directly from the journals or from the previous month's financial statements.

How to Make Accrual Entries
With a Cash Basis Accounting System

Cash basis and accrual basis accounting systems have been distinguished and illustrated in Chapter 3. The system illustrated in this chapter is a simple cash basis procedure. Every entry is made because cash was either received or paid out. Even the transfer entry shown, while not a cash transaction, was simply a transfer of fund balances without incurring additional income or expenses for the total program.

In a simple accrual basis sytem, however, certain entries will be required in addition to the recording of all the cash entries. The purpose of the accrual entries will be to generate more accurate financial statements which will reflect commitments of the organization not yet paid and income promised but not yet received.

Thus, a congregation may wish to record in its statement of operations and balance sheet its month-end bills due but not paid. Disclosure of these amounts will alert readers to those anticipated payments already committed by the congregation. In like manner, offerings which have been promised for the period but not yet received, can be shown as income and receivables.

Accrual entries are generally made monthly after all cash entries are recorded. The general journal is used and the entries are posted to the general ledger. There they will appear in the appropriate account balances and on the various financial statements.

For example, typical accrual entries that may be required by a congregation would be:

1. An entry to record unpaid bills.

2. An entry to record unpaid salaries.

3. An entry to record uncollected pledges.

4. An entry to record depreciation.

5. An entry to record prepaid expenses.

6. An entry to record accrued interest income on investments.

A sample entry to record unpaid bills would be as follows:

Journal Entry # 1

July 31

502 Administrative expense	200	
503 Repairs	100	
504 Supplies	50	
202 Accounts Payable		350

To record the liability for unpaid bills at month end and to charge the appropriate expense accounts.

But in the next period, when the bills are paid, there is a potential problem on just where to charge that payment. Obviously cash will be credited, but if the accrual entry remains as is and the bills paid are charged to expenses, there will be a double charge. Of course, payment of the bills could be charged to accounts payable, as would be correct.

In order to eliminate the potential problem of a double charge, the accrual entry can be "reversed" in the following period. Then, when the bills are actually paid, they may be charged directly to the expense account without fear of a possible double charge. As you will notice from the reversal entry below, each expense account will have a credit amount for the accrual in the following period, thus offsetting the debit charge when the bill is paid. In this way the expense is actually charged to operations in the previous period when accrued, but paid in the following month.

Journal Entry # 1

August 1

202 Accounts Payable		350	
502	Administration Exp		200
503	Repairs		100
504	Supplies		50

To reverse accrual entry # 1 set up July 31.

Accruals for other expenses or income should be created in the same manner and subsequently reversed the following period.

Journal Entry # 2

July 31

103 Pledges receivable		1000	
401	Offerings income		1000

To record unpaid pledges at July 31.

Journal Entry # 3

July 31

130 Prepaid Insurance		200	
502	Administration costs		200

To record as an asset prepaid insurance premiums.

St. Andrew's

articles donated to outreach —
never seen by the church
but legitimate — the $ value
of article is recognized as
special offering. Is this
a legitimate thing?

Chuck Margaret.
2ᵈ Jan 21.

nal Entry #4

July 31

| | 50 | |
| lepreciation | | 50 |

he month of July.

these reversal entries would be required:

nal Entry #2

August 1

| | 1000 | |
| ivable | | 1000 |

July 31.

ıal Entry #3

August 1

| | 200 | |
| ance | | 200 |

uly 31.

The depreciation entry would not be reversed.

If depreciation is in fact used, and I have suggested that it really has no appropriate place in church accounting, it will be necessary for your congregation to develop a fixed asset register listing all of your assets and a depreciation schedule showing all pertinent information with respect to depreciation being taken. Besides, a procedure for funding depreciation would be appropriate, also.

For congregations that wish to record unpaid bills and pledged income on the appropriate financial statements, these modifications to a cash basis accounting system should be sufficient. A full accrual basis accounting system would probably be both unnecessary and cumbersome to most congregational treasurers.

Recall the objectives for a bookkeeping system:

1. All transactions must be recorded in a systematic manner upon occurrence.

2. All transactions must be summarized so like transactions can be grouped together.

3. Comprehensible financial statements must be prepared from such summaries.

(left margin, vertical text) Accounts Normal Balance To Increas

A checkbook system and a full accrual system can be utilized to achieve those functions. But your treasurer's best job in achieving those goals will be realized when the system is as simple as possible yet provides the necessary data for meaningful financial reports. Normally a modified accrual basis double entry bookkeeping system will be quite satisfactory for most congregations.

Accounting for Payroll Taxes

One of the most confusing financial record keeping procedures for congregational treasurers can be payroll accounting. Whether records are kept on a strict cash basis or an accrual basis system, understanding what to do is not as straightforward as for other disbursements or even other accruals.

Whether or not your congregation is subject to accounting for payroll taxes is a matter you must determine. As explained more fully in a subsequent chapter on taxes for congregations, your congregation will be required to withhold Federal income taxes on all employees' wages except the minister's. If your congregation elects to withhold FICA taxes also, then your treasurer will follow the proper procedures used by all employers. Your congregation may be required to withhold local income taxes as well. And your congregational treasurer may even agree to make other withholdings, such as for a pension plan or the United Way. Seldom will your congregation pay the full amount of wages earned without some withholding.

The amount of Federal income tax to be withheld is determined from the proper Internal Revenue Service schedule in Circular E. Local income tax instructions booklets will provide necessary information on those withholdings. The FICA tax to be withheld is currently 5.85% of wages up to $16,500 salary. No withholding is required on amounts over the current year's maximum wage base. In addition, the congregation will match that FICA withholding by paying an employer's tax, which is not withholding of course, but a tax. Contributions to a pension plan are determined by the requirements of that plan.

No matter how the payroll is handled, a record must be kept of wages earned and withheld for every employee. Likewise, a payroll register for each payday must be maintained. Suggested forms for each record are illustrated.

In a strictly cash basis system, the amount recorded in the cash disbursements journal will be the net amount of the cash paid to each employee. For example, if gross wages for the church secretary for the month are $600, Federal income tax is $120, and FICA tax $35.10, net pay would be $444.90. A check for $444.90 would be written payable to the secretary. The amount charged (debited) to salary expense for the secretary would also be $444.90.

Whenever the withheld taxes are paid, their payment would also be charged (debited) to the salary expense account. In addition, though, since the congregation must match the FICA tax withheld, that additional $35.10 must be paid at the same time and charged to salary tax expense.

For a cash basis system, therefore, the entries would be recorded in the cash disbursements journal but in general journal form could appear this way:

Entry #1

July 31

Salary expenses—Secretary	$444.90	
Cash		$444.90

To record payment of monthly net wages to secretary computed as follows:

Wages earned	$600.00
FICA tax withheld	35.10
Federal income tax w/h	120.00
Net wages	$444.90

Entry #2

July 31

Salary expense—Secretary	$155.10	
Payroll taxes (match FICA)	35.10	
Cash		$190.20

To record payment of payroll taxes withheld and due for the month of July.

On the other hand, if a simple accrual basis accounting system is used, the payroll tax entries would appear in this manner:

Entry # 1

July 31

Salary expense—Secretary	$600.00	
Cash		$444.90
Payroll taxes payable—		
Federal income taxes withheld		120.00
Payroll taxes payable—		
FICA taxes withheld		35.10

To record payment of monthly payroll and to set up liability for taxes withheld.

Entry #2

July 31

Payroll taxes payable—		
Federal income taxes withheld	$120.00	
Payroll taxes payable—		
FICA taxes withheld	35.10	
Payroll tax expenses	35.10	
Cash		$190.20

To record payment of payroll taxes withheld and due for
the month of July.

The same type of individual payroll record for each employee would be maintained. The monthly payroll register would likewise be similar to that of a cash basis system.

Since payroll taxes withheld and due may not be payable in the same period as withheld, nevertheless, in an accrual system, the balance due in the payable account will always represent total taxes still due.

If taxes are not paid in the same month as withheld, then it is necessary to make an accrual entry for the employer's tax due so that expenses are charged in the proper month and the payable is properly noted among the month's liabilities.

Entry #2

July 31

Payroll tax expense	$ 35.10	
Payroll taxes payable—FICA		$ 35.10

To accrue employer's FICA taxes due.

Entry #1

August 1

Payroll taxes payable—		
Federal income taxes	$120.00	
Payroll taxes payable—FICA	70.20	
Cash		$190.20

To record payment of payroll taxes due.

Accrual entries for payroll taxes are not reversed since the payment is charged (debited) directly to the payable account.

Individual Payroll Record for _____

Address _____ S.S. # _____

_____ Exemption Allowances _____

Date	Regular	Over-time	Gross Wages	Fed FICA	Fed Inc	Local Inc	Other	Total Ded.	Net Paid
Jan									
Feb									
Mar									
1st Q									
YTD									
Apr									
May									
June									
2nd Q									
YTD									
July									
Aug									
Sept.									
3rd Q									
YTD									
Oct									
Nov									
Dec									
4th Q									
YTD									

Figure 14.1

Payroll Register for the Month of _____ Year _____

Date	Regular	Over-time	Gross Wages	Fed FICA	Fed Inc	Local Inc	Other	Total Ded	Net Paid

Figure 14.2

Chapter Fifteen

A Cash Basis System:
Simplified Record Keeping System
Without Benefit of General Ledger

In a previous chapter it was mentioned that no two congregational treasurers are likely to keep the same two sets of financial records for their congregations. That happens because treasurers come to their jobs with a variety of backgrounds and experiences. Many do not know what accounting for the congregation's financial transactions is all about.

For those who equate the church with a business, the typical small double entry cash basis business bookkeeping system will seem most appropriate. Perhaps it is. For those who see the congregation's financial record keeping as similar to other non-profit organizations, some kind of fund accounting system seems best. And it may be. For those whose experience with financial statements is limited to the family checkbook, a simple single entry, casual back-side-of-a-#10 envelope may seem suitable. It never is.

Accounting systems do vary. And the purpose of this book has been to describe and illustrate those variances as well as to suggest some possible uniformity in the system.

Because many congregations are relatively small and use inexperienced voluntary personnel, including church treasurers, neither the foregoing fund accounting system or a typical business-oriented system or even some other system will be easy to maintain or use in the preparation of meaningful financial statements.

In this chapter yet another system is illustrated. This system is not intended to be just one more system among many, but should be a very useful and acceptable system, especially for treasurers of smaller congregations. It is simple, it is precise, and it does provide all those controls deemed important in a good accounting system. Besides, it offers a good procedure for preparing periodic financial statements. Similar in many respects to the simplified cash basis system illustrated in the previous chapter, the illustration here is a specific step-by-step, line-by-line description of a system.

This system consists essentially of two books of original entry: a journal for listing all receipts, and a journal for listing all checks disbursements. When proper columnar headings are added to the spread sheets on each of these journals, it is possible to prepare appropriate financial statements directly from the journals. Eliminating the use of ledgers speeds up the record keeping process and tends to simplify the procedure.

The complete system is described and illustrated in this chapter with careful instructions about what amounts go on which lines in both journals and on all report forms. Congregations can develop their own forms from these illustrations by using columnar pad sheets available at any stationery store.

In addition to what is a cash receipts journal (Monthly Report of Offerings) and the cash disbursements journal of checks written, the system includes a weekly report of offerings, a statement of expenditures compared to the budget, a statement of fund activity and balances, a bank reconciliation form, employee payroll records, and simple records for recording individual contributions.

Line-by-line instructions for any system may at first glance seem overwhelming. So here. But an understanding of the flow of money through the system to begin with may help to make the detail more understandable. Please note the descriptive flow chart sketch.

The basic premise is that all offerings and other receipts must be recorded in the weekly and monthly cash receipts journal count of offerings, and that all checks written or other disbursements must appear in the cash disbursement journal. Every financial transaction for the congregation must appear in either one of those records. It may also appear elsewhere, either individually or combined with other amounts. But at the outset these two records will contain all financial information for the congregation in this system.

Information for the cash receipts journal comes from a similar report for each week. As offerings are received, they are listed by the counters on the weekly report form. A summary listing of each week's offering then is copied onto the month's cash receipts journal record.

In the cash disbursements journal every check written is listed and distributed to the proper expense column. At month-end all of the columns in both of these journals are added up, cross totaled and balanced.

Financial reports are important for telling the congregation what has happened to their gifts. Thus, the next step is to prepare a listing of all income, expenses, and cash on hand. This could be accomplished with one fund report, but

Flow Chart - Offerings

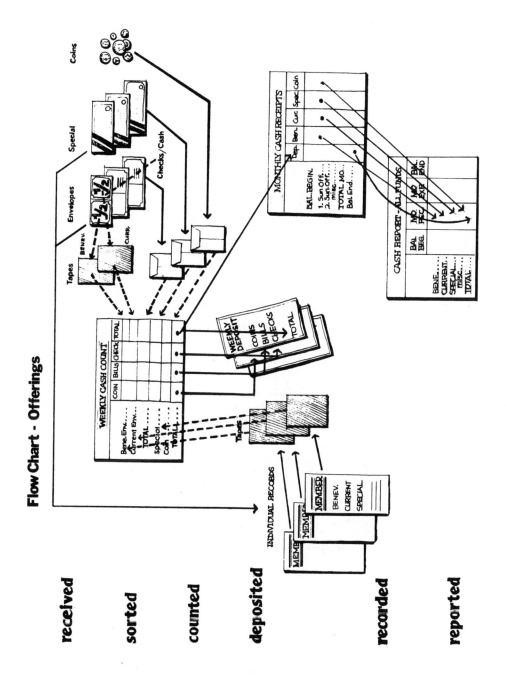

received

sorted

counted

deposited

recorded

reported

Flow Chart - Disbursements

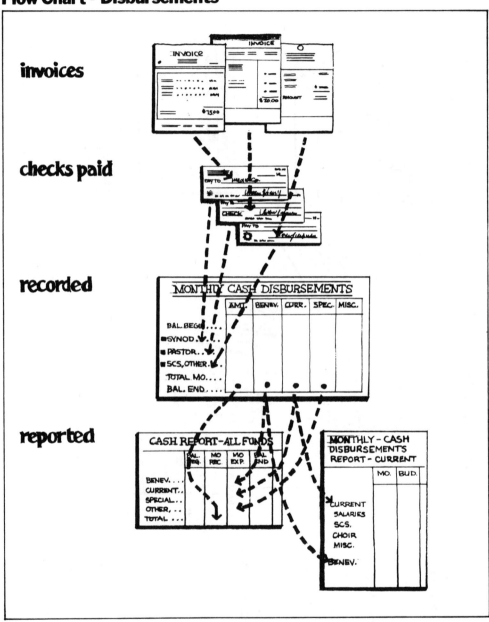

invoices

checks paid

recorded

MONTHLY CASH DISBURSEMENTS

	AMT.	BENEV.	CURR.	SPEC.	MISC.
BAL. BEGIN					
SYNOD . .					
PASTOR . .					
SCS, OTHER .					
TOTAL MO. . . .					
BAL. END. . . .					

reported

CASH REPORT - ALL FUNDS

	BAL. BEG.	MO. REC.	MO EXP.	BAL END
BENEV. . . .				
CURRENT . .				
SPECIAL . .				
OTHER . , .				
TOTAL . . .				

MONTHLY - CASH DISBURSEMENTS REPORT - CURRENT

	MO.	BUD.
CURRENT SALARIES SCS, CHOIR MISC.		
BENEV.		

to eliminate possible confusion with too many figures on one statement, one report is prepared listing all expenses by category or columns designation, while a second report is prepared noting beginning and ending cash balances, but reporting receipts and disbursements only in total, not in detail.

Information for these two reports is taken directly from the totals of the columns in both journals. When done correctly, the cash account is in balance when the reports are totaled, and cash on hand matches up to the bank statement reconciliation amount. A bank reconciliation report will verify the totals that should appear on the statements.

Finally, to keep tab on payroll records, an appropriate listing must be kept for all employees. And a record of all individual contributions may be kept as shown.

The system is best used by smaller congregations. Where several funds and many transactions are involved, larger congregations will find that systems described in the foregoing chapters using a complete set of ledgers as well as journals may be more appropriate for their record keeping needs.

The system illustrated here is adapted from our book *Money and Your Church,* Keats Publishing Inc., New Cannan, CT, and used here with permission.

A CHURCH ACCOUNTING SYSTEM*

by
Manfred Holck, Jr.

A complete financial record keeping system
for congregations

- Simple to use
- Easy to keep
- Step-by-step instructions
- Including monthly financial reports

---

*From the book *Money and Your Church* by Manfred Holck, Jr., published by Keats Publishing, Inc., New Canaan, Conn. Copyright 1974 by Manfred Holck, Jr. Used with permission.

Instructions for Using "A Church Accounting System"

Report #1—Counters' Report of Cash Receipts and Weekly Analysis of Deposits

1. Immediately following each worship service sort all envelopes, loose offerings, Church School offerings and any other offerings into separate piles.

2. Count money in each envelope making certain the amount enclosed is correctly marked on the outside. Enter coins, bills and checks in envelopes onto column 1, lines 5 to 9.

3. If the loose offering includes checks without envelopes, the check should be handled as though received in an envelope. Place a slip of paper properly marked with the name of payor, amount of check and purpose of offering with the envelopes. Enter amounts of coins and bills received in loose offering onto column 2, lines 5 and 6.

4. Enter amount of coins, bills and checks received in the Church School offering and other special offerings in appropriate columns on lines 5 to 9.

5. The total of coins, bills and checks listed in column 6, lines 5 to 9 must be the same as that listed on the deposit slip.

6. Some time after the offering is deposited, sort and tabulate envelopes. Enter proper amounts on lines 17 to 35. The total amount of money deposited and shown on line 9, column 6, must be the same as the total offering recorded on line 35, column 6.

7. Transfer totals on line 35 to Report 2, lines 1 to 10 for the proper week of the month.

Report #2—Monthly Report of Offerings

1. Complete columns 1 to 6, lines 1 to 10 for the month. Information for the respective weekly tabulations of offerings are on Report 1. The total of column 6 must be the same as the total deposits for the month.

2. Copy column 6, lines 1 to 10 onto lines 25 to 33 in column 1 and also onto Report 4, column 2, lines 1 to 11.

3. Copy last month's Report 2, column 3, lines 25 to 33 onto this month's report, column 2, lines 25 to 33. Enter totals of each line in column 3.

4. Copy column 3, lines 25 to 33 onto Report 4, column 2, lines 21 to 32 and also onto next month's Report 2, column 2, lines 25 to 33.

Cash Disbursements Journal (Complete This Journal Before Doing Report 3)

1. From information in the check book list in numerical order all checks written during the month. Distribute correct amounts to the appropriate expense column.

2. At the end of the month total all columns.

3. The sum of the totals of columns 1 to 5 must equal the sum of the totals of columns 6 to 25. (Columns 2 to 5 may have plus or minus or zero balances.)

4. Enter the sum of columns 2 to 5, line 36 onto Report 4, column 3, line 12.

5. Enter the sum of columns 2 to 5, line 38, onto Report 4, column 3, line 33 and column 4, lines 12 and 33.

6. Enter totals of columns 6 to 24, lines 36 and 38 onto the appropriate lines on Report 3, columns 4 and 5, respectively.

7. The sum of columns 6 to 24, lines 36 and 38, must be the same as line 41 on Report 3, columns 4 and 5, respectively.

8. Enter detail of column 25, lines 36 and 38 onto Report 4, column 3, lines 5 to 10 and 26 to 31 respectively.

9. Column 1, lines 36 and 38 of the Cash Disbursements Journal must be the same as Report 4, column 3, lines 16 and 37, respectively, for this bank account.

Report #3—Statement of Expenditures

1. Columns 1, 2 and 3 may be completed at any convenient time from information in the annual budget.

2. Columns 4 and 5 are to be completed from information in columns 6 to 24 of the Cash Disbursements Journal. Certain detailed analyses of columnar totals in the Cash Disbursements Journal may be necessary to provide the information required on Report 3. Total salaries, for instance, in column 7 of the Journal must be divided on Report 3 among pastor, office, music and others.

3. The totals of column 4 and 5 on lines 5 and 40 should be copied onto Report 4, column 3, lines 3 and 4 and lines 24 and 25.

Report #4—Statement of Fund Receipts, Disbursements and Balances; and Statement of Bank Account Changes

A. Fund changes, lines 1 to 13 and 21 to 32

1. Column 1, lines 1 to 13 and 21 to 32 are a repeat of the same lines from columns 4 and 1, respectively, of last month's report.

2. Amounts in column 2, lines 1 to 19 are copied from Report 2, column 1, lines 25 to 33. Lines 21 to 32 are from Report 2, column 3, lines 25 to 33.

3. Amounts in column 3, lines 3 and 4 and lines 24 and 25 are from Report 3, columns 4 and 5, lines 5 and 40.

4. On each line, add columns 1 and 2, deduct column 3, to determine the amount for column 4, which will be the balance in each fund and in each checking account.

B. Bank Account Changes, lines 15 to 19 and 36 to 40

1. Column 1, lines 15 to 19 are the same as lines 15 to 19 of column 4 last month. Column 1, lines 36 to 40 are the same as lines 36 to 40 in column 1 of last month's report.

2. Column 2 includes all deposits made during the month or year in each bank account, the same as line 33, columns 1 and 3, Report 2.

3. Column 3 includes the total of all checks written during the month or year on each bank account as recorded in the Cash Disbursements Journal, column 1, lines 36 and 38.

4. Column 4, lines 13, 19, 34 and 40 are the reconciled bank balances (see Report 5) at the end of the month and must all be the same. Lines 1 to 19 must be identical to lines 22 to 40.

C. Payroll deductions, lines 12 and 33

1. For column 1, lines 12 and 33: Repeat the same information from last month's report, column 4.

2. For column 3, line 12: If payroll deductions exceed cash payments during the month, then deduct the sum of columns 3, 4 and 5, line 36 of the Cash Disbursements Journal; if not, add the sum.

3. For column 3, line 33: If payroll deductions exceed cash payments for the year to date, then deduct the sum of columns 3, 4 and 5, line 38 of the Cash Disbursements Journal; if not, add the sum.

4. For column 4, lines 12 and 33: Do the opposite of what was done for column 3, line 33.

COUNTERS' REPORT OF CASH RECEIPTS

Year _____
Month _____
Day _____

REPORT NO. 1

	1	2	3	4	5	6

WEEKLY CASH COUNT OF OFFERINGS

	Envelopes	Loose	Church School	Other	Other	Deposit
Coins						
Bills						
Checks						
TOTAL						

WEEKLY ANALYSIS OF DEPOSITS

	Benevolences	Current	Other	Other	Other	Total
Envelopes:						
Benevolences						
Current						
Others (List):						
Total Envelopes						
Loose						
Church School						
Others (List):						
TOTAL						

MONTHLY REPORT OF OFFERINGS

Year _____

Month _____

REPORT NO. 2

		First Week	Second Week	Third Week	Fourth Week	Fifth Week	Total Monthly Deposit
1	THIS MONTH						
2	Benevolences						
3	Current						
4	Other						
5	Other						
6	Other						
7							
8							
9	TOTAL						
10	DEPOSITS						
11							
12							
13							
14							
15							
16							
17							
18	YEAR TO DATE						
19							
20							
21		Total This Month	Year to Date Last Month	Year to Date This Month			
22							
23							
24							
25	Benevolences						
26	Current						
27	Other						
28	Other						
29	Other						
30							
31							
32	TOTAL						
33	DEPOSITS						
34							
35							
36							
37							
38							
39							
40							

YEAR_____   CASH DISBURSEMENTS JOURNAL
MONTH_____
             Name of Bank_____

	Payee		Amount of check	Income Tax Withheld	Social Security Tax W/H	City or State Tax W/H	Other With- holdings	Benevo- lences	Salaries & allow- ances
1									
2									
3									
4									
5									
6									
7									
8									
9									
10									
11									
12									
13									
14									
15									
16									
17									
18									
19									
20									
21									
22									
23									
24									
25									
26									
27									
28									
29									
30									
31									
32									
33									
34									
35									
36	TOTAL THIS MONTH								
37	PRIOR MO. YR-TO-DATE								
38	TOTAL YEAR-TO-DATE								
39									
40									

Pulpit Supply, Substitutes	Taxes Pension Etc.	Office Supplies Postage	Miscel- laneous	Transfers	Worship, Music Bulletins	Christian Education SCS,VCS	Steward- ship, Evangelism	Youth Activities

Social Ministry	Personage Loan & Interest	Personage Utilities Taxes, Ins.	Personage Mntc., & Repair	Church Loan & Interest	Church Utilities Taxes, Ins.	Church Mntc.,& Repair	Other Items	Other Funds	
									1
									2
									3
									4
									5
									6
									7
									8
									9
									10
									11
									12
									13
									14
									15
									16
									17
									18
									19
									20
									21
									22
									23
									24
									25
									26
									27
									28
									29
									30
									31
									32
									33
									34
									35
									36
									37
									38
									39
									40

STATEMENT OF EXPENDITURES

YEAR _____
MONTH _____

REPORT NUMBER THREE

		1 Budget for Year	2 Budget for Month	3 Budget to Date	4 Actual for Month	5 Actual for Year	6	
1	**BENEVOLENCES**							1
2	District-Conference							2
3	Other							3
4								4
5	Total							5
6								6
7	**CURRENT OPERATIONS**							7
8	General Adm.							8
9	Salaries and Allow-ances — Pastor							9
10	Office							10
11	Music							11
12	Other							12
13	Pulpit Supply							13
14	Taxes, Pensions							14
15	Office Supplies							15
16	Miscellaneous							16
17	Transfers							17
18								18
19	Total							19
20								20
21	Parish Adm.							21
22	Worship, Music							22
23	Christian Ed;							23
24	Stew., Ev.,							24
25	Youth Activities,							25
26	Social Ministry							26
27								27
28	Total							28
29								29
30	Property Adm.							30
31	Par-son-age — Loan & Int.							31
32	Util., Taxes							32
33	Maint.							33
34	Church — Loan & Int.							34
35	Util., Taxes							35
36	Maint.							36
37								37
38	Total							38
39								39
40	Total Current							40
	BENEV. & CURRENT							

STATEMENT OF FUND RECEIPTS, DISBURSEMENTS AND BALANCES and BANK ACCOUNT CHANGES REPORT NUMBER FOUR			Beginning Cash Balances	Receipts	Disbursements	Ending Cash Balances	
1	THIS MONTH						1
2	FUNDS						2
3	Benevolence						3
4	Current						4
5	Other						5
6	Other						6
7	Other						7
8							8
9							9
10							10
11	Total						11
12	Payroll Deductions						12
13	Total						13
14							14
15	BANK ACCOUNTS (List)						15
16							16
17							17
18							18
19	Total						19
20							20
21	YEAR TO DATE						21
22							22
23	FUNDS						23
24	Benevolence						24
25	Current						25
26	Other						26
27	Other						27
28	Other						28
29							29
30							30
31							31
32	Total						32
33	Payroll Deductions						33
34	Total						34
35							35
36	BANK ACCOUNTS (List)						36
37							37
38							38
39							39

			BANK RECONCILIATION	YEAR		
			Name of Bank _____	MONTH		
			REPORT NUMBER FIVE	DATE		

1	
2	Balance shown on bank statement
3	Add: Deposits made but not appearing on bank statements
4	
5	
6	
7	
8	
9	Deduct: Checks which do not yet appear on the bank statement
10	List: Ck. number
11	
12	
13	
14	
15	
16	
17	
18	
19	Adjusted bank balance
20	
21	
22	
23	Balance shown on check book
24	Add: Deposits not yet recorded in check book or
25	on Reports No. 1 or No. 2
26	
27	
28	
29	
30	Less: Charges appearing on bank statement but not
31	yet recorded in Cash Disbursements Journal
32	
33	
34	
35	Adjusted check book balance
36	
37	
38	NOTE: Lines 19 and 35 must be the same. They must also be the same as lines
39	16 and 37, Column 4, Report Number 4 for this bank account.
40	

NAME
ADDRESS
SOCIAL SECURITY NUMBER

		Date	Gross Salary (1)	Income Tax Withheld (2)	Social Security Tax (3)	(4)	(5)	Net Amount of Check (6)
1								
2								
3								
4								
5								
6								
7								
8								
9								
10								
11								
12								
13								
14		Quarterly Total						
15								
16								
17								
18								
19								
20								
21								
22								
23								
24								
25								
26								
27								
28								
29		Quarterly Total						
30								
31								
32								
33		Total to Date						
34								
35								
36								
37								
38								
39								
40								

Chapter Sixteen

Computers in the Church: The Modern, Fast, Efficient Way To Keep Church Financial Records In Larger Congregations

The use of electronic data processing (EDP) equipment or management information systems (MIS) is a "way of life" for almost any business enterprise today. No matter its size, some phase of almost any financial record keeping system is dependent on the use of a computer. In fact, more and more enterprises are adapting all of their financial transactions to computerization. When used properly it is the modern, fast, efficient way to maintain financial records.

Congregations have been relatively slow in utilizing the computer. This may be due in large part to size, since the vast majority of all congregations have so few members and transactions that even the simplest data processing system is often much too sophisticated or expensive to justify the change. But many congregations, capable of converting, have failed to take advantage of the opportunity because key leaders do not understand computers nor the possibilities inherent in their use for creating more efficient, accurate and timely financial reports.

Nevertheless, continued technological advances make a computer of some kind attractive to more and more congregations each year. Size and costs continue to improve to the point where congregations which may have ignored the matter ten years ago, looked into it five years ago but voted negatively because of cost, may find that in today's market the size, capacity, and cost are right.

A computer system and the computer reports generated for a congregation must satisfy certain basic criteria before any decision to convert to EDP is voted.

To begin with, the capacity of the equipment used must obviously be appropriate for the congregation. It must be large enough to satisfy the system's needs, but not so large as to be unused most of the time. Larger computer capacity of course can be maximized by a congregation when the equipment is shared with other organizations. Time sharing allows each group the use of and access to much more capacity and speed than each one alone could possibly afford. The size of the computer, therefore, must be appropriate to the needs of the congregation.

Any computer purchased or leased must be useable by congregational personnel. Operating complexity is certainly an important consideration. Fortunately, learning the procedures for using computers effectively is not difficult.

However, lay leaders must first learn what a computer can do for their congregation, what they *expect* the computer to do for them, and then be certain that the computer selected will adequately perform all of the expected functions. Computers vary in their capacity to do what you might expect. A careful review of all expected applications is critical to the procurement of the right computer facility.

Cost is naturally all important. And it should be quickly determined which will cost the least, a computer or the current system. Personnel time, machine time, supplies and maintenance are all part of the costs no matter what kind of system is used. Of course, an expensive machine does not necessarily rule out its purchase. There may in fact be other considerations that prompt the conversion —efficiency, accuracy, timeliness of reports, internal control. All factors must be weighed, but cost still looms as one of the more decisive factors.

Finally, and perhaps most important, any computer used by a congregation must be easily adaptable to the needs of the congregation. There is not much point in buying or renting a computer that cannot realistically be programmed to the expressed record keeping and reporting needs of the congregation. Adaptability is crucial and obvious.

When Should a Congregation Consider a Computer?

Congregations seldom go into a complete computer use system all in one plunge, although they certainly can. There is frequently a gradual phase-in from one operation to another.

Thus, a congregation may begin its computer experience in the obvious high volume contributions record system. Computers can be used effectively for this function because they make the processing of a lot of routine tasks feasible in a very short period of time. For congregations, the largest routine financial record keeping activity is always the individual contributor's record. Many members give money frequently, and every contribution must be properly recorded. A hand-kept system for even 400 or 500 families could be quite time consuming and fraught with potential undetected errors.

Thus, maintaining that kind of record on the computer is often the starting point for a congregational computer system. From there a congregation may wish to add a simple feature that would provide a data processing produced record and report on all cash receipts. When the writing of checks becomes burdensome due to the number required each month, a computer can be utilized. Payrolls with many employees are easily converted to computer computation. Creation of the general ledger from the cash receipts and cash disbursements records is a natural next step with all posting done automatically. In fact, a cash receipts or cash disbursements journal as such would not then even be necessary. The final step in the conversion will be creation of financial statements and statistical data by computer.

In order for a congregation to utilize a full computer system, it must obviously be large enough to justify the cost. Again, depending on the size of the computer used, costs, personnel and perhaps other factors, congregations with less than 400 families may find computers useful for only a limited portion of their activities, if any. Congregations exceeding 2000 families will surely find a computer system valuable.

The computer can be a valuable tool to a congregation when it is used properly. But many factors must be considered before a firm decision to buy or lease or share is made. The following steps offer suggestions.

Suggested Steps for Developing
A Computer Based Accounting System

Computers should not be shopped for and bought the same way as an automobile. You don't just decide you need a computer and then go out and buy the cheapest model you can find. You develop specific plans and programs and a budget, defining precisely the kind and type of equipment, even the brand, that will fulfill your needs and fit your budget.

Besides, your congregation's needs may vary substantially from those of other organizations. So, don't buy what your neighbor has just because it looks good and does the job for him. Buy what you need, what will do the job for you, and what you can afford. Thus one organization's needs for a computer are generally never precisely the same as that for any other organization. Computer hardware needs, especially peripheral equipment, vary by system requirements and cost limitations. And programs for implementing desired systems and producing required reports are often unique to the particular organization. While hardware, systems, and programs can be standardized, a congregation should first seek that combination that suits its needs, not what may have worked well for others. Then, once its own needs have been defined, it may well search out what others (whose needs are similar) have done. There is no need for a congregation to "reinvent the wheel" in developing its computer system, but it must know its own needs first. Needs will determine hardware and software.

Once a decision has been made to utilize a computer system, but before specific hardware has been selected, a system developed, or programs written, a plan for implementation must be prepared. Congregational leaders charged with the responsibility of selecting equipment, developing a system, and implementing the programs should make conscious decisions on each of the following steps in the order listed:

1. A plan for a computer begins at the end by answering the question: What kind of financial reports does the congregation want from its computer? Presumably a computer has been voted to facilitate time-consuming record keeping functions. But before anyone goes out to buy a computer, a specific plan of reporting needs should be developed. The financial reporting format should be determined first.

So, which statements need to be produced, and what statistics reported, and in what form? Spell them out!

a balance sheet for each fund
a statement of revenues, disbursements and transfers by fund
a summary of fund changes report
an application and use of funds report
an analysis of giving and pledges
a directory of membership
address labels for mailings
plus anything else considered useful or needed.

2. A written working plan for implementing the procurement of on-line use of a computer is important. What are the steps required and the expected dates of beginning and completion for securing the computer and converting to its use. A timetable keeps everyone informed of what should happen when.

Specific responsibilities required of all personnel need to be assigned and listed. Schedule when each report will be produced. Put into a written memo agreed input data dates, programming times, parallel runs, and every other conceivable part of the conversion plan.

3. A system must be developed. With an understanding of reports to be expected and a knowledge of data required, a carefully designed system must be planned to get the data from its original source onto the final financial report. The system must be analyzed and preferably developed by an expert both knowledgeable about church accounting and familiar with the capabilities of a computer.

4. A computer facility must be located to satisfy the needs of the system and

the capacity required. A major decision cost-wise is obviously required here. A machine can be bought outright (as many smaller models are) or leased. Time can be purchased on someone else's computer by any one of several methods. The facility can be in the church building or located across the nation with telephone hookup.

The selection will not be easy because sales persons will all attempt to convince the congregation that their product is what is needed. However, because of the preliminary planning that must be done before equipment is purchased, congregational leaders ought to have a very good idea of the specific type of equipment that will satisfy their needs. The congregation may want to consider a mini-computer as described later in this chapter.

5. When the system has been described and equipment designated, computer programs must be written to tell the computer how to analyze the data, where to store it, what calculations to make and how to print out a final report. This is a job for professional computer programmers, obviously, people who know computer language and who can translate "plain English" instructions into that language.

6. Depending upon the decisions for access to a CPU (Central Processing Unit—the computer), various items of other equipment may be desirable. For example, if the system requires the use of punched cards, a keypunch machine may be desired using the congregation's own personnel for keypunching. Card sorting to arrange cards in the order preferred is done with a sorting machine. Perforated reports are separated with a burster. Carbon copies of computer processed reports are separated on a decolator.

Or if your system in "on line" with a larger computer somewhere, you may need a desk top CRT (Cathode Ray Tube) reader. Special telephone lines and head sets may also be required.

Knowing in advance just where all that equipment will be placed is good office management.

7. The written working plan of implementation will include a schedule for conversion. On one Sunday the old system is still in use, on the next the new is used. Everyone involved must be informed and prepared. Checks are hand written one day, processed by machine the next. Financial statements are delayed to nearly the end of one month, perhaps, because of hand preparation, but may be ready by the 5th day of the following month when the new computer is used. Expected dates for changing should be carefully listed.

8. In all of this, the congregation should be kept informed of progress. Many parishioners will not understand the procedures or the language or why so much money has to be spent to keep the records. But telling them what is happening avoids suspicions of secret, expensive, and unnecessary goings-on. Periodic progress reports help to gain support for the program.

9. No matter how sophisticated an accounting system may be, adequate internal control features are important safeguards for avoiding improper manipulations of the records. A computer does not guarantee accuracy or safety. Accuracy is no better than the information furnished to the computer by employees. Safety is no better than the audit checks used to guarantee control at each step. Thus all of the principles enunciated in the chapter on internal control are still applicable. Separation of duties, checks and balances over data entries, control of cash—these remain important. Systems development must include adequate checks and controls.

10. Finally, when the system is in use, certain "debugging" steps will be required to smooth out the rough places. Not everything may work out exactly as it was planned the first time around. A brief time period must be anticipated to get the kinks out of the system. It's a final, necessary step toward developing a computer system for a congregation.

Computer systems for congregations are probably as varied as the number of systems used, just as with most of church accounting. But the development of a system will be done best by those familiar with accounting procedures. The accounting procedures and reports illustrated elsewhere in this book offer a basis upon which to build such a computer system.

Some years ago an organization called Computer Assisted Church Programs developed a description for its computerized individual contributors record system. That description and accompanying illustrations are adapted in the following comments from an article in *Church Management* magazine, used here with permission. Of course, almost all church offering envelope manufacturers have developed similar systems.

How to Record Individual Contributions by Computer*

At a cost of only a few cents for each member each month, the entire individual contributions record keeping process of almost any sized congregation can be handled quickly, efficiently, and economically by computer. By using such an automated system, a congregation need do no more record keeping for contributions than to count the Sunday offering. All individual contributions record-keeping functions, including the mailing of quarterly and annual reports to each member, are done by the computer, automatically. Here's how.

As soon as possible after the Sunday services, a very brief report, similar to that illustrated, is completed by those who count the offering. This only requires that coins, bills and checks in all offering envelopes be counted, with the contents properly marked on each envelope. The total of an adding machine tape of the

---

Church Management: The Clergy Journal, Vol. 46, No. 10 ("How to Record Individual Contributions by computer," by Manfred Holck, Jr.), published by Church Management, Inc., Hopkins, MN 55343, used with permission.

envelopes must equal the total of coins, bills, and checks noted on the illustrated report in column one. Also, all loose offerings, if any, are tabulated and noted for each special fund in columns two to four, as needed. The total deposit—all coins, bills, and checks—is listed in the final column.

With this system there is no need for the counters to sort the envelopes by fund, name or number since the computer will do the sorting and total all contributions received for each fund automatically. All that is required on Sunday morning, therefore, is to count the loose plate offering and the money enclosed in each envelope, verifying the count of envelope money as equal to the amounts marked thereon. This procedure alone saves those responsible for counting money considerable time, eliminates many chances of error, and greatly simplifies the church's counting and record keeping procedures.

Then the envelopes, the adding machine tape of the total contributions, and the counting report are all placed in a pre-addressed, postage-paid mailing carton and mailed to the computer service the same day.

When received, the computer service will immediately keypunch appropriate cards for each envelope. The cards will be processed through the computer and a weekly report of all fund totals printed and mailed back to the congregation, all within the same week!

This weekly report will show total contributions to all funds this week, this month to date, and thus far this year. It will also show total pledges for the week, as well as for the year to date. In addition, each week the report will include for the week, month, and year to date the total number of contributors, the total contributions to every fund, the percentage of contributions to pledges, the range of average weekly contributions, and the totals of contributions to all special funds.

Few congregations using present procedures will have all that information readily available within a few days after counting the Sunday morning offering!

Then at the end of each month, a complete detailed report of the offerings by all individuals for the month will be sent to the congregation. This report will show every member's name, offering envelope number, and contributions to every fund during the month and the year to date. It will also show weekly pledge and pledge for the year to date.

Plus, at the end of each quarter, individual reports are mailed to each member showing all contributions each week for the past quarter, total contributions to each fund so far this year, and pledges for the quarter and year to date. Thus, every member will have a complete record, Sunday by Sunday, by funds, of every contribution made during the past thirteen Sundays. The congregation will receive for its own record a copy of each of these member reports.

All of this information can certainly be a tremendous help to harassed pastors, finance and stewardship committee chairmen, and church secretaries and treasurers who must often wait weeks for similar hand recorded information!

And all of this, of course, eliminates the time-consuming Sunday morning balancing of contributions to each fund, the weekly posting to each member's record, and the computation and mailing of quarterly reports. Besides, a complete listing of all contributions is available, if desired, every week, month, or quarter.

For added convenience, each weekly, monthly and quarterly report is prepared on letter-size 8½ × 11 report forms for easy filing in a three ring notebook.

Many congregations, no matter how large or small, will soon discover that their own time, forms and salary costs (not to mention inconveniences and inaccurate reports) for keeping these kinds of records is far more than the cost of modernizing their procedures in this up-to-date, convenient, and efficient way.

For many congregations, keeping only individual contributions records on a computer is an excellent place to begin the up-dating of record keeping procedures. Congregations eager to keep up with the times, save money, and conserve the energies of their membership for other tasks, may therefore well consider exploring the possibilities of using computer services for at least individual contributions record keeping. For a congregation this is the one obvious time-consuming operation that can be handled well by a computer.

CHURCH NAME   NUMBER   DATE
STREET
CITY   STATE   ZIP

WEEKLY COUNT OF OFFERINGS AND DEPOSIT

	All Envelopes	Loose Offerings (Specify Fund)		Total Deposit
Coins				
Bills				
Check				
Total				

1. Attach to this report an adding machine tape of all envelopes. Total of tape must be the same as total of coins, bills and checks in column one.

2. Indicate loose offerings for proper special funds; i.e., Sunday Church School, Thanksgiving, etc.

3. Be certain every envelope is correctly marked with member's number and amount of contribution. Each check received from a member but not enclosed in an offering envelope should be noted on a "Report of Check Without Envelope" form (illustrated below) and included on the adding machine tape of total envelopes.

4. Mail all offering envelopes (including information about checks without envelopes), adding machine tape of envelopes, and one copy of this form to service center.

Name of Counters _____

SAMPLE FORM REPORT
OF CHECK WITHOUT ENVELOPE

Account number _____
Member name _____
Amount of check $ _____
Fund _____

REPORT OF CONTRIBUTIONS

NAME OF CHURCH   NUMBER   DATE OF CONTRIBUTIONS
STREET ADDRESS   FEBRUARY 2, 1969
CITY, STATE, ZIP CODE   WEEK NO.   5
                                                   PAGE NO. 1

ENV. NO.	N A M E	S C	F C	WEEKLY PLEDGE	PAYMENTS	THIS MONTH PAYMENTS	YEAR TO DATE PLEDGE	PAYMENTS
TOTAL OF ALL ENVELOPES				XX.00	XX.00	XX.00	XX.00	XX.00
PERCENTAGE TO PLEDGES					52.6			84.7
TOTAL OF LOOSE OFFERINGS					XX.00	XX.00		XX.00
TOTAL OF ALL FUNDS AND DEPOSITS					XX.00	XX.00		XX.00
NUMBER OF CONTRIBUTORS					XX	XX		XX
AVERAGE CONTRIBUTION					XX.00	XX.00		XX.00
RANGE OF CONTRIBUTIONS (AVERAGE WEEKLY AMOUNTS)								
$50.00 AND OVER					XX	XX		XX
$25.00 - 49.99					XX	XX		XX
$10.00 - 24.99					XX	XX		XX
$ 5.00 - 9.99					XX	XX		XX
$ 1.00 - 4.99					XX	XX		XX
.99 AND UNDER					XX	XX		XX
NON-CONTRIBUTORS					XX	XX		XX

OPERATIONS FUND   A

	WEEKLY PLEDGE	PAYMENTS	THIS MONTH PAYMENTS	YEAR TO DATE PLEDGE	PAYMENTS
TOTAL OPERATIONS FUND ENVELOPE	XX.00	XX.00	XX.00	XX.00	XX.00
PERCENTAGE TO PLEDGES		83.9			92.3
TOTAL OF LOOSE OFFERINGS		XX.00	XX.00		XX.00
TOTAL OPERATIONS FUND		XX.00	XX.00		XX.00
NUMBER OF CONTRIBUTORS		XX	XX		XX
AVERAGE CONTRIBUTION		XX.00	XX.00		XX.00
RANGE OF CONTRIBUTIONS (AVERAGE WEEKLY AMOUNTS)					
$50.00 AND OVER		XX	XX		XX
$25.00 - 49.99		XX	XX		XX
$10.00 - 24.99		XX	XX		XX
$ 5.00 - 9.99		XX	XX		XX
$ 1.00 - 4.99		XX	XX		XX
.99 AND UNDER		XX	XX		XX
NON-CONTRIBUTORS		XX	XX		XX

REPORT OF CONTRIBUTIONS

NAME OF CHURCH   NUMBER   DATE OF CONTRIBUTIONS
STREET ADDRESS   FEBRUARY 2, 1969
CITY, STATE, ZIP CODE   WEEK NO.   5
                                                      PAGE NO. 2

ENV. NO. NAME	S F C C	WEEKLY PLEDGE	PAYMENTS	THIS MONTH PAYMENTS	YEAR TO DATE PLEDGE	PAYMENTS
BENEVOLENCE FUND	B					
TOTAL BENEVOLENCE FUND ENVELOPE		XX.00	XX.00	XX.00	XX.00	XX.00
PERCENTAGE TO PLEDGES			83.9			92.3
TOTAL OF LOOSE OFFERINGS			XX.00	XX.00		XX.00
TOTAL BENEVOLENCE FUND			XX.00	XX.00		XX.00
NUMBER OF CONTRIBUTORS			XX	XX		XX
AVERAGE CONTRIBUTION			XX.00	XX.00		XX.00
RANGE OF CONTRIBUTIONS (AVERAGE WEEKLY AMOUNTS)						
$50.00 AND OVER			XX	XX		XX
$25.00 - 49.99			XX	XX		XX
$10.00 - 24.99			XX	XX		XX
$ 5.00 - 9.99			XX	XX		XX
$ 1.00 - 4.99			XX	XX		XX
.99 AND UNDER			XX	XX		XX
NON-CONTRIBUTORS			XX	XX		XX

SPECIAL OFFERINGS ENVELOPE	F		XX.00	XX.00		XX.00
SPECIAL OFFERINGS LOOSE	F		XX.00	XX.00		XX.00
TOTAL SPECIAL OFFERINGS	F		XX.00	XX.00		XX.00
SPECIAL OFFERINGS ENVELOPE	G		XX.00	XX.00		XX.00
SPECIAL OFFERINGS LOOSE	G		XX.00	XX.00		XX.00
TOTAL SPECIAL OFFERINGS	G		XX.00	XX.00		XX.00
TOTAL OF SPECIAL OFFERINGS			XX.00	XX.00		XX.00
NUMBER OF CONTRIBUTORS			XX	XX		XX
AVERAGE CONTRIBUTION			XX.00	XX.00		XX.00

REPORT OF CONTRIBUTIONS

```
NAME OF CHURCH      NUMBER              DATE OF CONTRIBUTIONS
STREET ADDRESS                           FEBRUARY 2, 1969
CITY, STATE, ZIP CODE                    MONTH OF   MARCH
                                         PAGE NO. 1
```

ENV. NO.	NAME	S C	F C	WEEKLY PLEDGE	PAYMENTS	THIS MONTH PAYMENTS	YEAR TO PLEDGE	DATE PAYMENTS
0012	ADAMS JOHN	1	A	XX.00		XX.00	XX.00	XX.00
0012	ADAMS JOHN	1	D	XX.00		XX.00	XX.00	XX.00
0325	BAKER CHARLES	3	A	XX.00		XX.00	XX.00	XX.00
0325	BAKER CHARLES	3	S			XX.00		XX.00
0001	COLLINS MARY	2	A	XX.00		XX.00	XX.00	XX.00
0001	COLLINS MARY	2	B	XX.00		XX.00	XX.00	XX.00
0001	COLLINS MARY	2	E	XX.00		XX.00	XX.00	XX.00
0078	HANSON PAUL	1	B	XX.00		XX.00	XX.00	XX.00
0014	JACKSON HELEN	4	A	XX.00		XX.00	XX.00	XX.00
1262	MOORE HAROLD	1	C	XX.00		XX.00	XX.00	XX.00
1262	MOORE HAROLD	1	S			XX.00		XX.00
0244	SMITH JOHN	3	A	XX.00		XX.00	XX.00	XX.00
0244	SMITH JOHN	3	S			XX.00		XX.00
0006	THOMAS STEVE	1	A	XX.00		XX.00	XX.00	XX.00
0585	WALKER JOHN	1	B	XX.00		XX.00	XX.00	XX.00
0432	ZIMMERMAN C L	3	A	XX.00		XX.00	XX.00	XX.00
0432	ZIMMERMAN C L	3	C	XX.00		XX.00	XX.00	XX.00
0432	ZIMMERMAN C L	3	S			XX.00		XX.00
TOTAL OF ALL ENVELOPES					XX.00	XX.00	XX.00	XX.00

FUND CODE -S- DENOTES SPECIAL FUNDS WITHOUT PLEDGE

QUARTERLY REPORT OF CONTRIBUTIONS   THREE MONTHS ENDING DECEMBER 31, 1969

	WEEK 1	WEEK 2	WEEK 3	WEEK 4	WEEK 5	TOTAL
OPERATIONS FUND A						
MONTH OF OCTOBER	XX.00	XX.00	XX.00	XX.00	XX.00	XX.00
MONTH OF NOVEMBER	XX.00	XX.00	XX.00	XX.00	XX.00	XX.00
MONTH OF DECEMBER	XX.00	XX.00	XX.00	XX.00	XX.00	XX.00
TOTAL THIS QUARTER	PLEDGE	XXX.00		CONTRIBUTIONS		XXX.00
TOTAL YEAR TO DATE	PLEDGE	XXX.00		CONTRIBUTIONS		XXX.00
BENEVOLENCE FUND B						
MONTH OF OCTOBER	XX.00	XX.00	XX.00	XX.00	XX.00	XX.00
MONTH OF NOVEMBER	XX.00	XX.00	XX.00	XX.00	XX.00	XX.00
MONTH OF DECEMBER	XX.00	XX.00	XX.00	XX.00	XX.00	XX.00
TOTAL THIS QUARTER	PLEDGE	XXX.00		CONTRIBUTIONS		XXX.00
TOTAL YEAR TO DATE	PLEDGE	XXX.00		CONTRIBUTIONS		XXX.00
BUILDING FUND C						
MONTH OF OCTOBER	XX.00	XX.00	XX.00	XX.00	XX.00	XX.00
MONTH OF NOVEMBER	XX.00	XX.00	XX.00	XX.00	XX.00	XX.00
MONTH OF DECEMBER	XX.00	XX.00	XX.00	XX.00	XX.00	XX.00
TOTAL THIS QUARTER	PLEDGE	XXX.00		CONTRIBUTIONS		XXX.00
TOTAL YEAR TO DATE	PLEDGE	XXX.00		CONTRIBUTIONS		XXX.00
FUND D						
MONTH OF OCTOBER	XX.00	XX.00	XX.00	XX.00	XX.00	XX.00
MONTH OF NOVEMBER	XX.00	XX.00	XX.00	XX.00	XX.00	XX.00
MONTH OF DECEMBER	XX.00	XX.00	XX.00	XX.00	XX.00	XX.00
TOTAL THIS QUARTER	PLEDGE	XXX.00		CONTRIBUTIONS		XXX.00
TOTAL YEAR TO DATE	PLEDGE	XXX.00		CONTRIBUTIONS		XXX.00
FUND E						
MONTH OF OCTOBER	XX.00	XX.00	XX.00	XX.00	XX.00	XX.00
MONTH OF NOVEMBER	XX.00	XX.00	XX.00	XX.00	XX.00	XX.00
MONTH OF DECEMBER	XX.00	XX.00	XX.00	XX.00	XX.00	XX.00
TOTAL THIS QUARTER	PLEDGE	XXX.00		CONTRIBUTIONS		XXX.00
TOTAL YEAR TO DATE	PLEDGE	XXX.00		CONTRIBUTIONS		XXX.00
SPECIAL FUNDS						
MONTH OF OCTOBER	XX.00	XX.00	XX.00	XX.00	XX.00	XX.00
MONTH OF NOVEMBER	XX.00	XX.00	XX.00	XX.00	XX.00	XX.00
MONTH OF DECEMBER	XX.00	XX.00	XX.00	XX.00	XX.00	XX.00
TOTAL THIS QUARTER	PLEDGE	XXX.00		CONTRIBUTIONS		XXX.00
TOTAL YEAR TO DATE	PLEDGE	XXX.00		CONTRIBUTIONS		XXX.00

```
TOTAL ALL CONTRIBUTIONS THIS QUARTER    XXX.00
TOTAL ALL CONTRIBUTIONS YEAR TO DATE    XXX.00
```

```
        CHURCH NAME     NUMBER          CHURCH MEMBER NAME    NUMBER
        STREET ADDRESS                  STREET ADDRESS
        CITY    STATE   ZIP             CITY    STATE   ZIP
```

An Alternative Approach:
Using the Mini-Computer
for Church Record Keeping*

Mention computers and most of us think of giant complicated electronic machines, banks of tape drives, whirring motors, and noisy printers spitting out paper by the reams. But not all computers are such monsters as the IBM 270's, Honeywell 200's NCR Century 200's. The desk top mini-computer, like the mini-calculator, has come into its own, thanks to recent "chip" technology. Smaller organizations can now have their own computers at much less cost than was ever possible before. Even by sharing with others, the costs can be dramatically less than they were only a few years ago.

Indeed, before the advent of the mini-computer, religious organizations were limited to the use of data processing service bureaus, a bank, or a sympathetic business firm if they desired electronic processing of data. On the national scene several church-related service bureaus and publishing houses do offer centralized processing of data. Selected names and addresses of some of these are listed at the end of this chapter.

With the mini-computer, however, another alternative is now available and at a price range much more favorable for congregations and religious organizations. Not only are size and cost considerably less, but the new equipment makes possible the combining of several functions ordinarily requiring several machines. The mini-computer can be used as a calculator, bookkeeping machine, an addresser, an automatic letter writer, and is a file cabinet full of coded and uncoded information about membership and constituency.

This versatility opens the way to a whole new concept for the consideration of those responsible for the business-like conduct of the affairs of congregations and religious bodies. Where one organization might need the versatility of the mini-computer but not have enough work to justify the investment in dollars, it could join with one or several like-minded institutions and share the cost and time in order to have complete control and ownership.

This concept of ownership sharing is now used by many groups. Illustrative is the experience of the Southwest Texas Conference of the United Methodist Church and the Methodist Mission Home in San Antonio, Texas. As co-sponsors they have set up Church Data Processing as a service function of the Conference. For practical reasons the operation has been located in the Conference headquarters building.

Conference sponsorship was based on the premise that it was the logical

---

*Adapted from *Church Management: The Clergy Journal,* Vol. 53, No. 4 ("The Mini-Computer: Bane or Blessing for Your Church," Gayley, Harry K.), published by Church Management, Inc., 4119 Terrace Lane, Hopkins, MN 55343, used with permission.

organization to set up close-at-hand data processing services for local churches. The Mission Home had studied the installation of mini-computer equipment but its consultant had advised that it alone did not have enough work to justify the investment. However, by combining the Mission Home needs with the work of the Conference and the Travis Park United Methodist Church, the project became feasible and was initiated.

Commercial software with programs for all the functions desired was initially purchased and adapted to the kind of financial reports required by the sponsors and the local congregation. One month after installation of equipment, current reports were being generated.

However, about three months later it became apparent that commercial programs adapted to religious organizations may not be entirely satisfactory. So this initial phase of operations was followed by six months of designing and programming of a system using the distinctive features of the mini-computer and meeting the *specific* needs of the participating religious organizations.

The initial participants in this program have decided that Church Data Processing is not to become another centralized service bureau for use by others outside the bounds of the Conference. Even within the Conference area, congregations and religious organizations wishing to use the unique features of this system will be required to install terminals connected by ordinary dial telephone lines to the San Antonio office.

When immediate access to data is not required, an alternative to the telephone line is the use of cassette tapes. Users will install their own mini-computer with a dual cassette facility for entering data and updating files, composing letters or documents and then sending the tapes to the processing center specifying the type of output or reports to be produced. Either method provides low cost congregational access to a sophisticated system of data processing.

The Church Data Processing system as presently designed by these participants can produce several reports. For example, fund accounting reports for judicatories such as a Conference, Presbytery, or a Foundation are available. For an organization desiring to maintain a record of individual contributions, reports are generated showing amount of pledge, frequency of payment with the option of printing statements to all contributors, or only to those who have a balance due on pledge to date. For lists or mailing labels, name and address files are maintained with or without coding for special selections. Complete membership information files can be maintained with name, address, telephone number, geographical area, names of family members with their dates of birth, baptism, membership and with almost unlimited coding capacity for other purposes. Automatic letter writing and document generation from previously edited files in the system is an additional option.

Where to Get Help for Putting
Church Financial Records on the Computer

For more specific information on standard data processing services available on a commercial basis to congregations, the following companies may be contacted:

Lutheran Church Supply Store
Data Processing Program
P.O. Box 5512
Richmond, VA 23220

Religious Data Services, Inc.
697 Main St.
Farmingdale, NY 11735

Church Records Management, Inc.
1539 Round Table
Dallas, TX 75247

National Church Supply Co., Inc.
Box 269
Chester, WV 26034

Ministers Life Information Systems Company
3100 West Lake Street
Minneapolis, MN 55416

Part Four

Financial Reports, Church Audits, Internal Controls, and Church Management Techniques

Chapter Seventeen

Basic Financial Statements:
A Key to Meaningful Reporting
Of Church Financial Activity

The caliber of congregational financial statements runs the gamut—some are good, some are very good; some are bad, some are very bad. Yet, as congregations honestly try to convey their financial status to the membership, increasingly successful attempts are being made to do the job creatively, accurately, and informatively.

It is not an easy thing to do, to summarize a month's or a year's activities into a format easily understood by people who may have trouble even balancing their own checkbooks. But it is a challenge congregational treasurers accepted when they took on their record keeping jobs.

Fortunately, the accounting profession is finally recognizing the need for assisting congregations and other nonprofit organizations in the preparation of their financial statements.

One of the first attempts at publishing a guide to financial statement preparation was Malvern J. Gross, Jr.'s "The Layman's Guide to Preparing Financial Statements for Churches." Published by the American Institute of Certified Public Accountants, this small booklet is still a fundamental handbook for church financial statement formats.

Now, however, the AICPA has developed a more comprehensive set of illustrative statements. On the following pages are illustrative financial statements proposed in 1977 by the Accounting Standards Subcommittee on Nonprofit Organizations of the AICPA.* While these statements are applicable for a variety of

*See also "Highlights of the AICPA's tentative statement of accounting principles and reporting practices applicable to certain nonprofit organizations," Price Waterhouse & Co., NY 1977.

nonprofit organizations, they are also intended for congregations. Indeed, they are quite appropriate.

The AICPA Subcommittee urges organizations to develop financial statement formats that are most appropriate for their own circumstances and consistent with the reporting practices applicable to such organizations. These examples offer congregational treasurers significant helps for the preparation of financial statements.

Note that in the ten examples shown, four are for Balance Sheets in various formats, four for statements of activity reporting receipts and disbursements, and two relate to formats for changes in the financial position of the organization.

In due time, but after publication of this book, the AICPA will issue a final audit guide for nonprofit organizations that are not hospitals or colleges. (An audit guide specifically for hospitals and colleges has already been prepared.) Congregational treasurers are urged to write to the AICPA, 1211 Avenue of the Americas, New York 10036, requesting a copy of the final statement of accounting principles and reporting practices suggested for nonprofit organizations not covered by existing AICPA industry audit guides.

ILLUSTRATIVE FINANCIAL STATEMENTS*

*From the discussion draft on tentative accounting principles and reporting practices for nonprofit organizations that are not covered by existing audit guides, published by the Accounting Standards Subcommittee on Nonprofit Organizations of the American Institute of Certified Public Accountants, New York, 1977. Used with permission.

EXAMPLE I

BALANCE SHEET
December 31, 197X

| | Current | | | | Annuity/ Life | |
	Unrestricted	Restricted	Plant	Endowment	Income	Total
Assets						
Cash and temporary investments	XX	XX	XX	XX	XX	XXX
Pledges receivable, net	XX	XX				XX
Other assets	X					X
Investments	XX		XX	XXX	XX	XXX
Land, buildings, and equipment, at cost less accumulated depreciation of XXX			XXX			XXX
Total assets	XXX	XX	XXX	XXX	XX	XXXX
Liabilities and Fund Balances						
Liabilities						
Accounts payable and accrued expenses	XX	XX	XX			XX
Deferred restricted revenue		XX				XX
Bonds payable and other debt			XXX			XXX
Annuities and life income payable					XX	XX
Total liabilities	XX	XX	XXX		XX	XXXX
Fund Balances						
Unrestricted—designated	XX					XX
Unrestricted—undesignated	XXX					XXX
Restricted			XXX	XXX	XX	XXXX
Total fund balances	XXX		XXX	XXX	XX	XXXXX
Total liabilities and fund balances	XXX	XX	XXX	XXX	XX	XXXXX

EXAMPLE 2

BALANCE SHEET

December 31, 197X

Assets		Liabilities and Fund Balances	
		Current Unrestricted	
Cash and temporary investments	XX	Accounts payable and accrued expenses	XX
Pledges receivable, net	XX	Total liabilities	XX
Other assets	X	Fund balance:	
Investments	XX	Designated	XX
		Undesignated	XXX
		Total fund balance	XXX
Total	XXX	Total	XXX
		Current Restricted	
Cash and temporary investments	XX	Accounts payable and accrued expenses	XX
Pledges receivable, net	XX	Deferred restricted revenue	XX
		Total liabilities	XX
		Fund balance—restricted	—
Total	XX	Total	XX
		Plant	
Cash	XX	Accounts payable and accrued expenses	XX
Investments	XX	Bonds payable and other debt	XXX
Land, building, and equipment at cost less		Total liabilities	XXX
accumulated depreciation of XXX	XXX	Fund balance—restricted	XXX
Total	XXX	Total	XXX
		Endowment	
Cash	XX	Fund balance	XXX
Investments	XXX		
Total	XXX	Total	XXX
		Annuity and Life Income	
		Annuity	
Cash	XX	Annuities payable	XX
Investments	XX	Fund balance	XX
Total annuity	XX	Total annuity	XX
		Life Income	
Cash	XX	Income payable	XX
Investments	XX	Fund balance	XX
Total life income	XX	Total life income	XX
Total	XXXX	Total	XXXX

EXAMPLE 3

STATEMENT OF FINANCIAL POSITION
DECEMBER 31, 197X

	Expendable	Nonexpendable Fixed Assets	Endowment	Total
Assets				
Current assets:				
Cash	XX	XX		XX
Short-term investments	XX			XX
Accounts receivable, net	XX	`		XX
Inventories	XX			XX
Prepaid expenses	X			X
Total current assets	XXX	XX		XXX
Investments	XX	XX	XXX	XXXX
Land, buildings, and equipment at cost less accumulated depreciation of XXX		XXX		XXX
Total assets	XXX	XXX	XXX	XXXX
Liabilities and Fund Balances				
Current liabilities:				
Accounts payable	XX	X		XX
Accrued expenses	XX			XX
Deferred restricted revenue	XX			XX
Portion of long-term debt due currently		XX		XX
Total current liabilities	XXX	XX		XXX
Long-term debt		XXX		XXX
Total liabilities	XXX	XXX		XXX
Fund balances:				
Unrestricted	XXX			XXX
Restricted		XX	XXX	XXX
Invested in fixed assets		XXX		XXX
Total fund balances	XXX	XXX	XXX	XXXX
Total liabilities and fund balances	XXX	XXX	XXX	XXXX

EXAMPLE 4

BALANCE SHEET
DECEMBER 31, 197X

Assets

Current assets:

Cash	XX
Short-term investments	XX
Accounts receivable, net	XX
Inventories	XX
Prepaid expenses	XX
Total current assets	XXX
Investments	XX
Land, buildings, and equipment at cost less accumulated depreciation of XXX	XXX
Total assets	XXXX

Liabilities and Membership Equity

Current liabilities:

Accounts payable	XX
Accrued expenses	XX
Deferred dues revenue	X
Portion of long-term debt due currently	XX
Total current liabilities	XXX
Long-term debt	XX
Total liabilities	XXX
Membership equity: cumulative excess of income over expense	XXX
Total liabilities and membership equity	XXXX

EXAMPLE 5

STATEMENT OF SUPPORT, REVENUE, EXPENSES, CAPITAL ADDITIONS AND CHANGES IN FUND BALANCES
For the Year Ended December 31, 197X

	Current Unrestricted	Current Restricted	Plant	Endowment	Annuity/ Life Income	Total
Support and Revenue						
Fees for services	XXX					XXX
Investment income	XX	X				XXX
Current gains/losses	XX	X				XX
Contributions	XXX	XXX				XXX
Contributed services	XX					XX
Total	XXXX	XXX				XXXX
Expenses						
Program A	XXXX	XXX	X			XXXX
Program B	XXX	XXX	X			XXX
Program C	XX					XX
General administration	XXX	XXX	X			XXX
Fund raising	XX	X	X			XX
Total	XXXX	XXX	XX			XXXX
Excess (Deficit) of Support and Revenue Over Expenses Before Capital Additions	XX		XX		XX	XX
Capital Additions						
Contributions			XX	XXX	XX	XXX
Gains, losses, and investment income				XX	X	XX
Excess (Deficit) of Support and Revenue Over Expenses After Capital Additions	XX		XX	XXX	XX	XXX
Fund Balances—Beginning	XXX		XXX	XXX	XX	XXX
Transfers	(XX)		XX			
Fund Balances—Ending	XXX		XXX	XXX	XX	XXXX

228

EXAMPLE 6

STATEMENT OF SUPPORT, REVENUE, EXPENSES, NONEXPENDABLE CAPITAL ADDITIONS AND CHANGES IN FUND BALANCES

For the Year Ended December 31, 197X

		Nonexpendable		
	Expendable	Fixed Assets	Endowment	Total
Support and Revenue				
Fees for services	XX			XX
Investment income	XX			XX
Expendable gains/losses	X			X
Contributions of which XXX were expended for restricted purposes	XXX			XXX
Total	XXX			XXXX
Expenses				
Program A	XX	X		XXX
Program B	XX	X		XXX
Program C	X	X		XX
General administration	X	X		XX
Fund raising	X	X		XX
Total	XXX	X		XXX
Excess (Deficit) of Support and Revenue Over Expenses Before Nonexpendable Capital Additions	X	(X)		X
Nonexpendable Capital Additions				
Contributions		XX	XXX	XXX
Gains, losses, and investment income		XX	XXX	XXX
Excess (Deficit) for the Year	X	XXX	XXX	XXX
Fund Balances—Beginning	XXX	XXX	XXX	XXXX
Transfers	(XX)	XX	—	
Fund Balances—Ending	XXX	XXX	XXX	XXXX

EXAMPLE 7

STATEMENT OF ACTIVITY
For the Year Ended December 31, 197X

	Expendable	Nonexpendable	Total
Public Support and Revenue			
Fees	XXXX		XXXX
Investment income	XX		XX
Gains/losses	XX		XX
Research grants	XXX		XXX
Contributions of which XXX were expended for restricted purposes	XXX	_____	XXX
Total public support and revenue	XXXX	_____	XXXX
Expenses			
Program services:			
Program A	XXX	X	XXX
Program B	XXX	X	XXX
Program C	XX	X	XX
Total program services	XXXX	X	XXXX
Supporting services:			
General administration	XXX	XX	XXX
Fund raising	X	XX	XX
Grant solicitation	XX	_____	XX
Total supporting services	XXX	XX	XXX
Total expenses	XXX	XX	XXXX
Excess (Deficit) of Public Support and Revenue Over Expenses Before Nonexpendable Additions	XXX	(X)	XXX
Nonexpendable Additions:			
Contributions		XX	XX
Gains, losses, and investment income	_____	XX	XX
Excess of Public Support and Revenue Over Expenses After Nonexpendable Additions	XXX	XXX	XXX
Fund Balances—Beginning	XXXX	XXXXX	XXXXX
Transfers	(XX)	XX	_____
Fund Balances—Ending	XXXX	XXXXX	XXXXX

EXAMPLE 8

STATEMENTS OF INCOME, EXPENSES AND CHANGES
IN MEMBERSHIP EQUITY
For the Year Ended December 31, 197X

Income:

Membership dues	XXX
Publication advertising	XXX
Subscription fees	XXX
Miscellaneous publication sales	XX
Seminar fees	XXX
Sale of self-study courses	XX
Convention registration and exhibition fees	XXX
Investment income	X
Total income	XXXX

Expense:

Program services:

Membership services	XXX	
Information services	XX	
Continuing education	XXX	
Annual convention	XXX	
Publications	XXX	
Total program services		XXXX

Supporting services:

General administration	XX	
Membership development	XX	
Other	XX	
Total supporting services		XXX
Total expenses		XXXX

Excess of Income Over Expenses	XX
Membership Equity—Beginning	XXX
Membership Equity—Ending	XXX

EXAMPLE 9

STATEMENT OF CHANGES IN FINANCIAL POSITION
For the Year Ended December 31, 197X

	Current Unrestricted	Current Restricted	Plant	Endowment	Annuity/ Life Income	Total
Sources of cash:						
Excess (deficit) of support and revenue over expenses before capital additions	XX		(XX)			XX
Capital additions:						
Contributions			XX	XXX	XX	XXX
Gains, losses, and investment income				XX		XX
Excess of support and revenue over expenses after capital additions	XX		XX	XXX	XX	XXX
Add (deduct) items not providing cash—depreciation			XX			XX
Issuance of debt			XX			XX
Deferred restricted contributions received		XX				XX
Proceeds from sale of investments	XX		XX	XXX		XXX
Total cash provided	XX	XX	XXX	XXX	XX	XXX
Uses of cash:						
Purchase of buildings and equipment			(XX)			(XX)
Reduction of debt			(XX)			(XX)
Purchase of investments	(XX)	(XX)		(XXX)		(XXX)
Net change in annuity and life income payable					(XX)	(XX)
Deferred restricted contributions recognized as support and revenue		(XX)				(XX)
Increase in pledges receivable	(XX)	(X)				(XX)
Purchase of other assets	(X)					(X)
Decrease in accounts payable and accrued expenses	(XX)	(X)	(XX)			(XX)
Total cash used	(XX)	(XX)	(XXX)	(XXX)	(XX)	(XXX)
Increase (decrease) in cash	XX	X	XX	XX	XX	XXX

EXAMPLE 10

STATEMENT OF CHANGES IN FINANCIAL POSITION
For the Year Ended December 31, 197X

Financial resources were provided by:	
Excess of income over expenses	XX
Add (deduct) items not affecting working capital—depreciation	XX
Working capital provided by operations	XXX
Issuance of long-term debt	XX
Proceeds from sales of long-term investments	XX
Total resources provided	XXX
Financial resources were used for:	
Purchase of building and equipment	XX
Reduction of long-term debt	XX
Purchase of long-term investments	XXX
Total resources used	XXX
Increase (decrease) in working capital	XX
Changes in working capital:	
Increase (decrease) in current assets:	
Cash	XX
Short-term investments	XX
Accounts receivable, net	XX
Inventories	XX
Prepaid expenses	(XX)
	XX
(Increase) decrease in current liabilities:	
Accounts payable	XX
Accrued expenses	(XX)
Deferred dues revenue	XX
Portion of long-term debt due within one year	XX
	XX
Increase (decrease) in working capital	XX

Chapter Eighteen

Auditing the Church Financial Records: A Basic Procedure in the Modern Church Accounting System

Whether your congregation insists on an annual audit or not is a value judgment. Audits may cost money. They do take time. The values derived weighed against costs incurred must be carefully considered. Not every congregation has an audit annually. Some *never* do.

Generally, an audit is a series of procedures followed by those in charge to test, on a predetermined selective basis, the various transactions occurring in the last year, verifying internal control methods, and generally forming an opinion about the appropriateness or fairness of the financial statements presented. An audit does not guarantee that every transaction was accurately recorded. It is no proof that all funds were handled appropriately.

An audit is an opinion. Through a series of tests and inquiries and probing investigations, the auditor or auditing committee decides if, based on the information given to them, the financial reports do fairly represent the financial condition of the congregation. Based on a testing of selected transactions—checks written and deposits made—and on their own experiences of similar institutions, the auditors state as precisely as they can if things seem to be in order.

Let's be sure to understand one thing: an auditor cannot guarantee the accuracy of the financial statements. If someone contributed $100 but it was never recorded anywhere, an auditor cannot know that. Furthermore, if $100 is stolen somehow and the amount is really not material to the total sums involved, the auditor is not likely to discover that either.

Audits thus express opinions. And if your congregation has an external auditor prepare a statement for you, those financial statements will be attached to an "opinion" letter, not a guarantee. A typical nonqualified opinion letter would go something like this:

> In my opinion, the accompanying balance sheet and the related statement of income and expense present fairly the financial position of Christ Church at December 31, 19X1, and the results of its operations for the year in conformity with generally accepted accounting principles applied on a basis consistent with that of the preceding year. My examination of these statements was made in accordance with generally accepted auditing standards and accordingly included such tests of the accounting records and such other auditing procedures as I considered necessary in the circumstances. It was impractical for me to extend my examination of contributions received from the membership beyond accounting for amounts so recorded.

All of which means that an auditor is telling readers that these statements, so identified, do present fairly the financial conditions of the organization. Only the statements attached, none others, are so verified.

Furthermore, the opinion does not say the financial statements are accurate or correct. It simply states that there is no misstatement of facts that seriously distort the financial reports shown. (For further clarification see the American Institute of Certified Public Accountants Statement on Auditing Standards Number Five, "The Meaning of 'Present Fairly in Conformity with Generally Accepted Accounting Principles.' ")

The opinion defines those accounting principles which have been followed both in the preparation of the financial statements and in the auditing procedures—"generally accepted accounting principles." Such principles are those approved by the American Institute of Certified Public Accountants as those consistently used to record business transactions in similar organizations. Previous chapters in this book outline what some of those principles are for congregations.

Not only are appropriate principles used to record transactions and report those results, they are used consistently. If changes have been made in accounting procedures followed and for some reason these changes make comparisons with prior years impossible, the inconsistencies will be noted. Meaningful statements must be comparable to those of previous years if progress is to be noted. Recording transactions in a consistent manner is necessary if meaningful reports are to be prepared.

Auditing standards are those procedures used to check the transactions. Such procedures have been carefully defined and generally standardized. An auditor's opinion, therefore, which states that the examination was made according to generally accepted auditing procedures is actually describing precise methods used to test accuracy. It also implies a standardization of training, proficiency, and planning for audit engagements.

Auditors do their work primarily through testing. Since it would be unrealistic to examine every transaction for the year, auditors must use certain tests to verify as much as possible the accuracy of all transactions. Thus, the opinion states that those tests considered most important for verifying that accuracy have been done. If essential tests are not performed, such as the confirmation of contributions or pledges unpaid, the opinion will so state. Readers will then have been told that such tests were not made and that the results of the financial statements must be read with that understanding.

Opinions may be qualified when an auditor takes exception to some aspect of the financial statements. Or some contingency may create such an uncertainty about the validity of the financial statements and financial condition of the congregation that the auditor cannot express an unqualified opinion. This is sometimes referred to as a "subject to" opinion, and the auditor will carefully describe the condition that raises the question. Such a statement does not nullify the accuracy or the importance of the audit, but it does call to the attention of the reader that the financial statements may be affected in some way not shown because of the noted variance.

Audits Distinguished

The typical audit may be thought of as one conducted by an independent outside auditor, for a fee, similar to that used by business enterprises. Called an external audit, the examination of the financial records is done by someone hired for that purpose, usually a Certified Public Accountant. The auditor has no relationship to the organization and can review the records and procedures without any self interest in the outcome.

An internal audit, on the other hand, is generally performed by a committee of members selected for that purpose. The audit committee's function generally is to make certain, as best they can, that all receipts have been properly deposited in the bank and recorded and that all disbursements have been properly approved. The intensity of such an audit is much different than an external audit. In addition, an internal audit may be an ongoing process of frequent checks and reviews of procedures by the audit committee, not only on an annual basis.

A program audit reviews the attainment of program goals, variances from scheduled objectives. It attempts to evaluate program growth rather than only financial growth. When a master plan has been developed, progress toward those goals can be measured. A program audit checks it out.

As was noted in the chapters on planning programs and developing budgets, congregations must develop a plan of some sort if they are not just to drift along from one week to the next. Managing the congregation's activities and its finances means developing meaningful programs. The process to do that must be detailed; the objectives to be achieved carefully listed. The program audit monitors the progress.

Evaluating the Benefits of an External Audit

Audits may cost money, as was stated at the beginning of this chapter. An external, independent auditor will cost money. And whenever a congregation spends money it ought to measure the value to be received.

Such an audit does offer distinctive benefits.

1. A congregation can receive professional assistance in the preparation of its financial statements and reports from an outside expert. Too many church financial statements are quite unintelligible and virtually meaningless. A well intentioned treasurer may have struggled for long hours to put those statements together, but if they cannot be read by the membership, they serve no purpose. A professional accountant can often design those statements that will be accurate and most helpful to the membership.

2. Because internal controls are often lacking in a congregation's cash handling procedures, an independent auditor can make suggestions and initiate changes no member would think about or could ever achieve. Using an expert to give advice on the best internal control procedures can eliminate potential problems.

3. An opinion regarding the congregation's financial statements gains credibility when a Certified Public Accountant makes the audit. That opinion suggests that the statements presented are reasonably accurate and reliable. The accountant has staked a reputation on that statement. The responsibility is not taken lightly. The opinion can be counted on. The financial statements do reflect the true status of the congregation's financial resources.

4. Any payroll tax problems or unrelated business income reporting forms can be accurately completed by an independent auditor. Congregations do not get involved in the payment of many taxes, if any, or in the preparation of tax returns, but when they do, the availability of an expert helps.

The Professional Auditor

A professional auditor should be a Certified Public Accountant. Such accountants are professionals, as are lawyers and doctors. They are permitted to use the C.P.A. designation because they have successfully passed a rigorous national examination and attained a certain amount of accounting experience. They are recognized by other professionals, bankers and businessmen, as experts. They can generally offer a congregation the best help and advice.

Other accountants may be used, of course, But their acceptance as experts and auditors is open to much more question. Their training and experience is neither uniformly standard nor as stringently controlled.

Certified Public Accountants cost money—what service doesn't? To determine the potential cost in your community you will need to ask a Certified Public Accountant for an estimate of costs to audit your congregation's records.

It is not within the scope of this book to explain the auditing procedures to be employed by professionals. Their source books carefully detail the standard tests to be followed in any audit engagement.

Functions of an Audit Committee

Many congregations, especially smaller ones, do not feel that they can afford to pay a Certified Public Accountant and yet they, too, want to be certain that receipts and disbursements have been properly recorded and that the financial statements do reflect the true state of affairs. The audit committee, composed of selected members of the congregation, fulfills that function and, depending on the thoroughness of their investigation, ascertains the validity of the financial statements.

The audit committee, meeting periodically and seriously doing its job, can be of significant help in strengthening the congregation's internal control procedures. Lax procedures and ineffective separation of duties can be improved under the influence of a persistent and aggressive audit committee.

Unfortunately, too many audit committees are ineffective and ineffectual because they perform their duties perfunctorily and act merely as a rubber stamp. Too often the members are not sufficiently familiar with accounting techniques to know what to look for or check. Or the assignment is merely routine and no one expects more than the standard two line report assuring that everything seems to be in order and that the treasurer is to be commended for a job well done. A false sense of security based on the work of an audit committee could turn out to be disastrous.

The internal audit committee does have its limitations, but it is certainly better than no committee at all.

Procedures for an Audit Committee

Under the direction of the Finance Committee, the audit committee will have responsibility for examining and reviewing all records and accounts; examining and inspecting all insurance policies, records of securities, real estate records, inventories and records of other investments; preparing schedules and reports; and recommending changes and suggestions for improvements to the Financial Committee. Specific auditing procedures include the following steps:

1. *Cash receipts*

Your committee will need to review the methods for handling monies received from worship service offerings as well as in the mails, trace the amounts so received to the cash receipts journal, compare the entries in the journal with the duplicate deposit slips, and examine the transaction record for proper account classification.

The audit committee will also trace the deposits from the counter's reports to the journal and compare these entries with the deposits actually recorded by the bank. At the same time, it will check the timeliness of the deposit, check the account distribution in the cash receipts journal and check the use of the money received for specific purposes to make sure it got into the proper fund.

2. Cash expenditures

All cash disbursements (checks or cash) must be recorded in the cash disbursements journal showing the date, check number, the name of the payee, the amount of the check and the distribution to the proper account classification.

Then, the audit committee must test-check the bookkeeping entries in the journal for proper recording in the appropriate class of expenditure.

The committee will also foot (add) the journal for accounting accuracy; examine the authority for writing a check; the authority for approving the payment of invoices; the records of a minister's call, including the current salary and housing arrangements; the adequacy of contract agreements; the action of the official board in their minutes; and verify that the checks written for expenses were actually paid to the proper parties.

If prenumbered checks are used (and they should be), the committee must account for all checks used. If the treasurer has not already done so, the committee should prepare a statement of expenditures for comparison with the adopted budget for the year, as well as analyze expenditures for major improvements, refurbishings and new equipment for addition to asset accounts.

3. Bank statement reconciliation

The audit committee, rather than some other group or individual, should prepare the year-ending reconciliation between the bank balance and the balance shown on the books.

The reconciliation begins with the bank balance, to which is added deposits shown on the books but not yet credited on the bank statement. Outstanding checks are then subtracted to prove the book balance.

In the process of preparing the reconciliation, the committee must also verify on a test-check basis that proper endorsements are on the cancelled checks.

Furthermore, a request to the bank to confirm by direct written confirmation the balances held in the commercial and/or savings accounts is a normal and important procedure. An inspection of bank signature cards for approved signatures will make certain proper people are writing the checks.

4. Petty cash funds

Petty cash funds are difficult to control. Thus proper checks by the committee are important. The committee must determine that disbursement vouchers have proper approval, that reimbursements to the fund are made properly, that maximum figures for individual payments have been established and that there is adequate approval for advances to employees and for IOU's.

5. *Individual member contributions records*

The committee should compare "pledged amounts" with signed pledges, if any. A test-check of the financial secretary's posting of contributions to the members' records will verify accuracy.

6. *Insurance policies*

A check of all church insurance in force should be made. A schedule of coverages can be completed by the committee to show effective and expiration dates, kind and classification of coverages, maximum amounts of each coverage, premium amounts, and terms of payment. If there is an insurance appraisal, it should be compared with actual insurance coverage.

7. *Amortization of debt*

The committee must verify balances owing to all lenders by a direct confirmation, in writing. It must also review the terms of the loans and prepare a schedule of delinquencies, if any.

8. *Securities and other investments*

The committee must count all securities by the identifying number on certificates or accounts, and then prepare a schedule listing the numbers and amounts for each security. The committee must also make certain that all securities are in the name of the church. It will set forth the pertinent facts concerning other investments such as notes, mortgages and real estate.

9. *Finally*

The committee should prepare a letter of comment addressed to the official Board outlining their findings and their recommendations for any changes. The letter in Figure 18.1 is an example.

To: Members of the Official Board
From: Audit Committee
RE: Annual Audit

The purpose of this letter is to report to you on the Audit Committee's findings with regard to the internal control procedures as a result of the 19___ audit.

Receipts

(1) Counters are not making use of the official form titled "Report of Receipts for Sunday_____." The use of this form tends to facilitate the Treasurer's accuracy when posting to the Cash Receipts Ledger.

(2) We observed that no records are being posted to "Cash Receipts Detail Sheets." Such ledger sheets are very useful to identify readily all receipts.

Figure 18.1: Sample Letter of Comment*

---

*From the Diocese of Long Island, June 1976 Newsletter, Kenneth W. Miller, Treasurer, Garden City, N.J. Used with permission.

(3) Specific description of receipted items should be clearly stated on weekly reports of receipts. Such items are contributions by various organizations such as __________, __________, and others.

(4) We recommend the use of brackets (____) to indicate reverse entries for whatever reason, such as bad checks or bank adjustments due to miscount.

(5) Pencil should not be used. All entries should be recorded in ink. No item should be erased, but crossed out with a single line and re-entered correctly.

<u>Disbursements</u>

(1) Vendor receipts are missing on various items. We recommend that receipts be requested on all purchases of supplies and services. All other disbursements should be noted as approved in Executive Committee minutes.

(2) Checks for the month of August were listed against the wrong creditor in the disbursements ledger. These were corrected by the Audit Committee.

<u>General</u>

During the audit examination other internal control procedures, as noted below, were in order:

(1) Monthly financial reports to the Executive Committee and Denomination offices have been prepared and submitted.

(2) Bank accounts are reconciled at regular intervals.

(3) Two signatures are required on checks and on withdrawals from savings accounts.

(4) Two or more persons count the weekly collection.

(5) The Treasurer does not participate in the weekly collection process.

(6) All receipts are deposited intact.

(7) Pledge records are maintained by an individual other than the Treasurer.

(8) Pledge statements are sent periodically. Random audit of pledge records (over 10%) revealed no errors.

(9) Mail is received and opened by persons other than the Treasurer.

This concludes our comments and observations with regard to internal controls at <u>(Church)</u>. We recommend immediate corrective action to those areas noted in this letter which are lacking internal control strength.

We hope that the efforts which have been put forth by this Committee will be viewed as having best served the needs and objectives of <u>(Church)</u>. Further, we express our thanks for the opportunity to have contributed toward those objectives.

Respectfully submitted,

Audit Committee
John Jones, Chairman
Sue Simpson
Frank Brown

Figure 18.1 Sample Letter of Comment (cont'd.)

Bank Reconciliation Procedures

When the bank statement is returned to the church, a bank reconciliation should be prepared immediately. "The law is not unreasonable in holding that, when bank statements lie around untouched for long periods, those in control of the business should know that a risk is being run for which there is no valid excuse."*

The purpose of the bank reconciliation is to compare and check the accuracy of the checkbook with the church's actual cash balance in the bank. At the same time, it also provides a way to determine which checks have not yet been cashed. If the bank is requested to send the church's statement at the end of the month instead of at some other time, then the bank reconciliation will be much easier to prepare. And it is always better for someone other than the person responsible for depositing or disbursing funds to prepare this reconciliation.

The following steps are suggested:

1. Determine which checks have not yet been cashed. List and total them.

2. Determine which deposits, if any, do not yet appear on the bank statement. These are the deposits made after the last date shown on the bank statement.

3. Add to the bank balance as it appears on the bank statement (item 2 above). Subtract item 1 from this total.

4. Subtract from the checkbook balance the service charges or other charges made by the bank which are not yet recorded in the checkbook.

5. The bank statement and the checkbook should now be in balance. If so, the checkbook is correct. But if they do not balance, then the checkbook is probably in error. The bank statement is usually correct.

6. Repeat the procedure and check all additions and subtractions in the checkbook until any errors are located. Correct the checkbook balance accordingly.

7. The checkbook balance should also equal the cash balances in the journals. The service charges and other bank charges should be recorded in the cash disbursements journal, as well as in the checkbook. Also, errors in deposits must be noted in both the checkbook and cash receipts journal. Then, to determine the cash balance in the journals, add to the cash balance for the previous month (from the last month's financial statements), deposits for the current month and then subtract total checks written for the month.

8. Now, three amounts should be equal. (a) the adjusted bank statement, (b) the corrected checkbook, and (c) total cash balance on hand as recorded in the journals and as will appear on the financial statements.

---

*R. H. Montgomery, *Auditing Theory and Practice*, Sixth Edition (New York: The Ronald Press Co., 1940), p. 73.

Christ Church

Bank Reconciliation of Church Checking Account
As of July 31, 1978

Balance per Bank Statement		$2,341.56
Add: Deposits in Transit:		
Date	Amount	
July 30, 1978	$285.00	
July 31, 1978	150.00	435.00
Less: Bank Charges		(2.12)
Less: Outstanding Checks		
Check Number 211	$ 10.00	
Check Number 252	25.00	
Check Number 253	16.00	
Check Number 255	5.45	(56.45)
Balance per Books		$2,717.99
Balance per Ledger		$2,720.11
Corrections: Less Bank Charges		(2.12)
Balance per Books		$2,717.99

Figure 18.2: Bank Reconciliation

Christ Church
Minneapolis, Minnesota

Twelve Months Ending December 31, 1978

AUDITOR'S REPORT

1

Manfred Holck, Jr.
Certified Public Accountant
4119 Terrace Lane
Hopkins, MN 55343

February 15, 1979

Official Board
Christ Church
Minneapolis, MN

Accountant's Certificate

In accordance with your request, we have examined the balance sheet of Christ Church as of December 31, 1978, and the related statements of receipts, disbursements, and changes in fund balances for the year then ended. Our examination was made in accordance with generally accepted auditing standards, and accordingly included such tests of the accounting records and such other auditing procedures as we considered necessary in the circumstances.

Cash transactions are reported in the following statements, exhibits, and schedules.

Exhibit A—Balance Sheet	Page 2
Exhibit B—Comparison of Operating Fund Cash Receipts and Disbursements with Budget	Page 3
Exhibit C—Comparison of Operating Fund Cash Receipts and Disbursements for the Twelve Months Ending December 31, 1978 and 1977	Page 4
Exhibit D—Cash Receipts and Disbursements All Funds	Page 5
Schedule A—Bank Reconciliation	Page 6
Notes to Financial Statements	Page 7

In our opinion, the aforementioned financial statements present fairly the financial position of Christ Church as of December 31, 1978, and the results of its operations and changes in fund balances for the year then ended, in conformity with generally accepted accounting principles applied on a basis consistent with that of the preceding year.

_____

Manfred Holck, Jr. CPA

2

Christ Church
Balance Sheet
As of December 31, 1978

ASSETS

Current Assets		
Cash		$ 5,681.22
Fixed Assets		
Land—Cost	$ 208,456.00	
Parsonage—Cost	56,421.93	
Church Building—Cost	1,221,054.62	
Furnishings and Equipment—Appraised	195,500.00	
Total Fixed Assets		1,681,432.55
Total		$1,687,113.77

LIABILITIES AND NET WORTH

Liabilities	
Note Payable to Bank	$ 195,422.00
Net Worth	
Unappropriated Surplus	1,491,691.77
Total Liabilities and Net Worth	$1,687,113.77

Note: Unpaid pledges of $4,562.10 have not been included in assets because the congregation is on a cash basis.

3

Christ Church
Comparison of Operating Fund
Cash Receipts and Disbursements with Budget
Twelve Months Ending December 31, 1978

	Cash	Budget	Increase (Decrease)
Cash on Hand, January 1, 1978	$ 452.10	$ -0-	$ 452.10
Receipts:			
Previous Year Pledges	3,102.16		3,102.16
Current Year Pledges	251,421.15	265,400.00	(13,978.85)
Loose Plate Offerings	9,341.51		9,341.51
Special Service Offerings	4,712.10		4,712.10
Total Receipts	268,576.92	265,400.00	3,176.92
Total Cash Available	269,029.02	265,400.00	3,629.02
Disbursements:			
Benevolences	92,681.20	90,000.00	2,681.20
Ministers' Salaries	30,456.00	32,000.00	(1,544.00)
Administrative Salaries	25,941.62	32,450.00	(6,508.38)
Church School	21,265.92	20,000.00	1,265.92
Membership and Evangelism	1,471.10	1,500.00	(28.90)
Social Action Commission	221.14	500.00	(278.86)
Building Maintenance	27,456.10	26,000.00	1,456.10
Utilities	6,943.29	6,500.00	443.29
Insurance	4,521.44	4,800.00	(278.56)
Administrative Expenses	25,729.14	24,000.00	1,729.14
Music and Supplies	10,914.16	10,500.00	414.16
Debt Retirement—Note	14,922.10	9,922.00	5,000.10
Debt Retirement—Interest	7,441.26	7,228.00	213.26
Total Disbursements	269,964.47	265,400.00	4,564.47
Cash on Hand, December 31, 1978	$ (935.45)	$ -0-	$ (935.45)

4

Exhibit C

Christ Church
Comparison of Operating Fund
Cash Receipts and Disbursements
For Twelve Months Ending December 31, 1978 and 1977

	December 31, 1978	December 31, 1977	Increase (Decrease)
Cash on Hand—January 1	$ 452.10	$ 5,432.21	$ (4,980.11)
Receipts:			
Previous Year Pledges	3,102.16	2,945.21	156.95
Current Year Pledges	251,421.15	222,641.98	28,779.17
Loose Plate Offerings	9,341.51	9,241.68	99.83
Special Service Offerings	4,712.10	2,145.16	2,566.94
Total Receipts	268,576.92	236,974.03	31,602.89
Total Cash Available	269,029.02	242,406.24	26,622.78
Disbursements:			
Benevolences	92,681.20	88,539.16	4,142.04
Ministers' Salaries	30,456.00	27,321.45	3,134.55
Administrative Salaries	25,941.62	23,482.16	2,459.46
Church School	21,265.92	20,481.22	784.70
Membership and Evangelism	1,471.10	1,541.68	(70.58)
Social Action Commission	221.14	-0-	221.14
Building Maintenance	27,456.10	22,941.32	4,514.78
Utilities	6,943.29	4,568.91	2,374.38
Insurance	4,521.44	4,200.51	320.93
Administrative Expenses	25,729.14	24,941.16	787.98
Music and Supplies	10,914.16	8,421.57	2,492.59
Debt Retirement—Note	14,922.10	6,922.10	8,000.00
Debt Retirement—Interest	7,441.26	8,592.90	(1,151.64)
Total Disbursements	269,964.47	241,954.14	28,010.33
Cash on Hand, December 31	$ (935.45)	$ 452.10	$ (1,387.55)

5

Exhibit D

Christ Church
Cash Receipts and Disbursements of All Funds
Twelve Months Ending December 31, 1978

	Cash on Hand 1-1-78	Receipts	Disbursements	Transfers	Cash on Hand 12-31-78
Operating Fund	$ 452.10	$268,576.92	$269,964.47	$ -0-	$ (935.45)
Organ Fund	541.00	4,845.65	-0-	-0-	5,386.65
Easter Care Fund	75.42	259.65	321.69	-0-	13.38
Equipment Fund	100.62	1,150.00	45.00	(500.00)	705.62
Kindergarten	392.11	5,432.96	5,848.22	500.00	476.85
Missionary Fund	120.69	411.26	500.00	-0-	31.95
Miscellaneous Projects	45.22	22.00	65.00	-0-	2.22
Total Cash	$1,727.16	$280,698.44	$276,744.38	$ -0-	$5,681.22
Checking Account	$1,085.54	$274,702.79	$276,199.38	$ 500.00	$ (411.05)
Savings—Organ	541.00	4,845.65	-0-	-0-	5,386.65
Savings—Equipment	100.62	1,150.00	545.00	(500.00)	705.62
Total Cash	$1,727.16	$280,698.44	$276,744.38	$ -0-	$5,681.22

6

Schedule A

Christ Church
Bank Reconciliation of All Funds
As of December 31, 1978

Balance per Bank Statement $1,253.15

Add Deposits in Transit   Date   Amount

December 30, 1978 $1,223.41
December 31, 1978   68.00   1,291.41
2,544.56

Less Outstanding Checks:

Check Number	Amount	
10023	$ 62.21	
10045	3.45	
10046	681.62	
10047	1,345.22	
10060	421.66	
10061	321.45	
10063	20.00	
10064	100.00	2,955.61
Balance per Books		$ (411.05)

7

Notes to Financial Statements

History and organization

Christ Church was organized on September 10, 1956 as a nondenominational congregation. It has since become an influential church within the Twin Cities area.

Balance sheet

Exhibit A, page 1, presents the assets and liabilities.

Current assets - $5,681.22

A standard bank confirmation request was sent to the congregation's depositary bank and savings and loan associations. The amounts shown on their records conformed to those on the congregation's records or were reconciled. Schedule A, page 6, presents the bank reconciliation of the congregation's only checking account. Cancelled checks and deposits as well as withdrawals and deposits for the two savings passbook accounts were test checked to the books as necessary. Bank balances were as follows:

Organ Fund—First Federal Savings & Loan Association	$5,386.65
Equipment Fund—M & M Federal Savings & Loan Association	705.62
All other Funds—First National Bank	(411.05)
	$5,681.22

Fixed assets - $1,681,432.55

From original records of transactions the cost of land and buildings was obtained. No allowance for depreciation or obsolescence has been recorded.

Land costs are as follows:	
Original two acres—1960	$ 110,000.00
Additional acre—1965	85,000.00
Corner lots—1972	13,456.00
Total Costs	$ 208,456.00
Parsonage costs -lot and home—1958	$ 56,421.93
Church building costs:	
First unit—1962	$ 485,921.00
Second unit—1970	735,133.62
Total Cost	$1,221,054.62

8

It was impossible to verify the original costs of all furnishings and equipment since not all prior year records were available. An appraised value was used as approved by the congregation for insurance coverage.

Liabilities—$195,422.00

The remaining indebtedness on the church building is represented with:

(1) A $120,000 first mortgage loan held by the First Federal Savings & Loan Association of Minneapolis. The note is dated December 1, 1970, for 20 years at 8% interest, principal payable in annual installments of $6,000 plus interest. Prepayments are permitted without penalty.

(2) A second mortgage note of $100,000 held by the Church Fund Development Corporation, interest of 5% payable annually, no principal payments required until 1980.

Net worth—$1,491,691.77

The difference between total assets of $1,687,113.77 and total liabilities of $195,422.00 is $1,491,691.77.

Operating fund

A summary of operations is shown in Exhibits B, C, and D.

In *Exhibit B,* page 2, disbursements of $269,964.47 exceeded receipts of $268,576.92 by $1,387.55. Since the beginning fund balance was only $452.10, the operating fund was in a year end deficit position. Pledges for the year were balanced equally with the budget at the beginning of the year. However, even the $3,176.92 excess of receipts over pledges was insufficient to offset the $4,564.47 over-expenditure of budget amounts.

Exhibit C, page 3, compares operating fund receipts and disbursements for the fiscal year ending December 31, 1978 and 1977. Total pledges received for each year were:

	1978	1977
Current Year Receipts	$251,421.15	$222,641.98
Pledges Received after December 31, 1977	-0-	3,102.16
Pledges Received after December 31, 1978 to date of this report	1,451.68	-0-
	$252,872.83	$225,744.14
Disbursements:	$269,964.47	$241,954.14

9

Exhibit D, page 5, shows beginning and ending balances, total receipts, disbursements and transfers for all funds including the operating fund. Receipts for all funds totalled $280,698.44 with disbursements of $276,744.38. The cash balances in all funds at December 31, 1978 totalled $5,681.22.

Chapter Nineteen

Internal Control:

Safeguarding Assets, Detecting Fraud, Proving Record Accuracies, Improving Spending Efficiencies, Separating Responsibilities*

Thieves and burglars aren't the only ones who can steal your congregation's money. Given the opportunity and the right conditions, members of your congregation who are responsible for financial record keeping can steal it, too. We call that embezzling, appropriating funds for personal use that belong to the congregation. It does happen and it is a crime, even in the church.

There are, however, far too many persons who insist that, because church people are honest people, the principles of the business world do not and should not apply to the finances in the church. Many good and faithful church members are naive. While we may hope that things could be as we wish, it is not always so. Church members are subject to the same temptations when they are handling the congregation's money as when they are handling their employer's money.

And when it is easier to walk away with the church's money than the employer's money, because the controls may be less stringent in the church, the church's money may be taken.

It may be only an "honest" loan to tide the church member over to the next payday. But, the next payday comes and goes, the "loan" is not paid, another "loan" is soon required, and so the process goes. If discovered, the consequences

*Adapted from *Church and Clergy Finance*, Vol. 8, No. 2 ("Internal Control," by Manfred Holck, Jr.), published by Ministers Life Resources, Minneapolis, MN, used with permission.

can be serious. And all the while there was never any intention, really, to do something illegal. But it happened!

Very few embezzlers actually start out to be embezzlers. The illustration above is pertinent. A church official is placed in a responsibility of trust and opportunity, and when a personal crisis arises the temptation is just too much. If the opportunity is there, the funds may be inappropriately but conveniently used.

For example, in one congregation the same person has counted the Sunday morning offering for many years. Suddenly, that person, advancing in age somewhat, becomes seriously ill. A record of perfect church attendance is marred. And when the sickness continues, the absence goes on.

In the meantime, others are pressed into service to count that offering. And a few months later someone begins to compare the offering count for this year to a year ago. It is duly noted that offerings have taken a turn for the better, especially the loose offering. Where a year ago or even a few months ago, loose offerings were practically nil, suddenly the amount is much more. An average of $10 in loose coins and bills has suddenly jumped to a weekly average of nearly $50 in coins and bills. Envelope offerings are substantially the same as before, though up some, too.

The pastors and the church officials are mystified. There have been new members and that may account for the rise in envelope offerings, but visitors have not been any more numerous each Sunday on the average than before. It is difficult to understand why the sudden jump in loose offerings. Any change normally should be accounted for by those who have no envelopes, which are primarily visitors. And experience indicates that visitors aren't very generous in their giving.

A look at the records reveals that loose offerings in relation to envelope offerings was once approximately the same as now, but suddenly dropped down several years ago. The sudden increase now becomes suspicious.

No one can prove anything, but almost imperceptibly the sick, elderly, faithful member who so regularly and promptly counted the offerings all those years is suddenly suspected of appropriating that loose change. He could have! No one checked his work. And since he always counted the money by himself, it cannot be proved. But there are suspicions!

The point of that illustration is to show that given the chance, funds can disappear. Not only that, but since the loss cannot be proven, mistrust and suspicion of possible embezzlement is quickly fanned. Some defend the person, others attack, and soon there is division.

Three critical results have come out of all that: (1) the congregation has lost some money, perhaps a considerable amount, (2) a fellow member is being accused without proof of an actual embezzlement, and (3) the congregation is being divided.

All of which suggests that an adequate system of internal control might have alleviated a very serious problem for that church. Other illustrations of similar severity could be cited. And indeed, the most likely place for a misappropriation of money is precisely at the point of the illustration—counting the offering. A congregation's offering is most susceptible to being pocketed between the time the offering is placed in the plate and the time it gets to the bank.

But there are other points of control as well, places where the temptation to take without detection is quite evident.

A Definition

But, first, what is internal control?

Internal control is a plan of control, not only to detect error or fraud, but to safeguard assets; to check the accuracy and dependability of financial records and reports; to encourage operating efficiency and adherence to the rules, regulations and policies set by management. An accounting system for a church is essentially based upon the principles of internal control accepted by that congregation. The system reflects the principles accepted.

Thus, a good system of internal control will attempt to prevent loss of money or other assets by theft. It will keep honest members honest by removing the temptation to dishonesty. And, it will help to defend officials against claims of incompetence in the management of contributions made by the membership.

The assets of the congregation must be safeguarded from unauthorized use so that dollars are available when needed for programs. For not only would the loss of a large sum be a crime, but it might seriously jeopardize the programs of the church as well. Appropriate internal control features help to minimize those risks of loss.

There are, of course, many checks and balances which a congregation might develop to be certain that there is no intentional or unintentional misstatement of any transaction or account balance. And any system of internal control must account for that. But, the handling of cash is the most obvious place for the temptation to steal. And, it is that physical asset that is the thrust of the principles listed below. Receivables, inventories, securities, and other assets are not of as much concern, simply because churches don't have them often, although proper checks must be maintained for those assets as well.

In developing any accounting system so that internal controls are adequate, just plain, good common sense is important. The rule of the prudent man is quite appropriate. So any listing of controls will include those procedures that are probably rather obvious and elementary. Nevertheless to list them is important. You can check off your procedures by comparing what you do with what you "ought to do."

The purpose of this chapter, therefore, is to summarize the more obvious points of internal control. Some of these have been previously noted, especially in the chapters on income and disbursements. But here is a listing of generally accepted principles of internal control for any congregation.

Basic Controls

1. Don't assign the same person responsibility for more than one of the following tasks: counting the offering, writing checks, recording individual contributions, and reconciling the bank statement.

That separation is important to reduce the opportunity for any misappropriation. When one individual has responsibility for more than one function involving cash, the ease of misappropriation is greatly increased. For example, if the same person that counted the offering also kept the individual contribution records, false entries could be made to the member's account and the cash pocketed. A verification request to the members would reveal nothing amiss since the record would be accurate. Only an audit of all contributions and a determination that all contributions had not been properly deposited and recorded would reveal the discrepancy. But, that would be time consuming and would only be done upon suspicion of an irregularity.

Or, if the same person counts the offering and writes the checks, one set of records could be falsified to cover up a discrepancy in the other set. Bank statements reconciled by the person who writes the checks can be used effectively to cover up checks inappropriately written to the embezzler or a fake payee.

2. Make certain that at least two people are in custody of the offering until it has been safely deposited in the bank or placed in a night depository or safe.

It doesn't take much imagination to figure out what could happen to the loose coins and bills in an offering plate if only one person has access to them. Since receipts have not nor will not be given for those gifts, there is no accounting yet on how much money should be in that offering. The temptation is present to slip a few coins or bills out of the pile with no one the wiser for it.

When at least two people must be around that cash all the time until it is safely deposited, the chance of cash going into the wrong pocket is minimized. The two people may not watch each other, but the likelihood of two people entering into a collusion to defraud is less likely than for one person to do it, especially when someone may be watching.

Not only does this procedure protect the congregation's money, it also prevents unjustified accusation against an individual suspected of taking the money. Not only may funds be misappropriated if only one person is involved, someone may erroneously think that it has been misappropriated. No one should agree to handle the cash without a second person who is also assigned the task.

And the rule is important from beginning to end. It is not enough to have several people counting the offering (just because that gets the job done more quickly), but two people need to take the offering plates off the altar, go together to the counting room, count together, and together take the bag to the bank. Such togetherness is an essential element of internal control.

3. Promptly deposit all money—cash or checks—received on Sunday or during the week. A list of checks received should be compared regularly with the bank statement. Those responsible for record keeping should not have access to the mail.

The purpose of this control is to prevent any misappropriation of money after it has been received. Midweek mail is not likely to include any cash, but it may include a substantial number of checks. While it is supposed to be relatively difficult to endorse a check made out to someone else, with care it can be. Thus, checks received in midweek, or even those received on Sunday, should be promptly endorsed for deposit and payable to the bank.

Safeguards for protecting such midweek contributions include mail opening by someone not responsible in any way for record keeping. Checks should be promptly endorsed by that person and a list made of checks received. A copy of that list may be given to the treasurer and the financial secretary, the latter to make the deposit. The point of that activity is to prevent the opportunity for those responsible for record keeping from converting a check to their own use and marking the records as though it had been received.

A comparison of that list with the amount deposited as shown on the bank statement will confirm that the deposit and all the checks listed were received. That comparison may well be made by the person reconciling the bank statement. When confirmation of contributions recorded are sent out to members, it will quickly be evident if the person opening the mail has appropriated any checks.

The purpose of depositing the Sunday offering promptly and intact is to have a record of all receipts and disbursements. No payment for services should be made from that offering. Checks should be written to pay for any bills. Such a control will not prevent a person from claiming and getting an illegal payment from the church, but at least a check request will have to be made. All bills should be paid by check and all cash deposited intact.

4. Encourage all members to use offering envelopes. The purpose of this control is to make certain that each member's contributions are actually received by the congregation as intended. As noted in the chapter on accounting for income, as well as above, loose cash received can be easily removed for personal benefit without anyone else being aware of the loss. An envelope offering means a record will be made of the gift and a confirmation requested from the member. Members not receiving a report from the secretary would be expected to report that fact. When adequate procedures are followed, the use of offering envelopes can be a very effective internal control feature.

Another purpose for using offering envelopes is to provide the member with a record of gifts to the church for income tax purposes. Offerings made by envelope and verified by the congregation are acceptable to the IRS.

Some pastors prefer to know what the membership is giving. The use of envelopes makes that possible. And, statistical information about giving patterns as needed for reporting or projecting is easily available from offering envelope records.

Offering envelopes are especially useful when members insist on giving cash rather than writing checks. But, either way the envelope is useful. For their own record and protection of the gift made, all members should be encouraged, where possible, to make their contribution to the church by check.

5. Don't let just anyone have access to the offerings and to the checking account. Just as the same person should not have access to receipts and to the checkbook, access to cash should be carefully defined and limited to only those persons assigned responsibility for its care. Perhaps many people do assist with the counting of the Sunday offering, but if there is confusion in the procedure, then proper controls may be lacking. A selected group of people, thoroughly familiar with the controls and the procedures can make the counting process very efficient and accurate. Control of cash receipts involves careful screening of those who count the cash.

It is also better to limit those authorized to signing checks to a selected few rather than to several persons. There may be lack of control when only one person signs the checks as well as when the same person counts money and signs checks, too. But a half dozen authorized signers is generally unnecessary and does limit control. Since any two of these would presumably be authorized to sign, the other four, and notably the treasurer, could be unaware of checks written by the other two. Three or four authorized signers should be sufficient with the treasurer always in charge of the checkbook. Control involves efficient procedures as much as it may involve adequate safeguards.

6. Insist that all payments be by check. Adequate supporting documentation should accompany each check. The purpose of this control is to be certain that a record of all disbursements is kept and that only those authorized to make the payment have done so. A check is a permanent record of a payment. It verifies that a payment has been made, when it was made, to whom it was paid, the amount paid and even the purpose of the payment.

The only payments made by cash are those from the petty cash fund. Everything else should be paid by check. The supporting voucher designates the authority for the payment. The check signer verifies that authority by writing the check.

7. Require two signatures on every check. Since the treasurers of many congregations generally keep the financial record books and prepare and sign the checks, too, a second signature should be required. Anyone signing a check should examine carefully the support documentation and ascertain that the check is properly authorized.

This control also prevents the treasurer from writing a fraudulent check, absconding with the proceeds, and covering up the act by appropriate entries in the records. The second signer must verify the authority. Invoices are marked paid when signed to avoid a duplicate payment and another chance to misappropriate funds. Obviously, blank checks should not be signed in advance by anyone. The pastor should not count money, sign checks, or keep the financial records. A check protector machine and the use of prenumbered, imprinted personalized checks are desirable control features.

8. Assign someone other than those who handle cash or keep the financial records the responsibility for receiving and reconciling the bank statement. The purpose of this control is to prevent the treasurer from writing a fraudulent check, covering up the fraud in the books and destroying the cancelled check when it is returned by the bank. Another person designated by the Finance Committee should have the statement mailed directly from the bank and immediately reconcile that bank balance with the checkbook and journals of the congregation. It means securing the records from the treasurer, verifying all checks cancelled as those authorized, accounting for outstanding checks, and verifying all deposit slips with deposits shown on the bank statement.

The treasurer of a congregation should insist on this procedure, as inconvenient as it may be, if for no other reason than to prevent suspicion of wrongdoing.

9. Use a church budget effectively! The church budget can well be one of the most effective internal controls available to a congregation. By comparing budgeted amounts with actual expenditures, church officers can detect whether funds are being spent as authorized. Any deviations can be immediately investigated.

This kind of regular review is very important. Every member of the official Board should examine the financial statements and be prepared to question any serious deviations. Frequent and constant probing often uncovers potentially serious problems.

Of course, the effectiveness of this control depends upon timely financial statements. Monthly is not too often and by the tenth of the month probably not unreasonable.

This control also presumes that reports will be prepared in such a manner that comparisons can be made and marked deviations quickly noted, questioned and explained.

10. Unpaid pledges should not be written off by any financial officer. If a congregation records pledges as receivables, none should be written off without the explicit approval of the official Board. To permit such receivable write-off at will allows those with access to the records to cover up offerings received and not recorded. The write-off quite conveniently obscures the perpetration of that kind of fraud.

11. Keep marketable securities, notes, valuable personal property, cash (coins, bills, or checks) in a safe place. If a congregation has securities, notes and

valuable jewels or coins or other objects they should be kept in a safe deposit box. Keep cash in a checking or savings account.

The purpose of this control is to protect those assets from theft, fire, or improper appropriation. These should not be kept in a safe on the premises but in the custody of a bank for greatest protection. A bank safe deposit box requiring two signatures for entry is recommended.

12. Maintain an inventory of assets. This control is necessary to be certain that the congregation knows at all times precisely what assets it has and where they are located. A periodic count to verify the location of all items will determine which, if any, are missing.

Such a record should include a description of the item, cost, date of purchase, location, intended use, and eventually disposition and sale. Such information is not only valuable in keeping track of the assets but in case of fire will provide replacement cost information quickly. Such a record is also important in a congregation because employees and volunteers using that equipment come and go. A written record helps to verify what is available.

13. Make sure an annual audit is conducted. The purpose of this control is to have disinterested persons (persons not involved in the financial record keeping procedures) attest to the accuracy of the records and adherence to authorized procedures and generally accepted accounting procedures in the record keeping process. Chapter 18 explains in detail procedures for accomplishing this control.

14. Put all of your cash handling procedures into writing. The purpose of this control is to assure continuity in record keeping procedures and to provide an explanation to those assigned responsibility for what they are supposed to do. Consistency in record keeping and reporting is important in order to note and examine deviation. Control is maintained best by persistently using those procedures approved by the official Board.

15. Get a fidelity bond for all cash handlers! The purpose of this control is to make certain that the congregation will, in fact, be reimbursed if an embezzlement does occur. The insurance may also act as a deterrent to misuse because employees will be aware that an insurance company may press more severely for recovery of its loss than may the congregation.

Don't be fooled into an unrealistic dependence on this type of insurance, however. Good records are essential to prove a loss did occur. A suspicion of loss is insufficient for recovery.

Finally . . .

Anyone reading this chapter may suspect deep-seated suspicion of church members by the authors. Let us assure you that we no more suspect church members of fraud of the congregation's records than we would suspect anyone else of fraud who handles cash in any commercial firm. The purpose of this chapter is not to arouse doubts about the moral integrity of church members, but to recommend those procedures that are most likely to remove the temptation for fraud or embezzlement, eliminate mere suspicions of dishonesty, protect those responsible for financial records, and maximize the likelihood of discovery of a theft.

We have not expressed a lack of confidence. We have merely outlined reasonable procedures for the proper care and control of the financial records of a congregation. The larger the congregation, the more descriptive and lengthy such a list would be. Nothing here is new. Any accountant would confirm these procedures as appropriate for any congregation.

Chapter Twenty

Modern Management Techniques: Planning and Developing Effective Church Financial Record Keeping Systems

This book has been about church accounting—how to keep the financial records of a congregation efficiently and effectively. Every suggestion made and illustration shown has deliberately been included in these chapters to help your congregation do a better job of keeping track of all its financial transactions and reporting the results intelligibly to the membership. It has been a handbook of accounting principles and procedures. And that's why you read it.

By now you should have discovered that church accounting is more than just a matter of routinely listing offerings, checks and cash balances. To be sure, that is part of the process, but even the mechanics of keeping that kind of record can sometimes be somewhat complicated.

Church accounting is more than just a bookkeeping process. It is also a way of expressing the stewardship convictions of your congregation's membership. At the very beginning of these pages we started out by saying that how your congregation secures its resources, how it keeps a record of those resources, and how it spends and uses those resources will reveal the level of concern which your congregation may have for the program of the church.

In a very real way, we believe that a congregation can express its attitudes toward stewardship and its concerns for other people by the way it spends its money and keeps its financial records. Obviously, all the things—services, materials, programs, benevolences—for which your congregation's money is spent does indicate the priorities of its membership and its attitude toward the implied objectives of a congregation's reason for being. Keeping tab on how those resources are used reveals the emphasis of that congregation's thrust in its community.

Furthermore, the measure of internal control which your congregation insists upon, as outlined in Chapter 19, says something about your congregation's stewardship responsibility toward its monies and its people, too. The kind of financial reporting your congregation does tells not only how you spend the money, but what kind of example of stewardship your congregation practices, professes and preaches. Good financial records are the essence of good congregational stewardship practices. This, of course, has been the thrust of all these pages.

But all of that is accomplished only within the context of good church management practices and procedures. After all, the financial record keeping function of a congregation is only one phase of its total operational procedure, certainly an important part, but still only a part of a much broader concern.

In order to place this book and the church accounting principles which your congregation intends to use into proper perspective with the total management of your congregation's resources and program, these concluding pages are intended to be descriptive of church management in general, particularly as such principles may relate to the financial record keeping function of your congregation.

What is Church Management?*

Church management has been defined as "the guiding of human and physical resources into dynamic organizational unities that attain their objectives to the satisfaction of those served, and with a high degree of morale on the part of those rendering the service to the glory of God and by the power of the Holy Spirit." (John C. Horn, Church Management Services, Inc.) But the efficient management of congregations doesn't just happen! It is planned and organized, directed and coordinated by someone who is aware of what management is all about.

In the congregation, as in any organization, everything that is done must be managed somehow by someone. Whether planned or intended that way, it happens. And some things are managed poorly, others very well. But it must be managed.

Management experts define effective management as the process of planning, organizing, directing (delegating and controlling), and coordinating.

The application of proven management functions to the management of your own congregation can give your organization and your programs a boost of substance and a chance to bring order out of what may seem to be only chaos and confusion to you now.

1. *How planning improves efficiency.*

Planning is essential if you are ever going to do things efficiently and effectively. You simply cannot go from one situation to another waiting for problems to occur before you take action.

*Adapted from *Church and Clergy Finance*, Vol. 6, No. 22 ("What Is Church Management?" by Manfred Holck, Jr.), published by Ministers Life Resources, Minneapolis, MN, used with permission.

There are those who insist that Jesus was against planned management. He said, "Take no thought for the morrow; for the morrow will take care of itself." And indeed it will, particularly in those matters over which we have no control. Some things you just can't do anything about, so why worry about them.

But in other matters, the choosing between alternative objectives, policies, and programs may dramatically affect the outcome of other actions. Planning for anything will have a decidedly different impact on the future than if no plans were developed or those plans simply developed on their own accord.

The best laid plans may go wrong! Still, planning provides the guidelines for action that help make things happen that might not otherwise happen. If you don't plan, if the congregation just lets things happen, your program will probably eventually disintegrate and your members will surely be confused.

Planning is important! A careful plan of action, for example, lets the leaders of your congregation know what you want done and what the congregation expects of them. It will help them to coordinate their own activities and the plans of their committees.

Planning generally improves the efficiency of a program. You'll only stumble into the future unless you plan, and stumbling is inefficient, expensive and bad stewardship.

Planning gets people participating in the program of the church. And participation is one of the most effective ways to keep people there! You may not want to measure the effectiveness of your congregation's program by statistics (such as church attendance, membership, giving, etc.). Yet, it is generally true that congregations with the vital programs and the statistically impressive growth signs are well planned and efficiently organized. Their movement into the future is planned; it doesn't just happen.

Developing over-all objectives (planning) generates a cohesiveness among the congregation's power structures that tends to keep the forward momentum going in one direction.

Planning means every area of the congregation's life must be periodically examined and assessed. All the parts must fit into the overall objective of where the congregation expects to go. Unless you plan, every organization may go off on its own tangent and you begin to wonder why there is confusion and uncertainty in the life of your congregation.

Plan things well and you avoid activity for the sake of activity! When you do things because they fit into a plan that's expected to accomplish certain goals, you utilize the time, effort and money of participants more effectively. Good management is good stewardship!

Planning is not done by one person in the congregation. Everyone must plan, from the custodian to the pastor to the altar guild to the acolytes. A plan must be developed if all of these activities are going to get done when they need to be. When the pastor sweeps the steps on Sunday morning, or waits until midnight Saturday for the Spirit to come, or runs out of wine and wafers at communion, or lights the altar candles as the first hymn ends, it doesn't say much that's good about the management skills of that congregation's leadership.

Planning may not make every program you dream about successful, but without planning, your dream won't go very far either. Planning is a primary activity for accomplishing an objective previously set. Coordination, implementation, action all happen because they are planned in one way or another.

Planning involves the choice of alternatives. Each possibility is explored, examined, and a choice made for the best. Among the alternatives available for doing a certain thing, the most feasible is selected.

Planning means setting objectives. After all, the only way you'll ever know if your congregation is doing what it is supposed to do is if there is something by which to measure achievement. Objectives identify where you are going and the limits within which you expect to operate. When you know where you are going, you can plan how best to get there.

The primary objective of your congregation is whatever you expect the mission of your congregation to be. But you plan the kind of organization you need to achieve that mission. You establish goals by which your progress will be measured and you select the personnel you'll need to achieve those goals.

Planning avoids the chaos and confusion that may be associated with congregational programs. If no one knows where you're headed, if objectives are obscure or non-existent, things simply won't get done, at least not efficiently or effectively.

This means that the activities in your congregation must fit in with achieving those objectives. You simply cannot afford to waste time and money on irrelevant activity. Unless the women, the men, the youth, the choir engage in that which will be most useful in achieving the mission of your congregation, they are all wasting their time and yours. Using your facility for a day care center, for example, may or may not fulfill your objectives, but if it does not, you should not encourage it.

Planning is the responsibility of many people. Decisions by committee may not always be the best decisions, but a decision by the pastor alone may not be the best one either. An important principle of planning suggests the broadest possible base for planning, using as many people as possible to make those decisions.

Planning also involves the development of the simplest way possible for doing a job. Don't make the work any more difficult or complicated for your people than it already is.

Reviewing costs, eliminating inefficiencies, budgeting spending carefully are all important planning techniques.

Planning must be flexible. No budget, plan or objective should be so rigid that it can't be changed as required. Planning creates the opportunity for change and improvement as the plan develops. Effective planning requires the possibility of a different strategy when circumstances change.

Finally, church management planning is never easy. No one said it should be. But managing your congregation, developing policies and procedures to implement your objectives can be done most effectively when principles such as these are seriously considered.

2. How organizing achieves consistency and efficiency in program implementation.

You will get more done and achieve the objectives of your congregation quicker by having an efficient and well developed congregational organization structure. Organization is required if you expect to be efficient in the way you go about doing things. Unless you organize your congregation efficiently, you will be spending too much money, duplicating efforts, and generally have considerable confusion and chaos.

You can organize in a lot of ways. But whatever system you have, people must function as a group, as an organization. You simply cannot have the women's group, for instance, completely ignoring the structure of organization which your congregation maintains. Organizational structure requires considerable cooperation.

You may want to develop a very formal structure or something quite informal. Congregations run the gamut. In larger congregations a formal organizational chart may be useful to show the correlations between the people and the functions. In smaller congregations a simple chart by function of committee responsibility may be sufficient.

A formal organization chart may be helpful, but carefully planned informal structures can be efficient, too. Whatever the pattern, it is important to keep in mind just where the congregation is supposed to go and how the organizational pattern fits into accomplishing those objectives. Organizational structure should assist in achieving those goals.

However you organize for maximum efficiency, you should keep the plan simple. People react best when they understand the arrangement and know what goes where. Organize to assign tasks to people who are qualified to get the job done. Have people report to only one person. Organize so everyone knows what to do and to whom to report.

Good organizations keep the layers of management to a minimum. The closer you keep top management to the people, the better. Yet, the span of responsibility for any one person, including the pastor, must be reasonable. Too many people, too much work, too much responsibility can be disastrous to efficient management.

Finally, in any organization, people should be encouraged to make their own decisions within the sphere of their responsibilities. People are assigned jobs to do them and to make the decisions required to get them done.

An efficient organization doesn't just happen. It's developed and created by managers who are trying to achieve the congregation's objectives. Keeping mission in mind, organizational structure complements the tasks of planning, of getting things done.

3. *How directing by delegating and controlling implements the plan.*

How do you get the job done? How do you manage people so they will get on with it and achieve the objectives your congregation has agreed upon?

People react and respond for all kinds of reasons. It may be a physiological response or an emotional response, but whatever, people can be motivated to a response depending upon where they are.

A person's capacity to be motivated is arranged in a specific order depending upon the level of satisfaction achieved along the way.

A person's physiological needs must be satisfied before they can be motivated to do much else. Satisfy a person's need for safety, for example, and you can motivate for action on the basis of that person's need for love. Self-esteem can be stimulated when one is loved and needed. Self-gratification follows self-esteem and once the level is achieved, it's possible to motive a person toward a desire for self-perpetuation. That's where a church member is ready to give.

A congregation cannot normally stimulate or satisfy a member's physiological needs. It doesn't normally feed hungry members. But it is a good place to satisfy one's need for a normal, just, fair, and fear-free existence. When a person joins the church, for example, the need for safety is satisfied. Then, that person can be motivated to satisfy other desires through service in that congregation.

We all want to belong! We are social creatures. We all need to be loved! Thus, people can be motivated to become effective leaders when their social needs, their sense of belonging and love have been satisfied.

We all need to be needed! The satisfaction of doing something useful for others is a natural for the church to exploit; it can be a tremendous motivator for people.

Challenge your members to use their abilities and potential talent and you will satisfy that natural and persistent personal need for self-gratification.

Finally, church members often seek the self-perpetuation of their own desires and the needs of the church as well. Creative members who make significant contributions and who are remembered for that, offer a unique opportunity to the perpetuation of your congregation. They will give themselves and their money to satisfy that need.

Everyone is motivated by his own particular personality needs. These vary in degree of priority, intensity, and frequency. But whatever those needs, the congregation that is aware of them, that finds a way to satisfy those needs, will be able to motivate (manage) people toward making a stimulating and inspiring contribution to the work of the church. Don't let your pastor do everything. Delegate the work to all the other members of your congregation.

4. *How coordinating can make managing persuasive.*

Your congregation's leaders will never develop good management techniques until they have successfully coordinated the work of your congregation. People must know what's going on; they must develop a common direction, otherwise they will be falling all over themselves doing their own thing. Coordination is achieved when the management functions of planning, organizing and motivating are effectively worked together.

Successful coordination begins when people are willing to keep in touch, exchange ideas, discuss their prejudices and life purposes. It is a way to begin to understand how others respond, react and think. It helps people work together and coordinate their own plans with others.

Effective coordination requires that appropriate standards be developed so everyone knows what has to be done. Check points must be agreed upon to determine progress of plans and deviations from the standards set. And everything that is done must frequently be reviewed.

Communication, therefore, becomes the key to effective coordination. Failure to communicate properly can be a disastrous blow to the efficient management of a congregation's program.

When the managers in your congregation communicate well, they have much less difficulty coordinating the planning, organization, and direction of a congregational program. And only then will they move toward accomplishing the congregation's objectives in such a way that the membership responds enthusiastically in its service to God.

Good church management is good stewardship!

Putting the Church Business Manager To Work Managing the Church

The efficient financial management of a congregation doesn't just happen. It takes persons with the necessary skills to carry out those management functions. Your congregation's management team is the key to effective church management. How it plans, organizes, coordinates, and directs programs, including financial record keeping procedures, makes a difference.

Generally, in most congregations, the key professional person on the local church staff is also the only employee, the minister. Overall management of all of the congregation's activities becomes the responsibility of that professional person.

However, even in the smaller congregations the minister is supported by a group of key lay leaders, many of whom are key managers in their professional careers. And they bring their expertise to their congregation. While not paid as professionals, nevertheless, they are part of the management team.

Larger congregations soon find that the pastor alone and the volunteers who help cannot keep up with all the tasks required, at least not in an efficient manner. When budgets exceed $100,000 and membership tops 1,000 congregations often consider adding another key professional manager, a church business administrator.

The position is important not only as a key member of the management team, but also because a church business administrator's primary function most often has to do with the management of money and property. And that includes keeping the financial records of the congregation.

As outlined below, a church business administrator is typically assigned all responsibilities for cash management—offering counts, bill paying, fund raising, insurance, financial record keeping, financial reports. Duties may be shared by volunteers, but the administrator is often assigned the total management responsibility.

Congregations of appropriate size and budget should consider the possibilities of employing such a person. Responsible stewardship of congregational resources requires proper trusteeship and accounting of the congregation's money.

Each congregation makes its own assignments of responsibility. But typically the church business administrator would assume these duties:*

1. *Finance.* He takes charge of offerings and supervises all accounting. He gives professional direction to the every member canvass or visitation. He guides all special appeals. He helps prepare the budgets and exercises continuous budget control.

2. *Property Management.* He is the purchasing agent for the church. He supervises maintenance and keeps the insurance program up-to-date. He is responsible for the schedules permitting use of the building. He processes recommendations for building and furnishing improvements and all matters pertaining to the proper care of real property, furnishings and supplies.

3. *Office Management.* He maintains all records of the church or sees to it that they are in proper order. He supervises all mailings and keeps office equipment in good order. He recommends changes in procedure for the sake of efficient operation.

4. *Personnel Supervision.* He interviews and recommends employment of applicants for the nonpastoral church staff. He supervises and provides for training of the office, custodial, and food-service staffs. He cooperates closely with the pastoral staff in the supervision of secretaries assigned to them. He recommends, whenever necessary, the release of personnel, and discharges the employee concerned. He exercises concern for the welfare of all members of the staff and their service to the church.

5. *Public Relations.* He is responsible for church printing, newspaper contacts, radio and TV contacts. He participates in civic affairs and interprets by his presence and actions the church of Jesus Christ.

6. *Coordinator and Consultant.* He helps coordinate the activities of the church

---

*As suggested by the National Association of Church Business Administrators from *Managing the Church* by Robert N. Gray, published by the Phillips University Press, Enid, Okla. 1971.

through maintenance of schedules and understanding of the church program.

7. *Future Development.* He gives leadership and guidance to any planning of the congregation in terms of expansion of facilities. He gives professional direction to capital finance campaigns. He works with the architects in developing building plans. He works with the builder during the actual time of construction.

The situation and the person will determine the tasks to be done. But modern management techniques in congregations require capable and knowledgeable staff persons if mission is to be accomplished.

Thus, the kind of person selected to be part of that management team is important. The qualities required—personal, intellectual and emotional—for a church business administrator are endless and will vary among dispositions. But at least, as a minimum, the person best able to contribute to the management tasks of the congregation will have these qualities:

1. A spiritual commitment to the job assigned as one of Christian vocation and within denominational policy.

2. A personality and character that command respect and inspire confidence.

3. A capacity for effective communication, both verbal and written, with particular ability to interpret accurately and clearly complex data and detailed plans.

4. A positive understanding of managerial principles with a capacity for planning, organizing, motivating, and coordinating.

5. A fertile and imaginative mind set.

Such a person may be difficult to locate. Training centers in several locations now offer formal college credit courses in church business administration. Graduates of these schools are in demand by congregations seeking top-level, qualified, and trained personnel.

Also, among the large cadre of successful business persons, now retired, there may be those with management experience and expertise who will fit perfectly into a church administrative leadership role. Their experience in financial management can be particularly helpful to a congregation in its attempt to use modern management techniques for church financial record keeping.

The National Association of Church Business Administrators offers help to any congregation considering the addition of a Church Business Administrator to its management team. Write to the NACBA, P.O. Box 7181, Kansas City, MO 64113.

A Stewardship of Church Accounting*

How your congregation secures its funds, how it keeps a record of those funds, and how it spends those funds can indicate the level of concern your congregation has for its financial program. In a very real way, your congregation can actually express its own church accounting philosophy and its stewardship attitudes by the way it keeps its financial records and spends its money.

What your congregation spends, for example, may well indicate its concern and interest in particular areas of the church's program. Adequate salaries and allowances may indicate a healthy concern for staff members' welfare. Sufficient funds allocated to the church schools may show a strong concern for your educational program. Advertising accounts may indicate an active public relations program. Increased amounts for janitorial services may show a concern for the upkeep of the physical plant of the church and the proper maintenance of its property.

Attitudes toward a stewardship of church accounting may also be discovered in the actual financial records your church keeps. Inaccurate, messy records show little concern for a proper accounting or reporting to the congregation. If your congregation is vitally interested in the work of the kingdom of God, then its financial system must necessarily be good. Even mailing "statements" to members about their contributions may reflect misconceptions about what church fund-raising is supposed to be all about.

Then, how your congregation's financial records are kept, how your congregation's money is spent, and how your congregation is kept informed about its giving demonstrate, in a large part, your congregation's concern over its financial resources. That concern is reflected in the impact your congregation makes on the life of its members and the community it serves.

Whenever money is received or paid out or when services or merchandise are received or purchased, a business transaction takes place in the accounting sense. When funds are received by the church and expanded for benevolences, services, supplies, debt payments, or for any other purpose, business transactions are involved. The administration and maintenance of a congregation is a business operation. Obviously, then, your congregation has a responsibility to use the best-known business procedures available to administer its affairs.

Good business procedures are important, for example, when funds are borrowed for the purchase of land or building construction or where credit is needed for other purposes. Banks will require certain information about your congregation's financial situation before making a loan. Business establishments may require credit ratings. Only adequate and accurate records can provide this required financial information promptly. Thus, your congregation should operate its finances in a business-like manner. That is just good stewardship!

---

*Adapted from *Church and Clergy Finance*, Vol. 6, No. 24 ("A Stewardship of Church Accounting," by Manfred Holck, Jr.), published by Ministers Life Resources, Minneapolis, MN, used with permission.

Planning

Among other things, good financial records will enable your congregation to project its plans for growth and outreach into the future. For example, on the basis of previous financial records you can anticipate seasonal fluctuations in offerings. If July has been a low month in the past, then it will likely be a low month in the year to come. Obviously you will need to keep financial commitments to a minimum during that time of year.

Perhaps December is an exceptionally good month. Then some plans might be made for setting aside a portion of these excess funds to meet contingencies or other expenditures in a low month. Seasonal fluctuations occur in every congregation. Proper planning is necessary to meet those problems. Good financial records provide the basis for better management and a better stewardship of resources during the peaks and valleys of a year's offerings.

That same kind of planning holds true with expenditures. Insurance premium payments, for instance, may be due and payable annually, but a congregation can save money by paying those premiums once every two or three years instead. Yet, unless the congregation has made plans for doing so, it may be unable to meet the larger payment when it comes due. Adequate financial records will help to anticipate when such payments are due.

It is certainly desirable for your congregation to anticipate receipts and expenditures over the years carefully, to plan for them, and then to adhere to adopted procedures in meeting obligations. "Seat of the pants" planning and spending is neither successful nor wise, nor good stewardship!

Cash

The profit principles of business are not appropriate for church accounting. This is especially true when church leaders attempt to maintain large cash balances in the congregational treasury. Some congregations even try to make a cash profit to prove they are in business to make money. But the church is not in business to declare a 20% dividend each year! Church offerings are contributed for a specific purpose and they should be put to work to accomplish that aim as soon as possible.

To be sure, a contingency fund to meet emergencies is a necessary part of any congregation's financial record keeping process. But large amounts constantly on hand seem unnecessary. Proper planning with the use of "cash forecasts" and other accounting tools can suggest anticipated cash needs far in advance of any requirements to pay.

This means that if a congregation is fully aware of its responsibilities, it will develop some plan, some goal, some system for using its resources to the best of its ability. It means that a definite program will be outlined, that the *what* and *why* of projected goals will be thoroughly discussed, and that a business-like order will be maintained.

Internal Controls

One of the basic principles of any good accounting system is a plan for separating the duties of those persons recording funds received and spent and those having access to such funds. Different individuals should be responsible for counting, recording, and disbursing funds.

While no system of internal control guarantees complete control of cash, the spreading of cash functions among several persons does tend to insure its safe handling and accurate reporting. Systems of internal control are set up in such a way that access to the records is denied those who handle cash. The system normally provides for separation of the receiving and paying functions.

The basic characteristics of a system of internal check as explained more fully in Chapter 19 are: (1) Separation of handling and recording cash receipts, (2) Daily deposit of all cash received, (3) Internal audit at irregular intervals, and (4) Voucher system to control cash payments.

For church accounting this means the assignment of a different person for counting the offerings, for recording the individual contributions, for writing checks, and for recording deposits and disbursements in the journals. Good stewardship insists that business-like precautions be followed in order to provide maximum security of the congregation's cash funds.

Generally accepted accounting procedures insist that no one person should ever be left alone with uncounted cash. Obviously, the misappropriation of cash is greatly reduced if two or more people must conspire in an embezzlement. For the protection of both the individual and the congregation, at least two people ought to be present to count, handle or otherwise dispose of cash funds on all occasions, from the moment the offering is removed from the altar to the time it's placed in the bank.

Regardless of size, almost every congregation maintains, or should, at least one checking account. In fact, modern methods of paying and receiving require the use of bank accounts.

However, not all congregations use their bank accounts effectively. For example, if several checking accounts are kept, record keeping is more complicated and funds less effectively controlled. Extra costs are likely, due to several bank service charges on the various accounts. And, if bank reconciliations are not prepared on every one of those accounts, there is little, if any, check on the accuracy of the congregation's records as compared with the bank records. With only one checking account, problems like these are avoided and the danger of any mishandling or theft of funds is greatly reduced when all checks are issued by the same officer on the same bank account.

Through the proper use of banking facilities a better control of the congregation's cash funds can be maintained. Cash received should be deposited in the bank intact, as frequently as possible, preferably right after each worship service. (Using the night depository prevents the likelihood of a theft of church funds.) Offerings are to be deposited as received, and disbursements are to be made only by check and then by proper authority—never out of the offering plate!

As an ordinary precaution against loss, no well-run business keeps any more cash than the minimum required for making change. Apart from petty cash and change funds, usually only nominal in amount, and the current day's receipts, all cash will be represented by bank accounts.

To afford the best internal check and control, many businesses now require that checks be signed and countersigned; one of those signatures should be that of the treasurer or a representative. It's a good rule for your congregation, too!

To safeguard the issuance of checks, checks should all be serially prenumbered so all may be accounted for. A random use of plain blank checks doesn't provide the proper kind of control over cash. Checks should bear the name and address of the church so they may be quickly and easily identified.

All checks should be written with care to prevent their fraudulent alteration. It is a serious business to write checks! It's especially incumbent upon church officers to exercise more than ordinary care for those funds that have been contributed for the specific work of the Lord. Checks carefully written in ink avoid possible embarrassment and provide for more accurate records.

An accurate record of checks written and deposits made can be kept on the stubs of a checkbook. Then, an up-to-date cash balance will always be available. But the check stubs should not become the only source of information for expenditures and receipts. A journal or other record for cash disbursements needs to be prepared to summarize the various entries noted on the stubs.

Where checking accounts are properly used and augmented with other records, a month-end bank reconciliation must also be prepared. It's the only way an accurate comparison can be made between the bank's records and the congregation's records. Errors can be detected and corrections made in the books of either, as the case may be.

Spending

Strict control of the congregation's funds also requires proper authorization for spending. Accounting principles insist that all disbursements should be supported by the proper authority and appropriate documentary evidence. Checks should be prepared only on the basis of a properly authorized written instrument such as invoices, vouchers, payrolls, contracts, etc.

Invoices, statements, and other papers signed by properly authorized individuals can be the basis for payment by the treasurer, providing such disbursements were also previously authorized by the budget or board.

Contracts for salaries, utility bills, and other fixed monthly expenditures would be authorized by the congregation when it adopted the budget.

Usually the pastor will be responsible for more purchases than anyone else, but that spending must also be controlled by the budget and the Board. As a safeguard to the pastor and the treasurer, every congregation should adopt a definite policy for purchasing goods and authorizing spending.

As you well know, congregations don't always have funds available to meet all obligations. In order that proper consideration be given to paying all congregational obligations, a specific policy ought to be established by the Board to designate priorities of payments.

Accounting principles, of course, only specify that payments should be properly authorized, disbursed and recorded, but Christian principles of stewardship insist on a different order of priority. The Bible teaches that upon the first day of the week a person should lay aside a portion of what has been earned accordingly as God has blessed them. It also promotes regular, proportionate giving—week by week, a definite percentage. It encourages giving to God of the first fruits, not the leftovers! It emphasizes that the mission of the church is to help others.

In establishing an order of priority for making payments, therefore, even a congregation should first determine a definite, proportionate amount of its offering to be used for benevolences each month.

Following in preference, should be the pastor's salary. Since the pastor has been called by God and the congregation to serve as the leader of this particular congregation, those needs should be met to help the pastor serve effectively in the community.

Only then would other legal contractual obligations be met, such as mortgage payments, notes, utilities, etc. Other bills would be prorated according to due date, discounts, credit ratings, etc.

There are no "theological grounds" for church accounting procedures. There are no biblical references to validate any accounting procedures. God's people are to be honest in all things. Principles of good accounting should determine a church accounting procedure.

Modern, tested, and proven methods of keeping account of the church's finances should be used in today's churches. To do so is simply good stewardship!

Chapter Twenty-One

Taxes That Matter for Congregations: Income Taxes, Social Security Taxes and Other Taxes

All individuals and all corporations, with few exceptions, are subject to an income tax as required by the Internal Revenue Code. Those organizations not required to pay a tax (thus exempt from the law) are called "exempt" organizations. Most "nonprofit" organizations are exempt if they meet specific requirements of the law.

Generally all of the income received by a congregation is exempt from Federal income tax because of the provisions of the Internal Revenue Code Section 501(c)3. That section provides exemption from income tax for

> Corporations, and any community chest, fund or foundation, organized and operated exclusively for religious, charitable, scientific, testing for public safety, literary, or educational purposes, or for the prevention of cruelty to children or animals, no part of the net earnings of which inures to the benefit of any private shareholder or individual, no substantial part of the activities of which is carrying on propaganda, or otherwise attempting to influence legislation, and which does not participate in, or intervene in (including the publishing or distributing of statements), any political campaign on behalf of any candidate for public office.

Tax on Unrelated Business Income

However, congregations are subject to normal corporate income taxes on

281

unrelated business income. The problem, of course, for congregations is in knowing precisely what is unrelated business income. According to Section 513(a) of the
Internal Revenue Code:

> The term 'unrelated trade or business' means . . . any trade or business the
> conduct of which is not substantially related . . . to the exercise or perfor-
> mance by such organization of its charitable, educational, or other purpose or
> function constituting the basis for its exemption . . .

In addition, Section 512(a)1 of the Code states in part that "the term 'unrelated business income' means the gross income derived by any organization from
any unrelated trade or business . . . regularly carried on by it, less the
deductions . . . which are directly connected . . . "

The key words in these rules are "regularly carried on" and "unrelated." Both
must be present to subject the net income of the activity to tax. It's not difficult to
determine what is regular, but knowing what activities are unrelated can be more
difficult. For assistance from the Internal Revenue Service on this issue, see their
publication #598 "Taxes on Unrelated Business Income of Exempt Organizations." Specific examples are cited.

There are some exemptions to the rule. For example, income from an activity
in which substantially all of the people working for the organization are volunteers
who receive no compensation is exempt providing the activity's income is donated
to the organization. Income from dividends, interest, royalties, and rents from
real property as well as gain on the sale of property are all exempt from the tax.
However, if your congregation owns a parking lot and you receive a percentage of
the gross revenues as rent, that is unrelated business income, hence taxable. Rents
based on a percentage of the net income of a property are considered unrelated. A
straight monthly rental is not.

The 1969 Act establishing this tax specifically stated that advertising income
was an unrelated business activity. Such advertising certainly may help to support
the organization, but the advertising income is still considered unrelated. The
activity must not only support the exempt organization, it must also be part of the
exempt function to escape the tax.

Thus, if your congregation sells advertising space in its Sunday bulletin or
monthly parish paper or annual directory, any net income from such advertising is
subject to income tax. It is important, therefore, to identify the specific costs
associated with that advertising in order to reduce as much as possible the amount
subject to tax. And the costs must be directly related to securing the advertising,
printing the ads and distributing them to readers. The total cost of the activity
may not be applicable since the entire activity is not intended to secure, sell, and
distribute advertising space.

If you show a loss operation, then obviously you pay no tax. But it is up to
your congregation to prove the reasonableness of that loss. IRS takes a dim view of

such operating losses. They will assume that you did not intend to sell advertising space in order to incur a loss. You must be ready to prove that you did.

According to one interpreter of the law (See: Malvern J. Gross, "Churches and the Tax on Unrelated Business Income," *Church Management: The Clergy Journal,* Vol. 52, No. 8, July 1976), a congregation will have minimum exposure to the tax on unrelated business income if it:

1. Sells merchandise which has been donated versus merchandise which has been purchased or produced.
2. Uses unpaid volunteers (versus paid employees) when engaging in otherwise taxable activities.
3. Receives royalties versus the development of the property on its own initiative.
4. Avoids debt-financed property, unless the property is clearly related to the exempt function or unless it is real property covered by the 15-year rule (church use within 15 years of acquisition).

If your congregation happens to earn (gross income) more than $1000 from such unrelated business sources, then your treasurer is required to file a Form 990-T promptly after the end of your fiscal year (within 2½ months). Tax rates are the same as for corporations, 20% on the first $25,000 of net income, 22% on taxable income over $25,000, and 48% on taxable income over $50,000 (1976 rates).

Obviously, your congregation needs competent professional tax advice if you believe you may have unrelated business income or expect to enter into an income-producing activity.

Federal Tax Forms Required for Filing

All nonprofit organizations exempt from income tax are nevertheless required to file an annual information return Form 990, except churches, exclusively religious activities of any religious order, and certain organizations with gross receipts of less than $5000. As noted above, however, unrelated business income must be reported on a Form 990-T whether or not the organization is required to file a Form 990.

How to Handle Payroll Taxes for Congregational Employees*

Wages paid by congregations to employees are exempt from the FICA tax. Wages paid to ministers are exempt from FICA tax withholding. Simply put, your congregation is not involved by law with Social Security taxes.

*Adapted from *Church Management: The Clergy Journal,* Vol. 53, No. 4 ("Social Security: The Law and Your Church," by Manfred Holck, Jr.), published by Church Management, Inc., 4119 Terrace Lane, Hopkins, MN 55343.

On the other hand, your congregation is required to withhold income taxes on all employees except the minister.

Probably, congregational treasurers would heave a sigh of relief if that was the way things really are. At least, any congregational financial officer or secretary who has ever tried to comprehend the complexities of Circular E and Form 941, not to mention Forms W-4, W-3, and W-2, would be relieved if they had nothing more to do with FICA withholding and all that goes with Social Security.

Truth of the matter is, though, that congregations are often involved with Social Security, but only because that was their choice. Congress has not imposed the Federal Social Security tax on congregations. To require employees of congregations to participate in the Social Security program would require the imposition of a Federal tax on the congregations to match the employee contribution. To tax the church, even in this way, would probably be unconstitutional. For a congregation to agree to be taxed is one thing; but to have a tax imposed on the church without choice is something else. Your congregation should have filed a Form SS-15 with the Internal Revenue Service if you are in fact actually withholding Social Security taxes now. That form said you wanted to waive your exemption and be covered henceforth by FICA.

If, however, your congregation never actually got around to filing a request to waive exemption, but you have been witholding Social Security taxes anyway, under the 1976 Tax Reform Act you will be deemed to have filed the waiver and are thus covered. It's a good idea to discuss the matter with your local IRS District Director or the Social Security Administration office near you.

Nevertheless, if you consciously made the choice, you probably did so because you wanted to give the employees of your congregation (exclusive of the minister) the opportunity to share in the benefits of the Social Security program. It is a commendable objective but not without certain obvious financial consequences.

Since not all of your employees may have originally taken too kindly to the idea of paying ever more taxes on their wages, there may still be some on your payroll who are not covered. Form SS-15a should have been filed at the same time your congregation filed Form SS-15. The SS-15a form includes the names of all employees who agree to be covered at the time your congregation asks for a waiver of exemption. These are those employees who want to pay the Social Security tax and have it withheld from their wages. Those who aren't interested don't sign.

Those who sign are then, henceforth, included in the program as long as the congregation continues to be covered by FICA regulations. Nonsigners have 24 months to sign up or else will be excluded from Social Security tax withholding during the rest of their employment with that congregation.

Once that certificate has been filed by the congregation (or the congregation is deemed to have filed a waiver of exemption) any new employees or rehired employees must be included in the program.

The congregation may be permitted to drop out of the program (just why, no one seems to know) for financial reasons. Your congregation must prove that you can no longer afford to pay the employer portion of the tax. But, normally there's at least a maximum ten year "membership" period anyway.

Check your congregational records. If you are withholding and paying that Social Security tax, then somewhere back in the musty records of your congregation, there should be a yellowing copy of Form SS-15. A Form SS-15a ought to be there, too, with signatures. It's a good idea to know where those forms are located.

For example, if some former employee retires and files a claim for Social Security benefits, but has no record of those early payments, it could be that that employee did not sign your Form SS-15a when the congregation filed its certificate (employee was hired prior to SS-15 filing). Your congregation withheld no taxes and therefore there was no coverage for that employee. Your records will prove why there was no withholding.

On the other hand, if the form was signed and you failed to withhold taxes, for whatever reason, your congregation could be required to cough up those back taxes, not just the congregation's share, but the employee's share, too! Could get a little sticky and a bit expensive. Knowing where you stand in the matter helps in any case.

If none of your employees signed the SS-15a form when you filed your SS-15 waiver of exemption request and you haven't hired anyone since then, you are still off scot-free. You don't do anything about it; in fact you can't.

However if you do have employees who now qualify for coverage, your congregation must follow all the same regulations required of any employer for withholding and paying the tax. Read Circular E for instructions.

Here's what to do if you have elected to pay the Social Security tax and withhold a matching amount from your employee's wages. First, request an Employer's Identification number from the Internal Revenue Service if you don't already have one. You will need that number to identify all the forms you will file in connection with the FICA program. No problem to get it—just write and ask your nearest IRS office for information.

Next, you will need to have every employee file a Form W-4 with your office. That will give your congregational treasurer the employee's Social Security number as well as indicate the number of exemption allowances and additional tax withholdings requested, if any. You will determine both Social Security tax and Federal income tax to be withheld by using the appropriate tables in Circular E.

If your total withholdings and the matching Social Security tax your congregation has to pay exceeds $200 a month (but less than $2,000), you must pay that amount by the 15th of the month following. You make a deposit at an approved depository bank. You will receive a data processing punch card to identify your congregation's payment.

At the end of each calendar quarter your congregation must file a Form 941. You will get the form automatically from IRS. Follow the instructions carefully, remit any balance due, and file the form within 30 days after the end of the quarter.

At the end of the year it is also the end of the fourth quarter, so Form 941 goes in as usual. But Form W-3 goes in, too, with copies of all those Form W-2's. January is a busy month for payroll people.

Form W-2 is the familiar wage earnings statement that all employees receive and must attach to their own form 1040's. So it's the congregation's business to make one out for each employee showing gross pay, wages subject to FICA tax, FICA tax withheld, income taxes withheld, etc. The IRS copy of all those W-2's is attached to a W-3 form and sent by your congregational treasurer to your IRS District Director. After that your treasurer will take a quick breather and get ready to start the process of filing forms all over again by April.

If you or your congregational treasurer have any questions about procedure, your local IRS District Director's office is the place to go for answers.

Procedures for including the minister are somewhat different and are explained further in the paragraphs below.

How to Withhold the Minister's Taxes

According to the Internal Revenue Code, wages paid to a minister are not subject to withholding of income taxes. Furthermore, a minister's wages are not subject to withholding of Social Security taxes, either. In fact, a minister must pay the Social Security tax personally and at the self-employment tax rate besides.

Thus, a minister is required to file a declaration of estimated tax due each year, file a form 1040ES by April 15, and pay any tax due on a quarterly basis. That is, of course, the minister's personal responsibility and in no way involves the congregation's treasurer.

Furthermore, having received wages not subject to withholding, the minister should not receive a W-2 form at year end from the treasurer, at least not for Federal taxes withheld. A local tax withholding may require the issuance of a W-2 to the minister for filing with that taxing authority's tax form.

Instead, a minister should receive a Form 1099MISC from the congregational treasurer. This form is used by a business to report to the Internal Revenue Service payments made for services rendered which are not subject to withholding. The issuance of a 1099 will then require an annual summary Form 1096 to be filed by the congregational treasurer with IRS. The 1099 form will not be attached to the minister's tax return but is an information report that should be kept in the minister's files.

Unfortunately, not all congregational treasurers understand the implications of issuing the wrong form to the minister. Tax-wise, the minister is going to pay the same tax, but if financial record keeping is going to be done in an orderly manner and correctly, congregational treasurers should maintain and issue the correct report forms.

Ministers normally report their income on Schedule C of their tax returns, the same as self-employed professional people. However, if a W-2 form is issued by the congregational treasurer, then the minister has no choice but to include the total income shown on the W-2 form on page one of Form 1040, attaching the W-2 form to the tax return. Professional expenses will still be listed on Schedule C along with any other miscellaneous income.

Ministers receiving a Form 1099 or no report at all will, as stated, include their income on Schedule C, certainly not on page one of Form 1040. To include income on page one without a corresponding W-2 form, or to have a W-2 form and not include the income on page one, can only cause problems with the Internal Revenue Service for the minister. W-2's are checked against the amount on page one and vice-versa. It is important to put the amount in the right place, although tax liability is the same either way.

In recent years certain District Directors, however, have made it possible for ministers to have their income taxes withheld if that is agreeable to a congregational treasurer. For ministers who simply want to avoid the hassle and the discipline of filing an estimate and accumulating the necessary money for a quarterly payment, having taxes withheld out of each pay check is certainly a much more convenient way of paying those taxes.

This method happens to be more expensive for the minister, however, if it is the alternative selected. Ministers with good money management habits will not want taxes withheld but instead will make their own monthly deposit into a savings account and then withdraw the sum to make the quarterly payment. That way, a few extra interest dollars can be earned. Payroll withholding eliminates that possibility.

If the minister is the congregation's only employee, withholding of taxes will mean additional work for the treasurer in maintaining a record of taxes withheld, remitting those sums to the Internal Revenue Service, filing necessary quarterly and annual reports, and preparing a W-2 form.

But under the rubrics permitting employees to request additional withholding of taxes, some District Directors, as noted, are permitting the procedures described here. The matter is handled in the following way.

The minister must sign a W-4 form indicating the number of exemption allowances permitted. Any additional taxes which the minister may want withheld from each paycheck, such as to cover estimated Social Security tax liability, must also be indicated on the W-4 form. The form is then signed by the minister *and* by the congregational treasurer.

Both signatures would be required as evidence that neither party was forcing the other into an undesired arrangement. The minister must agree to have taxes withheld; the congregational treasurer must agree to withhold those taxes. Neither can require the other to have taxes withheld.

The congregational treasurer then withholds the proper amount as determined from the withholding tables in Circular E plus the additional withholding requested. If the amount withheld exceeds $200, a deposit must be made with an authorized depository bank. Of course, the congregation must secure an employer's identification number and the necessary form from the Internal Revenue Service before withholding begins.

Each quarter the treasurer will file a Form 941E if no Social Security taxes are being withheld from other employees or a Form 941 if there are other employees and both income and Social Security taxes are being withheld. At the end of the year, the treasurer will prepare a W-2 form for the minister, and for any other employees as well, submitting a summary Form W-3 to the Internal Revenue Service.

There is no legal requirement that a minister's income taxes must be withheld, but they can be, as described, if mutually agreeable. Social Security taxes can never be withheld, although additional income taxes can be withheld to cover that potential tax liability, too. The process is up to the minister, with the consent of the congregational treasurer.

Other Taxes Congregations May Have to Pay

Churches do not come under the law requiring the payment of unemployment compensation taxes. However, other exempt nonprofit organizations may be covered even though they may elect to reimburse the state employment agency for any benefits paid to their former employees rather than paying the tax.

Employees of congregations who are terminated or quit may, however, seek relief under the special Supplemental Unemployment Compensation regulations. This is only a temporary program and may not be extended, but while in effect it covers clergy and other persons who have worked for noncovered employers.

Workmen's compensation taxes or insurance are generally required by all states for congregations. Congregations employing one or more persons, including the minister, are included in the regulations. In some states self-insurance by the employer is an option. But, since the program is insurance rather than a tax, there is little hesitation by governmental authorities to require church participation.

Generally congregations are exempt from paying any state or local sales taxes. An application for such exemption may, however, be required.

Bibliography

Audits of Voluntary Health and Welfare Organizations, American Institute of Certified Public Accountants, New York, NY, 1974.

Bramer, John C., *Efficient Church Business Management*. Philadelphia, PA: The Westminster Press, 1960.

Burkhardt, Godfrey F., *Accounting for Parishes*. Latrobe, PA: The Archabbey Press, 1954.

Crockett, N. David, *Sound Financial Stewardship*. New York: Morehouse-Barlow Co., Inc., 1973.

Ditzen, Lowell R., *Handbook of Church Administration*. New York: Macmillan, Inc., 1962.

Espie, John C., *Handbook for Local Church Financial Record System*. Nashville, TN: Abingdon Press, 1977.

Gray, Robert N., *Managing the Church* (Business Methods and Church Business Administration). Enid, OK: The Phillips University Press, 1971.

Gross, Malvern J., Jr., *Nonprofit Organizations, Financial and Accounting Guide*. New York: Ronald Press, 1972.

Gross, Malvern, Jr., "Layman's Guide to Preparing Financial Statements for Churches." Price-Waterhouse Review, Winter 1966.

Holck, Manfred, *Accounting Methods for the Small Church*. Minneapolis, MN: Augsburg Publishing House, 1961.

Holck, Manfred, ed., *Church Management: The Clergy Journal*. Church Management, Inc., 4119 Terrace Lane, Hopkins, MN 55343.

Holck, Manfred, *Money and Your Church*. New Canaan, CT: Keats Publishing, Inc., 1974.

Holt, David R., *Handbook of Church Finance*. New York: Macmillan, Inc., 1960.

Kantonen, T.A., *A Theology of Christian Stewardship*. Philadelphia, PA: Muhlenberg Press, 1956.

Leach, William H., *Handbook of Church Management*. Englewood Cliffs, NJ: Prentice-Hall, 1958.

Lindgren, Alvin J., *Foundations for Purposeful Church Administration*. New York: Abingdon, 1965.

Page, Harry R., *Church Budget Development*. Englewood Cliffs, NJ: Prentice-Hall, Inc., 1964.

Peterson, Robert E., *Handling the Church's Money*. St. Louis, MO: Bethany Press, 1965.

Strickland, Stanley P., "Some Possibly Desirable Computer Characteristics, Based on Some Data Input and Output Requirements, in an Hypothesized Church Management Information System." Unpublished paper, 1972.

Walker, Arthur L., *Church Accounting Methods*. Englewood Cliffs, NJ: Prentice-Hall, Inc., 1964.

Wixon, Rufus, ed., *Accountants' Handbook*. New York: Ronald Press, 1970.

Index